D1315409

The World in a Skillet

The World in a Skillet

in a

Skillet

A Food Lover's Tour of the New American South

Paul & Angela Knipple

THE UNIVERSITY OF NORTH CAROLINA PRESS   CHAPEL HILL

Textured background, © iStockphoto.com/Bill Noll; skillet, © iStockphoto.com/
Soubrette

Photographs by Paul and Angela Knipple

The paper in this book meets the guidelines for permanence and durability of the
Committee on Production Guidelines for Book Longevity of the Council on Library
Resources. The University of North Carolina Press has been a member of the Green
Press Initiative since 2003.

Library of Congress Cataloging-in-Publication Data
Knipple, Paul.
The world in a skillet : a food lover's tour of the new American South /
Paul and Angela Knipple.
p. cm.
Includes index.
ISBN 978-0-8078-3517-3 (cloth : alk. paper)
1. Cooking, American—Southern style. 2. Cooking, International. 3. Southern
States—Emigration and immigration. 4. Cookbooks. I. Knipple, Angela. II. Title.
TX715.2.S68K64 2012   641.5975—dc23   2011020425

16 15 14 13 12   5 4 3 2 1

To my daddy for being willing to sample anything once and
to my mom for teaching me that just because something doesn't
turn out the way you thought it would doesn't mean it won't
still be good. —Angela

To my father, with whom I never shared enough meals, and to
my mother, who makes every meal an adventure. —Paul

To Patric for being open-minded enough to go along for the ride
and openhearted enough to enjoy the journey. —Mom and Dude

I'm Chinese by birth, but I'm southern just by growing up here.
—Wally Joe, Chinese restaurateur, Memphis, Tennessee

I think one of the beauties of all this is that I'm an Israeli
person cooking regional Italian food in the south of America.
I would say that America is such a wonderful place because it
allows this type of stuff to happen.
—Alon Shaya, Israeli restaurateur, New Orleans, Louisiana

CONTENTS

In Praise of Korean Barbecue and Indian Fried Okra

A while back, the Southern Foodways Alliance, the organization at the University of Mississippi that I direct, organized a field trip for grown-ups on Buford Highway, a deliriously multicultural corridor that stretches north, beyond Atlanta's interstate beltway. Our tack was to showcase the future of southern food by taking a close look at its ongoing evolution.

What ensued was a two-day bacchanal of Cajun crawfish, boiled in lemongrass broth by Vietnamese cooks. And barbecue chicken, smoked on charcoal-fueled pits by Mexican pitmen. And garlic chicken, hacked into shards of flesh and bone by Cantonese fry masters.

The message in that programming was straightforward: The South can no longer be defined by the tensions and complements of people with roots in western Africa and western Europe. Like the rest of our nation, the South is shaped by global exchanges, among a myriad of people from places both far flung and nearby.

Despite what the moonlight-and-magnolia fabulists would have you believe, the region is not static. Southern culture is not a concept to fix in some time past and preserve in amber. Instead, southern culture—especially culinary culture—is dynamic.

Today, after a long interregnum when the South was deemed inhospitable to immigrants, the region teems with a diversity of new arrivals from new places. The region is richer for it. And so are the foodways of the region.

In The World in a Skillet, Paul and Angela Knipple employ reportage and recipes to showcase that dynamism and diversity. Their work is not an exercise in exotica. It's an honest portrait of a modern South, where *horchata*-flavored popsicles are everyday convenience store fare, and old guard snack manufacturers market their pork rinds as *chicharones*.

The Knipples live in Memphis, Tennessee. They speak fluent barbecue. They know their way around a kitchen stocked with cast-iron skillets and mason jars of bacon grease.

But they are not wholly provincial. The Knipples know Buford Highway, too.

They've eaten their weight in venison jerky, sold by an Atlanta strip mall retailer who also makes a market in Catholic reliquaries. At nearby broom closet bodegas, they've slurped Mexican soups that bob with offal and burn with cayenne.

As you will discover in the pages that follow, the Knipples eat like citizens of the world. On the road, and on paper, they serve as culinary diplomats, intent on forging a coalition of inquisitive eaters who comprehend time at table as a passport to building common bonds.

Travel the region with them and you will gnaw on Haitian-style oxtails in Georgia. Join them for *mofongo* at a Dominican restaurant, set in a onetime Wendy's in North Carolina. In the company of Paul and Angela, at the first sushi bar to open in Mississippi, you will sample maki rolls, stuffed with deep-fried catfish.

Between bites, you will come to know the people behind these restaurants and cafés, the butchers who hone their identity each time they heft a cleaver, the cooks who claim their place each time they season a wok. At their tables, you will glimpse a true New South in the making, where the best barbecue in Kentucky is grilled by a first-generation Korean restaurateur, and the best okra in Tennessee is fried by a recent Indian immigrant.

JOHN T. EDGE

We Are All from Somewhere Else

The South today is a far different place from what it was for most of the twentieth century. As John Egerton says in his classic *Southern Food: At Home, on the Road, in History*, "By any measure, it is a new and different South in the world of food, a South that has gained much in the postwar age, but also lost much. In both directions, it would be beyond the recognition of Captain John Smith or President Thomas Jefferson or General Robert E. Lee. When change finally came to the South, it came with a mighty rush."

New opportunities have brought new people into the region, people from around the world, people who are enriching southern culture by sharing elements of their heritage with their new communities. These people are the inspiration for our culinary tour of the South and for the chronicle of discoveries that appear in this book. You will be introduced, by way of food, to some of the fascinating immigrants making the South their home.

The United States is a nation of immigrants. The tired, the poor, the huddled masses come to the United States every day. Economic conditions in the South have brought larger waves of immigrants to the region than ever before, and the changes brought by these new arrivals are obvious. We find immigrants working in restaurant kitchens of every genre, bringing touches of their culinary traditions into the food they serve there. We find street vendors who carry the food of their homeland to areas where working people appreciate a taste of home. And we find restaurateurs who seek to introduce new flavors to the region.

Why look at these cultures through the lens of food? Culinary traditions form some of the strongest ethnic ties. Recipes are handed down through generations and are sources of national pride. When immigrants come to the United States, they bring these recipes with them. While these recipes may change over time, they are often the longest lasting ties to immigrants' original homes, remaining long after many other ethnic traditions they brought with them have disappeared.

Before we start on our food journey in today's South, however, it is important to reflect on the history of food in the South and on how the region developed. Southern food cannot be attributed to any single source. Long before the first Europeans arrived, Native Americans in the South were taking advantage of both the wild bounty and the fertile land. In the temperate climate, the Native Americans—truly the first southerners—hunted, fished, and gathered from the wild, but more important, they cultivated corn. This corn was shared with those first Europeans and is still one of the most essential parts of southern food today.

The contributions of the Europeans, to both ingredients and techniques, further defined what southern food is. During the period of exploration, the Spaniards brought pork. As settlers, the English dominated the food and culture of the thirteen colonies under their rule, introducing new grains such as wheat and barley. They also brought tea, still the most common drink on tables throughout the South. In Louisiana, where the French and Spanish ruled, the influences of their cuisines are evident even today.

As the United States grew, the divide between the North and the South was driven by climate. In the North, the shorter growing season led to an economy based on industry, but in the South, riches were derived from the land. The enslaved Africans who were forced to work in the fields of the agriculture-dependent South were the greatest influence of any on southern cuisine. Because of their contributions to techniques, flavors, and ingredients, southern cuisine became the most distinctive regional cookery in America, both then and now.

The first immigrants to North America arrived 14,000 to 16,000 years ago. They were hunter-gatherers, leading harsh lives as they followed herds of game across the land. Over time, they transitioned to a more agrarian lifestyle once they learned to cultivate corn. With a stable food supply, bands of Native Americans grew, becoming great tribes, including the South's so-called Five Civilized Tribes—the Chickasaws, the Choctaws, the Cherokees, the Creeks, and the Seminoles.

Life for the Native Americans began to change with the arrival of European explorers and settlers. The most common image of Native Americans and food in American history is the one we all learned in elementary school—the first Thanksgiving with turkey and corn shared by the Pilgrims and Native Americans. While that image glosses over the actual strife between the Europeans and the Native Americans, corn was indeed shared, and for the colonists it became one of the foods that helped them survive in the New World during the early days.

As familiar as corn is in the South today, the most iconic food of the South is not native to the New World at all. In 1540, Hernando de Soto played a major role in introducing pork to the New World. Somewhere near Tupelo, Mississippi, de Soto encountered the Chickasaw tribe. De Soto had a herd of pigs to butcher for his men during the winter, but he negotiated a tentative, hostile treaty with the Chickasaws to secure additional food.

When spring came, de Soto prepared to leave, but he had worn out his welcome well before then. Through the winter, he had demanded much from the Chickasaws, forcing their acceptance by taking hostages. As he was leaving, he made one demand too many. Rather than give him two hundred Chickasaw women to act as slaves, the tribe attacked and nearly wiped out de Soto's men. His pigs escaped during the conflict and remained in the region. Their descendants are the wild boars that still roam the woods of the South.

Where the explorers led, settlers followed, and their need for land led to many injustices for the Native Americans. The gradual evolution of treaties between the United States and the Native Americans shows a pattern of increasing disregard for the rights of the people who had been here first. From 1786 to 1805, treaties between the United States and the Chickasaws involved peace and protection. The treaties that followed, however, forced the Chickasaws to give up more and more of their lands and led ultimately to the removal era.

The forced removal of Native Americans from the South in the early nineteenth century was certainly one of the worst moments in American history. The Cherokees call the removal *Nunna Daul Tsunny*—The Trail Where They Cried or, more familiar to most Americans, The Trail of Tears. Many died from the harsh conditions on the march west, but many more died from cold, disease, and starvation in the concentration camps along the way.

In spite of the removal, some Native Americans remained on their land but at a cost. Prior to the Civil War, free Choctaws in Mississippi had fewer rights than slaves. They were not recognized as American citizens and had no recourse to the law. After the war, Choctaws were subjected to the same Jim Crow segregation laws as African Americans. It was not until the 1930s that the tribe was recognized by the federal government and granted protected status.

European settlement of the New World began another key and troubled chapter of American history. The British brought the first enslaved Africans to Virginia in 1619. From there, slavery spread throughout the English colonies. Slavery ended in the North by 1800, but by 1863, when the Emancipation Proclamation ended slavery in the Confederate states, over 50 percent of the population of the South was made up of enslaved Africans, and in the rice- and sugarcane-growing areas along the coast, that figure was up to 90 percent.

Throughout the South, African cooks were shaping southern food. Even in the distinct foods of New Orleans, the influence of enslaved Africans can still be seen and tasted along with the region's French and Spanish roots. This blending of cultures created the Creole cuisine that is uniquely the flavor of New Orleans. Perhaps the nuances of Africa in New Orleans foodways are different from those of the rest of the South because the practice of slavery there was as unique to the South as is the city itself.

New Orleans has always been a city unlike any other. The city and the Louisiana Territory were founded and claimed by the French and then were ruled by the Spanish before returning to French control. Continental culture and language distinguished Louisiana from the rest of the South. New Orleans was also the largest city in the South and much more similar to European cities.

As a major port in the slave trade, New Orleans had its issues with slavery like the rest of the South. Still, there were significant differences. Slavery began in Louisiana in 1706 with the enslavement of Native Americans. Enslaved Africans first arrived in 1710, and slavery in the territory increased dramatically after the Louisiana Purchase in 1803.

In 1724, the French rulers of Louisiana adopted the Code Noir, a formalized system listing the rights and restrictions for slaves, slave owners, and free people of color. Portions of the Code Noir remained in effect even after the Louisiana Purchase. A provision of the Code Noir allowed slaves to earn money. This had an impact on the lives of enslaved people in New Orleans because another provision of the code stated that if a slave could meet his or her owner's asking price, that owner was required by law to free the slave. This provision gave rise to the largest and most integrated population of free people of color in the United States, a population that flourished throughout the Civil War and until the withdrawal of Union troops from the city in 1877.

In the rest of the South, where nothing like the Code Noir existed, southern food was coming into its own. The contributions of enslaved Africans to the kitchens where they worked cannot be overstated. Foods like black-eyed peas, okra, yams, and many others came to the South on slave ships. Their preparation in southern kitchens and appearance on southern tables created an enduring legacy that, through the span of generations, became inseparable from any description of southern food.

Still, life for most southerners before and after the Civil War was very different from portrayals in popular film and literature. Many people think of such romanticized images as the barbecue at Twelve Oaks that Margaret Mitchell described in *Gone with the Wind*, a lavish spread prepared by slaves and enjoyed by the social elite. A more accurate picture would show that less than half of white southerners owned slaves. The disparity of wealth between the majority of the southern population and the minority of rich plantation owners reflected a system of poverty that still endures in some parts of the rural South.

Though slavery had existed in the South for 250 years, there was little change in the class structure of southerners both rich and poor, black and white, in the years after slavery. After emancipation, the great plantations still existed and still produced income for the landowners, but now those landowners had to find new laborers. This need fueled a new wave of immigration into the South. In the Mississippi Delta, the foodways brought by Mexican, Italian, and Chinese immigrants came to stand alongside and even merged with the foodways already in place to create changes in southern food that are still recognizable today. It was from this merging of cultures that foods like the Mississippi Delta hot tamale were born, a food with only a passing resemblance to the Mexican tamale that may have inspired its creation.

The need for laborers also gave rise to the system of sharecropping that forced impoverished people of every race and nationality into a situation that was exploitative and paternalistic. Sharecroppers farmed the land in return for food and shelter for their families, but a poor harvest or a family illness could leave sharecroppers deep in debt, reducing them to a level of poverty that many could never escape. The sharecropping system made no investment in the laborers and could easily replace them immediately with other poor families if the laborers left.

The food and shelter provided for the sharecroppers was often minimal. Hunger was a fact of life for many of the children who grew up in sharecropper shacks. While the Great Depression had a huge impact in the cities of the North and West, life was no worse than it had been before for far too many people in the South.

The period lasting through Reconstruction, the Great Depression, and up to World War II fundamentally changed the southern experience of food. The lines between poor food and rich food blurred, becoming what we know today as country cooking. Children were taught that all food was precious and that wasting any of it was asking for hunger. Those children taught the same lessons to their children and grandchildren. The principles of putting food away and of not wasting any part of animals or vegetables were an integral part of southern foodways. After World War II, the industrialized food system began to remove the need for these measures, and country cooking became endangered.

In the 1960s, amid the movement for African American empowerment, "soul" became an important term. Soul expresses many concepts, foremost being a particular quality of survival and strength that is celebrated in African American culture. For African Americans in particular, the foods that evolved from the days of slavery and the following days of poverty mean something more. Their legacy of "making do" suffuses southern cuisine and culture to this day. Thus in the 1960s, soul food came to the table, helping to preserve the uniqueness of southern cuisine.

The 1960s also saw a long-ignored southern food tradition make its way into the minds and onto the tables of America. Justin Wilson brought Cajun cooking and stories to prominence with the publication of his first cookbook, *The Justin Wilson Cook Book*, in 1965. He followed the success of that volume with the syndication of his cooking show in the early 1970s. While Wilson's authenticity as a Cajun was questionable at best, his recipes and voice were the first Cajun experience that many Americans, including southerners, learned.

It could be argued that Wilson's success enabled the acceptance and success of other iconic Cajun and New Orleans chefs. Paul Prudhomme, owner of K-Paul's Louisiana Kitchen, original blackener of redfish, and the face behind the Magic Seasoning Blends, came to national attention in 1979. His signature technique is now seen in restaurants with no other connection to Cajun food or culture. His spice blends are sold not only all over the United States but in foreign markets as well.

Perhaps because of the influence of Wilson, Prudhomme, and others, the images that come to mind when we think of Cajuns today are far removed from the first Acadian immigrants who found their way to Louisiana. The denizens of the bayous seem so at home there that it's hard to imagine that their ancestors first chose to settle in eastern Canada when they came to the New World.

French immigration to the area known as Acadia began in 1604, starting in present-day Maine. Between disease and British invasions, attempts at colonization failed until 1632, when immigrants settled in present-day Nova Scotia. The colony there thrived until 1710, when it was conquered by the British. Even then, the Acadians and the British peacefully coexisted until the renewal of British-French hostilities in

1744. The Acadians tried to remain neutral, but in 1755 the British governor of what was by then called Nova Scotia ordered the expulsion of the approximately 13,000 Acadians living there. Some were scattered along the Atlantic coast, while others were sent to England or France. Some fled to Quebec, and others went into hiding in Nova Scotia. Many Acadians traveled to the Louisiana Territory to live under French rule. They arrived there in 1763 only to learn that the territory had been turned over to the Spanish.

Few if any Cajuns today have a strictly Acadian lineage. Most include the heritage of the Spanish, Germans, British, French, and Native Americans. Cajun food is as reflective of this heritage as are the people themselves. The truly Cajun dishes, the ones made only in homes, show the nuances of the Acadians' French technique with the flavors of the other people who made the bayous their homes. And underlying it all are the native flavors of the region, the ingredients that thrived there and created a unique melding that is the true flavor of Louisiana.

Like the Cajun cuisine born in the bayous of Louisiana, another tradition of southern cuisine was born in the Appalachian Mountains. Approximately 250,000 Scots-Irish immigrants made their way to America in the early eighteenth century. Most of those immigrants made homes for their families in the mountains, and many of their descendants remain there today.

To say that those early settlers were isolated is a gross understatement. They were living in a mountainous region on the frontier of the American colonies that had few roads or established towns. Families were completely dependent on the food they could raise themselves or on what they could trade with other families. Using what they could raise and what they could gather, they created culinary traditions that have quietly contributed to southern cuisine. While the dried apple stack cakes and leather britches beans stayed in Appalachia, other dishes that we recognize as classic southern cuisine can trace their roots to those Scots-Irish mountain cooks. Chow chow, chicken and dumplings, cornbread pudding, and apple butter started out in the mountains.

Gardens and smokehouses were common features of family homes in Appalachia until the 1930s, when coal mining became a better source of income for many in the region. As those family farms were abandoned, the food of Appalachia began to vanish. It took a dedicated effort to save those traditions in the face of modern conveniences that were more readily available thanks to the roads and electricity that finally became common in the region with the coal mines.

The southern food that we cherish is a product of all these people—

the immigrants who made the South what it is today. The South and its foodways continue to grow and evolve with new generations of immigrants who are redefining southern cuisine one dish at a time.

While we hope you enjoy reading about the people included here, we also hope their recipes become favorites in your home. As given, they produce wonderful dishes, but they are only reference points for you in your kitchen. After many recipes, you will find a section called "Kitchen Passport," where we provide suggestions for variations on the recipe. Some will help you substitute for hard-to-find ingredients; others will help you think about ways to adapt the recipe for dietary restrictions; and others simply give you suggestions for different but equally delicious approaches to the dish. Don't feel that you have to use these suggestions, but do consider them and perhaps let them inspire you to try your own variations.

In each chapter, you will also find a section called "Culinary Tour Guide." Some ingredients and techniques are key to the cuisine of a particular part of the world, and in order to understand their significance in the recipes, you need to understand their cultural significance as well. The tour guides give you an overview of these ingredients and techniques that we hope will pique your curiosity to learn more about them.

The World in a Skillet

Keepers of the Flame

The new global South, with its rapidly increasing international business trade, has opened the region to new culinary influences as well as to a greater awareness of the influences that past immigrants have had in the South. In our travels, we saw signs of earlier generations of immigrants—and not just in monuments or historical markers but in flesh and blood, in people with stories, including some stories that reach back beyond history itself. To introduce you to this book, we want to introduce you to four people who are preserving the culinary history of their part of the South in their own unique ways.

During most of the year, Robert Thrower, Poarch Creek Tribal Historic Preservation officer, works collecting artifacts and documents that chronicle the history of his people. He also travels the globe speaking about their history and the ways in which he preserves it. Two days a year, during the tribe's annual Thanksgiving Pow Wow, he gives talks and leads tours in a former house-turned-school-turned-cultural center. The small building barely contains his passion and almost frenetic energy as he retells the story of the Creek nation in Alabama from before the arrival of Europeans through today.

Robert Thrower,
Poarch Band of
Creek Indians,
Atmore, Alabama

Robert's pride in his people shows as he leads the tour into a room where archaeological artifacts are displayed. Pointing to a case of sharpened stone points, he asks the group what they are. "Arrowheads," someone answers.

"That is what people call them, but think about it. Put something that heavy on the tip of an arrow, and the arrow will fall straight to the ground," he replies. "These are spear points. The bow and arrow was a European invention. We used spears to hunt. The spear might have been held to finish a wounded animal, but more likely, it would have been thrown."

At this point, Robert puts a long, slender piece of wood on the table. One end of the wood is slightly larger and hollowed out. "Now, I can throw a spear a fair distance, but with this, I can throw it much farther and much faster," Robert continues. "This is an *atlatl*. Way back then,

we understood physics enough to know that you could increase your leverage by extending the length of your arm with one of these. That was very innovative. Folks say they were primitive people, but look at these tools. Clearly there was some serious intelligence there." ⬚

THREE SISTERS SOUP

Active cooking time: 40 minutes | Total cooking time: 2 hours | Yield: 12 main dish servings

Native American ingenuity extended from hunting to agriculture and cooking as well. The three sisters are corn, beans, and squash—three key ingredients in the Native American diet.

Corn was planted and the stalks were allowed to grow. Next, beans were planted and allowed to climb the corn stalks. Finally, squash was planted among the corn so that the beans and corn shaded the squash from the harsh summer sun.

Many Native American tribes prepare these ingredients as a hearty soup. Versions of this dish were made even before the creation of pottery, when cooking and serving vessels consisted of hollowed gourds. Robert explains how a tribe could not only cook soup in flammable vessels but eat as a group from them as well.

"There was one item that every Creek woman had with her at all times. It was one of her most precious possessions." Robert puts a plain brown stone, smaller than a fist, on the counter in front of him. "To us, it just looks like a rock, but this was no ordinary stone. It was smooth, hard, and wouldn't shed grit in water."

Robert goes on to explain why a stone like this was so important. "She would heat this stone in the communal fire along with the stones of all of the other women. Then when it was time, she would add the hot stone to the cooking pot for her family. The heat from the stone would cook the soup. All of the families would cook their soup this way at the same time so that they could enjoy meals together."

Since variations of this recipe have been served in North America for thousands of years, it could easily be said that this soup is the truly iconic American meal. The simple spices allow the vegetables to add their own flavors. This dish is a great celebration of the harvest with the various squashes, onions, peppers, green beans, and tomatoes all ripening together.

Kitchen Passport There is no set recipe for this soup, which can become a base for other soups. If one of the vegetables isn't to your liking, replace it with something that is. Add meat if you want or replace the water with broth or tomato juice. Smoked peppers or canned chipotles in adobo will add extra heat. This is also a soup that only gets better with reheating, so freezing any leftovers will make wonderful meals later on.

1 large butternut squash (about 2 pounds)

1 acorn squash (about 1 pound)

1 tablespoon olive oil

1 medium yellow onion, diced (about
⅔ cup)

2 cloves garlic, minced (about 1 teaspoon)

½ medium green or red bell pepper, cut
into short, narrow strips (about ½ cup)

½ rib of celery, chopped (about ¼ cup)

2 (28-ounce) cans yellow or white
hominy corn

2 (15-ounce) cans pinto beans

4 medium red potatoes, peeled and
diced (about 1 pound unpeeled)

½ medium tomato, chopped (about ½ cup)

1 medium zucchini, quartered then sliced
into ½ inch rounds (about ¾ cup)

2 cups fresh green beans, trimmed
and snapped into 1-inch pieces
(about ½ pound)

¼ teaspoon crushed red pepper,
or more to taste

1 teaspoon rubbed sage

2 tablespoons unsalted butter, softened

2 tablespoons all-purpose flour

2 teaspoons salt

½ teaspoon freshly ground black pepper

Preheat the oven to 400 degrees.

Cut the butternut squash and acorn squash in half lengthwise and remove the seeds and fibers. Place the halves, cut side up, in a shallow baking dish and cover with aluminum foil. Bake the squash for 45 minutes or until easily pierced with a knife but still firm.

When the squash are cool enough to handle, scoop out the pulp from the skin and cut into pieces no larger than 1 inch by 1 inch. Reserve the pulp and discard the skins.

Heat the oil in a large skillet over medium-low heat.

Add the onion and cook, stirring frequently, for about 5 minutes or until the onion is translucent.

Add the garlic, bell pepper, and celery to the skillet and continue to cook, stirring frequently, until the onion is golden, about 3 minutes.

Add the hominy and beans to a large stockpot. Add the reserved squash pulp and the cooked vegetables to the hominy and beans. Add the potatoes, tomato, zucchini, green beans, crushed red pepper, and sage to the pot and add water to cover all of the vegetables.

Bring the soup to a boil over medium-high heat. Reduce the heat to low and simmer gently, covered, for 30 minutes or until all the vegetables are tender.

Combine the butter and flour into a thick paste. Stir the paste into the soup.

Increase the heat to medium-high and cook for an additional 15 minutes to allow the soup to thicken.

Season to taste with salt and black pepper.

Poppy Tooker,
New Orleans,
Louisiana

*Calas, calas, belles
calas, toutes chaudes,
madames, belle calas,
toutes chaudes!*
—Cry of the New
Orleans calas women
in bygone days

Under the Code Noir, slaves in New Orleans were given at least one day off each week. Many of them used this day to earn money by making calas, sweetened rice fritters, and selling them in the streets of New Orleans. Calas were very important to slave women. The income from the calas allowed women to buy not only their own freedom but also the freedom of their families.

Even after slavery ended, calas were sold by street vendors until they vanished from the streets of New Orleans during World War II. While no one can pinpoint an exact reason, this may have been because of food rationing or because of the other income opportunities that the war created for the calas makers.

Calas needed a champion, a savior, and Poppy Tooker stepped up to be just that. Poppy, a New Orleans native, has worked for years to preserve the culture and cuisine of Louisiana. As one of the driving forces behind Market Umbrella, she has promoted local farmers and farmers' markets as well as the White Boot Brigade, a project that has brought Louisiana shrimpers to national attention. She also works with Slow Food USA's Ark of Taste to highlight the importance of preserving the nation's endangered foods. The Ark of Taste's motto is "Eat it to save it," and that's how Poppy is saving calas.

"It almost became extinct because it was only a street food tradition. It was never sold from a stand like beignets. The only way you would know about the calas was if you had them as a tradition in your family," she says.

Poppy remembers how she fell in love with calas and decided to start the work of saving this important piece of New Orleans history. "I just thought they tasted good, and they were a lovely thing, and they were a lot easier to make than beignets. I didn't really begin to investigate their cultural significance or realize how important they were to the city's history until I did a festival at the Audubon Zoo," she says.

She was asked to make classic New Orleans food and serve it at the festival, so she chose to serve frozen Creole cream cheese and calas. "On the very first day, one of my very first customers was an older gentleman who came up to the booth and bought some calas." This man made Poppy realize just how important calas are. "He took a few steps away and took a bite. Then he came back to the booth with tears in his eyes, and he said to me, 'Lady, my mama used to make these for me all the time when I was a little boy. I had completely forgotten all about this until just now. Could you please tell me how you did this?'" she recalls.

"And that was my life-changing food moment, because it was so clear that the taste of the calas brought this man's mother back alive to him. It so illustrated that the sense of taste, the sense of smell—these are the things that are most evocative to the human spirit, the things that tie us all together and make us human." 🙶

CALAS

Active cooking time: 30 minutes | Total cooking time: 1 hour | Yield: 12 calas

Calas are, in many ways, the perfect metaphor for New Orleans. They originated in Africa and Europe independently but didn't truly flourish until they reached New Orleans. Despite their rich history, calas fell on hard times and were almost lost to us. Like their city, however, calas are resurgent as people like Poppy Tooker bring them back to the table.

2 cups cooked white rice

6 tablespoons all-purpose flour

4 teaspoons granulated sugar

2 teaspoons baking powder

½ teaspoon salt

¼ teaspoon freshly grated nutmeg

2 large eggs

¼ teaspoon vanilla extract

Peanut or soy oil

Powdered sugar

In a large mixing bowl, combine the rice, flour, granulated sugar, baking powder, salt, and nutmeg. Stir the eggs and vanilla into the rice mixture until thoroughly combined. Refrigerate the rice mixture for 30 minutes.

Using a deep pot or a deep-fat fryer, heat at least 3 inches of oil to 360 degrees.

Carefully drop the chilled rice mixture into the hot oil by spoonfuls. Fry the calas for 5 minutes or until they are brown on all sides.

Drain the calas on paper towels and sprinkle with powdered sugar.

Kitchen Passport Calas are wonderful treats alone, but there are some delicious variations. Mix cocoa powder or cinnamon into the powdered sugar before dusting the hot calas, or thin your favorite jelly by heating it in a pot over low heat with a small amount of water and glaze the hot calas with it as soon as they come out of the fryer.

Try making a chocolate sauce by mixing equal parts of sugar and unsweetened cocoa powder. Gradually stir in hot water until the sauce reaches the desired consistency. Serve it alongside the calas for dipping.

B. J. Chester-Tamayo was born in the small town of Meridian, Mississippi. While she's been cooking soul food professionally in her downtown Memphis restaurant, Alcenia's, for over twelve years, she says that she's been "dibbling and dabbling" with cooking for at least twenty-five years.

She was brought up on "good southern cooking" that her mother prepared, feasts that celebrated the seasons and local flavors. Some of the dishes she remembers best include fresh corn, yams, potato salad, roast with gravy, fresh crowder peas, buttermilk, cornbread, and apple cobbler that was so good it "would make you want to slap somebody."

B. J. learned to cook by watching her mother. In her restaurant today, she uses many of the simple dishes she learned to make growing up, serving them as soul food to her customers. She explains soul food as food cooked with intention. "Soul food is about how you really feel about what you want and what you want people to take away from that meal. That's what food here is to me; making it is an action to show how you care about people, how you love them." 🍵

GREENS

Active cooking time: 30 minutes | Total cooking time: 3 hours | Yield: 4 1-cup servings

Collards. Mustard. Turnip. A mess o' greens.

The first greens cooked by enslaved Africans in the South were likely cast-off turnip greens or the collard greens they brought to the South with them. Other greens were available, though, and did become part of the slave diet in part because they grow well in the South, even well into the winter. In addition to turnip and collard greens, mustard greens are very popular, and all of them are a great part of southern cuisine today.

Collards are the mildest greens with an almost creamy flavor. Turnip greens are more bitter and also tend to be stringy. Mustards are also more bitter, but they tend to have a spicy flavor.

A mess o' greens is defined as a serving of greens large enough to feed your family.

This recipe can easily be doubled if you have a big family or a family of big eaters. The recipe works well for any of these greens or a combination of the greens. Even spinach works, but cut the cooking time back to about ten minutes for spinach because it is so much more tender than the other greens.

According to B. J., you really can't overcook greens as long as you don't let the water cook away. When you are seasoning your greens, err on the side of caution. As she says, "You can always add more, but once it's in there . . ." Greens can obviously be prepared as a vegetarian dish, but B. J. always prepares her greens with meat. "Some people say they don't use any meat in their greens. I don't know how they do that."

2 pounds collard greens or mixed
   turnip and mustard greens
   (about 3 bunches)
1 medium yellow onion, chopped
   (about ⅔ cup)
1 ham hock or 1 pound smoked
   turkey pieces
3 teaspoons Greek seasoning blend
½ teaspoon crushed red pepper
4 teaspoons salt
Pinch of sugar

TO SERVE
Chow-chow (tomato relish)
   or pickled tomatoes

Wash the greens thoroughly and remove the tough stems and ribs.

Slice the greens into 1-inch wide ribbons or keep the leaves whole. Place the greens in a stockpot and add the onion to the greens.

Rinse the ham hock in cold water to remove any excess salt and add it to the pot with the greens and onion. Add the Greek seasoning, crushed red pepper, salt, and a pinch of sugar. Add 1 gallon of water to the pot.

Cook over medium heat until the greens are tender, about 2½ to 3 hours.

Season to taste with salt.

Serve in bowls with plenty of potlikker, the cooking liquid, for sopping with cornbread. Serve chow-chow or pickled tomatoes on the side.

Kitchen Passport So you've tried greens before and didn't like them? You're not alone. They're an acquired taste.

The younger your greens are, the less bitter they will be. To reduce bitterness, you can pour off some of the cooking liquid and replace it with fresh water halfway through the cooking time. Don't pour off too much liquid, though, because that liquid, the potlikker, is as valuable a taste treat as the greens themselves. All you need are some hoecakes (recipe follows) to soak up the potlikker. This is one of those cases where sopping is not only acceptable but encouraged.

Another way to cut the bitterness is to add more sugar—just a pinch at a time because a little can go a long way and no one wants sweet greens. Make them spicier if you like. Experiment with using different fresh peppers or hot sauces instead of the crushed red pepper flakes.

If you want to prepare your greens without using meat, add a tablespoon of vegetable shortening or butter to give the greens the richer flavor that the fat from the meat provides in this recipe.

If you're still not a fan of greens and potlikker, try this method. Bring a large pot of salted water to a boil. Blanch the greens by cooking them in the boiling water for 2 minutes and then immediately transferring them to a bowl of ice water. This way you'll have tender greens after only a brief time in the skillet. Cook 4 to 6 slices of bacon in a large skillet over medium heat. Transfer the bacon to a paper-towel-lined plate, leaving the grease in the pan. Cook the greens, stirring constantly, in the skillet with the bacon grease for 10 minutes. Crumble the bacon back into them and finish them with a pat of butter for a decadent treat.

HOECAKES

Active cooking time: 20 minutes | Total cooking time: 20 minutes | Yield: 12 hoecakes

Cornbread is a cornerstone of southern cuisine. It was originally considered a food of the poor in the South because cornmeal was much less expensive than the wheat flour used to make biscuits. Today, cornmeal is as prized as wheat flour; truth be told, stone-ground cornmeal is even more of a delicacy and is worth searching out.

The cornbread most of us eat today is not the same as the cornbread of the past. We bake cornbread in cast iron skillets or as muffins or sticks. Our cornbread is light and fluffy because we leaven it. When feeding themselves, slaves did not commonly have access to ovens or pans or leavening agents. Their cornbread was typically in the form of crispy flat cakes, consisting only of cornmeal, salt, and water. It would have been baked on any available hot, flat surface.

Typically, these flat cakes are called hoecakes. One theory on the origin of the name is that the hoe blade, used when working in the cotton fields, also provided a surface on which to cook these cakes. Having no access to even a skillet, a slave would have held the blade over an open flame. These cakes are also called hot water cornbread. Because of the quick cooking time, the hot water is needed to help partially cook the cornmeal before the batter is poured on the griddle.

Even though we have kitchens full of modern conveniences, there is still a place for hot water cornbread. Baking it on a griddle or in a skillet gives it a crisp, flavorfully browned exterior while the interior is dense and moist, perfect for munching on by itself or for sopping up potlikker with a big mess o' greens.

Potlikker

Simply enough, potlikker is the juices that come from greens while they are cooked. So why does something so simple have such a major role in the culinary traditions of the South?

It originated as a way to get the most from the greens. Because they cook for so long, a great deal of the nutrients in greens ends up in the cooking liquid. For the well-fed plantation owners, only the greens, not potlikker or homely cornbread, were served at the fine tables of the antebellum South. The potlikker went to the slaves who prepared the greens, and for them, these nutrients were important.

For those who got only the potlikker, cornbread was crumbled into it to make a tasty, nutritious, and filling meal. Even for those who had greens as well, it would not have been uncommon to use extra potlikker to make a second meal in this way.

After slavery, potlikker and cornbread were the foods of the poor in the South, both black and white. Poverty doesn't know color, and neither does hunger. In the era of sharecroppers and through the Great Depression, this simple meal was all too often the only food that kept children from starvation.

Potlikker was also a cure. In the days before pharmaceutical companies, doctors

2 cups stone-ground cornmeal

2 teaspoons salt

3 cups boiling water

4 tablespoons shortening or bacon
   drippings

Mix the cornmeal and salt in a large bowl. Carefully pour the boiling water onto the cornmeal mixture. Stir until a soft batter forms, adding more boiling water if necessary.

Heat the shortening or bacon drippings in a heavy skillet over medium heat.

Carefully pour ¼ cup batter into the heated shortening as you would to make pancakes. Cook for 2 minutes or until the edges start to brown.

Flip the hoecakes and continue cooking an additional 2 minutes or until both sides are golden brown. Repeat until all of the batter is used.

Serve alone with softened butter or with greens (previous recipe) and potlikker.

> **Kitchen Passport** Hoecakes don't have to be so simple. You can add chopped green onions to the batter for extra flavor, fresh sweet corn for texture, or cracklings (also known as "cracklins") for both.
>
> What are cracklings? They're pieces of pork fat and skin, fried until they're crispy and golden. If you don't have access to cracklings, you can crumble in pork rinds or cooked bacon.

actually prescribed the nutrient-rich liquid to treat a host of ailments. Considering the vitamin content of the potlikker, it certainly didn't hurt those for whom it was prescribed and in fact probably did a great deal of good without costing a great deal of money.

Later on, potlikker became political. Sharing potlikker was a way for a politician to show that he was no better than his constituents. He was just a normal person who understood what it was like to have nothing more to eat. He was one of them, and he would stand up for them. Potlikker reached its peak in politics when Senator Huey Long of Louisiana spoke on it elo-quently in 1935 during a fifteen-and-a-half-hour filibuster.

Potlikker came to be embraced at all social levels of the South as a way of expressing pride in being southern, pride despite poverty. It finally found its place on the fine tables of the South where once it was as unwelcome as the people who first prepared it. Most important, it became a food that was shared by all southerners, regardless of race or class, a food that brought everyone to the table together.

Jim Romero owns a bakery, Jim's Kountry Pies, in Coteau, Louisiana, south of Lafayette, deep in the heart of Cajun country. Jim's bakery is on Romero Road on land granted to his ancestors by the king of Spain in the 1600s; however, he has stronger ties to his Acadian ancestors who settled in Louisiana in the late 1700s.

Jim calls the exodus from Acadia "the Deportation." It was the largest migration of the Cajun people until Hurricane Katrina in 2005. "Families were busted up and a lot of the men were killed because they didn't want to leave, and yet twenty years later they were all in south Louisiana. Most families here know of it, but they don't know much about it," he says.

That was the start, though, of Cajun life in southern Louisiana. The same people who had adapted to life in Nova Scotia adapted quickly to life along the bayous. They blended with the Spanish who had settled the region as well as with the Native Americans already there and the Africans and Germans who came later.

You can hear all those influences in Jim's soft, lilting voice. His connection to this place, like that of many of the families in the region, goes deep. "We're just ordinary people, just happen to have our roots here, and we're not leaving. We want to stay here and continue our lifestyle and our method of cooking," he says. And it's that method of cooking that has brought the region onto the international stage as a culinary destination.

While Cajun traditions have been a part of Louisiana for centuries, the Cajun people were one of the most isolated and forgotten minorities of the South until the last half of the twentieth century. Both of Jim's grandmothers spoke only Cajun French, never having had a reason to learn English. As he tells it, "I never really looked at being different until I went into the service. Then I could speak the language of the people in Europe where I was." That was because Cajun French is a patois language, importing words from the languages of other immigrants who came to southern Louisiana.

At his bakery, he makes some of the best pies in the United States. Jim also keeps Cajun culinary traditions alive everyday in his meals. He reminds us that Cajun cooking is not about spiciness. "We would rather put in the trinity over the high seasoned stuff." The trinity is celery, green bell pepper, and onion. It is such a staple in the region that it's sold in local supermarkets in pre-cut, pre-measured packages. And it truly is the backbone of flavor in every savory Cajun dish.

Jim comes from a line of cooks. "I remember not having sliced bread until I was maybe ten or twelve years old. Mama would bake biscuits, bread, pancakes. And that's where I learned to do for me, too, when I'd come home from school. I still love pancakes today. But all made from scratch. There was no mixes. I had to make do with what I had. That's what a cook does."

Even now, his family gathers every Sunday at his godmother's home, everyone bringing a dish to share—and nothing picked up from a store. Those dishes are a part of their shared heritage, a part of what keeps them connected to the past. "You lose touch when you quit making something," Jim says.

With his pies and his stories, Jim makes everyone he meets feel just a little bit Cajun and a little bit like family. He makes you feel privileged to get to spend even a few moments in his world, a place where "being Cajun is just a part of life." The names of the Cajuns who brought their heritage into the cooking world's spotlight are well known: Justin Wilson, John Folse, Paul Prudhomme, Marcelle Bienvenu. But Jim is as much an emissary of his way of life as they are. As he says, "I just enjoy time with people. That's where we can touch one family at a time." 🐚

CRAWFISH ÉTOUFFÉE

Active cooking time: 1 hour, 10 minutes | Total cooking time: 1 hour, 45 minutes | Yield: 8 main dish servings

When early humans were searching for food, certain choices seem obvious: a juicy berry on a bush, small game struck down with a stone from a slingshot. Other things? Well, not so much. For instance, what intrepid soul first took it upon himself to find a way to crack open an oyster? And who decided to go face-to-face with a swamp beast that makes the alligator seem tame? Yes, who ate the first crawfish?

No matter what name you call them— crawfish, crayfish, crawdad, or mudbug— they are fearsome beasts with lightning-quick claws that freely express their displeasure with your dining intentions. Still, whoever first made a meal of mudbugs did us all a favor.

Today, Louisiana produces 90 percent of the domestic crop of crawfish, anywhere from 75 million to 105 million pounds annually. Some crawfish are pond-raised. Others are harvested from natural wetlands, primarily in the Atchafalaya Basin, the heart of Cajun country. Louisiana also produces the finest recipes utilizing crawfish, from simply boiled to the richness of an étouffée.

Although, in French, *étouffée* literally means "smothered," "enrobed" is a good word for the dish. "Swaddled" may be an even better word. A Cajun étouffée is a sometimes-spicy, roux-based dish. It is cooked down more than a gumbo and thus is thicker. This luxuriant gravy clings to the crawfish like a delicious blanket.

Jim is quick to correct a common misconception about crawfish étouffée. "If you go to New Orleans, everything they got is red. Jambalayas, crawfish étouffées, everything is red. Down here, the tomatoes are left out. We like our fresh tomatoes over putting it in the dishes. I fix crawfish étouffée for people when they come to visit and they tell me, 'Well, there's something missing.' I say, 'Taste it, and then tell me if there's something missing.' The only thing missing is the color. The flavors are wonderful. And no cornstarch in it like I know some of the people do. It's all made with a roux."

3 pounds whole fresh crawfish or 2 pounds
     crawfish tails, thawed if frozen
½ cup vegetable oil
1 medium yellow onion, diced (about
     ⅔ cup)
½ medium green bell pepper, seeded and
     minced (about ½ cup)
2 ribs celery, minced (about 1 cup)
2 cloves garlic, minced (about 1 teaspoon)
½ cup all-purpose flour
1 tablespoon unsalted butter
4 cups crawfish stock or chicken broth
1½ teaspoons salt
½ to ¾ teaspoon ground cayenne pepper
¼ teaspoon freshly ground black pepper
½ cup green onions, chopped
     (3 to 4 onions)

TO SERVE
Cooked white rice
Fresh parsley, chopped

If you are using fresh crawfish, separate the heads from the bodies and remove the meat from the tail and reserve. Make a crawfish stock by boiling the heads, claws, and shells from the tails in 5 cups of water for 15 to 20 minutes. Strain the liquid and reserve.

Heat the vegetable oil in a large, heavy pot over medium heat. Add the onion, bell pepper, and celery to the oil and cook, stirring constantly, for 5 minutes or until the onion is translucent.

Add the garlic to the pot. Stir in the flour until smooth. Continue cooking over medium heat, stirring constantly, for 20 minutes or until the roux is a light brown, about the color of peanut butter.

Add the butter to the vegetables, stirring until melted.

Gradually stir in the reserved crawfish stock or chicken broth ¼ cup at a time, being sure the first ¼ cup is thoroughly combined before adding the next ¼ cup. If you add all of the liquid at once, the roux will form lumps and will not thicken the sauce properly.

Stir in the salt, cayenne pepper, and black pepper.

Bring the mixture to a boil over medium-high heat, stirring constantly. Reduce the heat to low and simmer the mixture, uncovered, for 20 minutes or until the sauce has thickened.

Stir in the green onions and crawfish tails and simmer for another 5 minutes.

To serve, ladle a generous portion of the étouffée around 1 cup cooked rice. Garnish with freshly chopped parsley.

Roux

One of the basic ingredients in many Cajun recipes is roux. Roux is very simple on the surface but very complex in its usage. Simply put, a roux is nothing more than equal parts of flour and fat, stirred until smooth and cooked until the flour loses its raw flavor. It's the same technique used in French cuisine to thicken béchamel sauce, but Cajun cuisine takes roux to whole new levels.

It's all about the color of the roux. A white roux is over the heat just long enough for the flour to be cooked but not so long that it darkens. It adds very little flavor but has the most thickening power. The darker the roux, the less it thickens; however, the darker the roux, the more flavor it adds.

The next step is a blond roux where the flour has only slightly browned. Blond roux doesn't add a lot of flavor, but its presence in a dish is more obvious than a white roux. Next is a peanut butter roux, named because the finished version is the color of peanut butter. At this stage, the roux will add a nutty flavor and noticeable color.

A good fat for most roux is butter, since the roux won't cook long enough to worry about the butter burning. This is not true for chocolate roux. This roux adds even more flavor, but until you have had a lot of practice, it should be made with vegetable oil because butter will burn easily before the roux reaches the desired color. A final stage of roux is called brick. A product of a roux master, this roux stops just short of the next stage, charred.

There are two schools of thought on how to cook a roux. On one hand, you will be told to cook your roux slowly over low heat. On the other, you're told to cook your roux quickly over high heat. Both methods require you to stir the roux constantly. So why not take the quick method? Well, it's very easy to burn a roux over high heat, and once it has burned, it's not going to be usable. Quick may sound better, but it takes practice to get it right.

Roux can be made in advance and refrigerated in a sealed container until you're ready to use it. Just heat it up before using it in your recipe.

Hearing firsthand from these keepers of the flame about some of the trials and tribulations that have affected their lives, we recognize that the growth of the United States came at a high price for many. Complex issues don't find easy solutions. Troubling ideas don't vanish. Nonetheless, time moves on and change comes. Immigration continues because the South today has unprecedented opportunities for change and for growth. New generations of immigrants are coming to the United States not just to take advantage of these opportunities but to drive them, to create them. We see this change all around us, and it heartens us. That is why we undertook this journey—to see what is becoming of our beloved home and to get a glimpse of what the future holds.

The people you will meet in the next chapters will be part of that future. Immigration to the United States as a whole has increased dramatically since the end of the Vietnam War, and the South has become a home for many of the people who come for a new life, a better life. As the southern cuisine we know today evolved from the contributions of past immigrants, these new immigrants will leave their mark on the southern cuisine of the future, and a tasty future it will be.

Part I
Seeking the American Dream

In Mexico, no money, no honey, no funny.
In America, sí money, sí honey, sí funny.
—Traditional Mexican saying shared by Antonio,
an illegal Mexican immigrant, Tennessee

Mexico Up by the Bootstraps

"Have you eaten with us before?"

Pepe and Jonathan Magallanes greet every guest at Las Tortugas Deli Mexicana with brilliant smiles and that simple question. Pepe doesn't look at the restaurant as a place where he serves customers; for him, it's an extension of his home. Visitors are guests, not customers. He is as likely to be sitting at a table with one of his guests as he is to be behind the register or the grill. When he's sitting at a table, though, he's not taking a break. He's educating that guest about authentic Mexican cuisine and about why he chose to serve his version of the street food of Mexico City.

Pepe and Jonathan Magallanes, Germantown, Tennessee

One story goes that a guest once walked into the restaurant for the first time and tried to order without looking at the menu. He asked for a bean burrito. An hour later, he left the restaurant with a full stomach and a new appreciation for the fresh flavors of authentic Mexican cuisine. He's been a regular customer ever since.

After meeting Pepe, that story is not so hard to believe. When asked about his restaurant, the first thing he'll tell you is that he is not a chef. A retired mining engineer with no formal culinary training, he comes at food from a different angle from most restaurateurs. As he tells it, "The reason for our success was my lack of knowledge of the restaurant business. That's it." If he had known more about the restaurant business, he might have been tempted to take shortcuts. He might have considered his profit margin over quality. He might have tried to cater to the existing tastes of his customers instead of trying to offer them something unique.

He and his team prepare every item from scratch every day with an eye for excellence and exactitude. That eye comes from Pepe's engineering training and expresses his philosophy of quality above every other concern. They create food inspired by the simple fare of the taqueria but worthy of any fine dining restaurant. As Pepe says, "What we do on the grill is not difficult. What's difficult is to do it right always and to care. If we don't care, we don't need to be here."

That level of care is why Pepe's son Jonathan shops personally to choose fresh ingredients every day instead of ordering ingredients in bulk that could be delivered to the restaurant door. It's why he and

Pepe and Jonathan Magallanes at Las Tortugas Deli Mexicana.

Pepe work with local farms to serve beef, pork, and eggs of the highest quality while supporting other businesses in their community. It's why their specials come from the recipes Pepe learned as a child.

Unlike many immigrants, Pepe didn't open a restaurant because he needed a source of income. He had retired and was living comfortably. The restaurant came about because of his love of great food. He missed the fare of Mexico City, and he knew that if it were prepared with quality ingredients and traditional methods, other people would learn to love it as much as he does.

He taught those same values to Jonathan, who now owns the restaurant. Like his father, Jonathan had never planned to be a restaurateur. He had been working in sales and was looking for a career change not long after Pepe opened Las Tortugas. As he tells it, "In my downtime, I started helping him out and just eventually sort of fell in love with it."

Unlike Pepe, Jonathan did have some restaurant experience, as both a server and as a manager. "All those things I learned about service, and all the things I learned about the way that you talk about the food and present the food to people and the way you don't take orders but you lead people to what they should order—all of those things that I had accumulated, what I had thought were basically useless skills—I'm using all of them now," he says. "And that was a revelation to me because I realized that it's so beautiful, that God has a plan for your life, and you don't even know what that plan is until it starts happening to you. And so I felt like it was meant to be."

Jonathan sees several possibilities for the restaurant's future, including expansion of the existing location or a second location. But for him, those are lesser concerns. "I would say that the future is to remain obsessed with the quality of the food. That's what I'm certain the future is about, to never really rest on your laurels."

He takes his philosophy from his father and also from his friend Chef Kelly English, a James Beard Foundation Award nominee. "Kelly tells his staff, 'The only thing we've done is set a level of expectation for people when they come in here. That's it. We haven't done anything else,'" Jonathan says.

Jonathan was raised in Memphis and is a true southerner. He recalls an early dining experience that has stayed with him: "When I was young, my mom would cook salmon croquettes with black-eyed peas and cornbread. And to me, that's just my most memorable meal. That's it." Since then, he's eaten plenty of fabulous dishes in some of the best restaurants in the United States, but there's one aspect of his mother's cooking that those meals can never match for him. "The person cooking it for you doesn't love you. There's something about food that's being made with love for the person who's being served that makes it memorable."

Love is the secret of the success of Las Tortugas. Pepe opened the restaurant to serve the food he loves, and Jonathan came to love it just as much. That passion is as much a part of the flavor as any seasoning. And as Jonathan says, "There's something about when your heart is tied in." 🐢

COSTILLAS DE DON FELIX (Don Felix's Pork Ribs)

Active cooking time: 1 hour | Total cooking time: 3 hours, 30 minutes | Yield: 6 servings

Memphis, Tennessee, is widely recognized as the pork barbecue capital of the world, but when Pepe thinks of ribs, he doesn't consider the smoked and seasoned ones he can get where he is today. As he says, "I love the ribs in Memphis because they're different from what I'm used to, and they're really good. But a lot of what you're enjoying is the sauce that somebody makes." He thinks instead about the pork ribs he learned to prepare with his grandfather Don Felix at his ranch in Aguascalientes, Mexico.

Everywhere in the world, stories are shared with children in kitchens and over fires while recipes are passed along. The stories become a part of the recipes. Don Felix told Pepe about being part of the Mexican revolution, and Pepe shared this same story with Jonathan.

Pepe says, "My grandfather actually fought in the revolution for Mexico with Francisco Villa, called Pancho Villa. Francisco Villa in Mexico is a hero. For American people he is not because they were fighting against each other, so . . . But everybody has his opinion, and that's why America is so great. The ribs are named for Don Felix. That's the name of them because my grandfather taught me how to make these when I was about nine years old."

You may want to sit down before you read this recipe. As Pepe puts it, "It's a matter of health. The more we cook them, the more the fat of the pork gets burned out of the ribs." So that's good. However, this is not everyday food. After all, the first thing Pepe says about his grandfather's *costillas* is, "The most important ingredient that goes into the *costillas* is pork lard."

Yes. Lard. And this is not a recipe where you would want to use anything else. Vegetable shortening or peanut oil won't give you the same results. The ribs just won't taste right. If it helps, think of this as a French confit translated to the cuisine of Mexico. After all, a confit is simply cooking a meat slowly in its own fat, and that's really all you do here.

One thing to keep in mind is the quality of the lard. You never want to buy shelf-stable lard. It has additives that change the flavor, and not in a good way. Instead, you want to find refrigerated lard. Ask for it at the butcher's counter in your local supermarket or for *manteca* in a Hispanic market.

8 pounds pork lard

2 racks meaty pork baby back ribs,
    separated into 4-bone sections

2 whole oranges

2 whole limes

2 bay leaves

2 whole jalapeño peppers

4 limes, halved

Salt to taste

TO SERVE

Fresh salsa

Corn tortillas

Kitchen Passport There's not a lot to change in the technique of preparing these ribs. The main variations in flavor are going to come into play after they've cooked. If you would like to accent the pork with a sweet flavor, consider using mango, peach, or pineapple salsa with them. If you like spicier food, try drizzling over a chile paste or Mexican hot sauce.

Don't throw out the darkened lard, either. According to Pepe, the ribs taste better the more times you use the lard. It can also make for some excellent fried chicken. Just strain it and refrigerate it in a sealed container. Use it within a month or freeze it to last up to six months.

Melt the lard in a deep, heavy pot over medium heat, about 10 minutes.

Add the rib sections to the lard along with the whole oranges, whole limes, bay leaves, and jalapeño peppers. Keep the heat at medium and cook for 2 hours.

Remove and discard the fruit, bay leaves, and peppers. Lift out the rib sections and place them on a tray to rest for at least 30 minutes.

Skim off and discard any solids that have risen to the surface of the lard. At this point, you can refrigerate the ribs and lard separately to finish the process another day, if desired.

When you're ready to continue with the recipe, prepare a tray with a cooling rack positioned over it for the finished ribs. Place the lime halves and salt close to the rack.

Increase the heat to medium-high and cook the lard for 15 minutes or until it turns a deep brown. This will produce smoke, so be prepared.

Working in batches of no more than 2 sections, carefully return the ribs to the darkened lard. Cook the rib sections for 7 to 10 minutes or until crisped, depending on the thickness of the ribs.

Carefully lift out the rib sections and transfer them to the cooling rack. Immediately squeeze the juice of a halved lime over each section and sprinkle with salt. Repeat until all of the ribs have been crisped.

Spoon fresh salsa over each rib section and serve with hot corn tortillas.

Armando
Rodriguez,
Mobile,
Alabama

Entering any of Armando Rodriguez's Mobile area restaurants is like stepping into a different world for a little while. Armando has taken great pains with the decor in his Hacienda San Miguel locations to create an environment reminiscent of the beauty of his homeland.

Armando came to Mobile in 1990 from Queretaro, Mexico, a historic city north of Mexico City. For him, opening a restaurant was a natural step. While most children aren't thinking about their future employment, much less actually working, Armando began his culinary career at the age of nine when he took a job in a small restaurant in Queretaro. He's been cooking ever since. "I've been a cook a long time, and most of my family—well, part of my family—are in the business. I have a cousin in Louisiana who came with me to the Mobile area. He is in the same business in the Hammond region. So I think it's part of my family."

Even though Armando's family works with food and he got his start cooking Mexican cuisine, he learned restaurant management skills not in a small local establishment but in a U.S.-based chain restaurant. When he was seventeen, Showbiz Pizza in Queretaro sent him through its management training program and gave him his first experience as a manager in a large restaurant. He laughs now thinking about working in a pizzeria, but he learned valuable skills there that would help him when he opened his own restaurant, especially the skill of successfully selling a type of food that the people of a city might not be used to eating.

Armando had family in Mobile before he arrived, but the city does not have a particularly large Mexican immigrant community. When Armando opened Hacienda San Miguel, he wanted to serve authentic Mexican cuisine but knew most of his customers were familiar only with Tex-Mex food like hard-shelled tacos, burritos, and chimichangas. "As we've grown our business, we've been trying to include some part of the most authentic dishes of Mexico. So I think it has changed what people here are willing to try."

Now Armando has found a middle ground between the food locals expected and the food he wants to serve in his restaurants. In buildings made with stone imported from Queretaro, diners can choose well-prepared Tex-Mex food or opt for more authentic dishes like mole poblano or *huachinango a la veracruzana*. He takes pride in being able to say, "All those authentic Mexican dishes that you can only eat in Mexico? Now you can enjoy those dishes here in our restaurants."

Of course, freshness is paramount to good food, but the real element that sets Armando's food apart is care. The only difference between food at the restaurant and the food he eats at home is the level of

Armando Rodriguez at Hacienda San Miguel.

spiciness and the amount. "At home we use the same spices, just not as much. And of course, right here in the restaurant is where I tell my cooks that everything we cook has to be cooked as if it was going to be for us." ❧

TEX-MEX ENCHILADAS

Active cooking time: 1 hour, 35 minutes | Total cooking time: 2 hours | Yield: 12 enchiladas or 4 servings

Any Tex-Mex menu is sure to feature enchiladas, but really great Tex-Mex enchiladas are hard to find. They're worth the search, though. While the enchilada has been a favorite food in Mexico for cen-turies, those enchiladas are not the same as the ones with which most Americans have become familiar. Armando's recipe is a favorite of his customers in Mobile.

Making your own enchilada sauce makes

all the difference. You'll notice that the flavor is much richer than canned or jarred sauces from the supermarket. This recipe produces savory enchiladas that aren't too spicy. Serve them with refried beans and guacamole for a perfect Tex-Mex meal.

FOR THE ENCHILADA SAUCE

1 tablespoon corn oil
1 medium white onion, minced
　(about ⅔ cup)
1 clove garlic, minced (about ½ teaspoon)
1 teaspoon ground cumin
1 teaspoon ground chipotle pepper
1 teaspoon salt
1 cup chicken broth
2 bay leaves
1 (15-ounce) can tomato sauce
4 tablespoons all-purpose flour
5 tablespoons water
Juice of half a lime (about 1 tablespoon)
　(optional)

FOR THE FILLING

1 tablespoon corn oil
1 medium white onion, diced (about
　⅔ cup)
2 cloves garlic, minced (about 1 teaspoon)
1½ pounds ground beef or 1½ pounds
　shredded cooked chicken
½ teaspoon ground cumin
1 teaspoon Mexican oregano
1 teaspoon salt
½ teaspoon freshly ground black pepper
½ cup water

TO PREPARE THE SAUCE

Heat the corn oil in a large saucepan over medium-high heat.

Add the onion, garlic, cumin, chipotle pepper, and salt to the corn oil and cook, stirring frequently, for 3 minutes or until the onion is translucent.

Carefully pour in the chicken broth, stirring to loosen any stuck bits of onion. Add the bay leaves and bring the broth to a boil, stirring frequently. Reduce the heat to low and allow the broth and onion mixture to simmer for 30 minutes.

Remove the bay leaves and stir in the tomato sauce.

At this point, the enchilada sauce can be refrigerated or even frozen for later use. Bring the sauce to room temperature before completing the sauce recipe.

In a bowl, whisk the flour into the water. Be sure to whisk thoroughly to remove all lumps. Stir the flour mixture into the tomato mixture. Add the lime juice if desired.

Raise the heat to medium and bring the sauce to a boil. Cook the sauce, stirring constantly, for 15 minutes or until the sauce is thickened.

Keep the sauce over low heat until ready to use.

TO PREPARE THE FILLING

Heat the corn oil in a large skillet over medium-high heat.

Add the onion to the corn oil and cook, stirring frequently, for 3 minutes or until the onion is translucent.

Add the garlic to the onion and cook for an additional 2 minutes.

1 cup corn oil

12 corn tortillas

1 cup sharp cheddar cheese, shredded
   (about 4 ounces)

TO SERVE

½ small red onion, minced (about ⅓ cup)

½ cup fresh cilantro, chopped (about
   1 ounce)

Kitchen Passport For a twist on the enchilada sauce in this recipe, replace the tomato sauce with an equal amount of salsa verde, salsa made with tomatillos. If you want a spicier sauce, try using an equal amount of salsa picante found in most Hispanic markets.

For fillings, consider shrimp or shredded beef. Cook them using the same method that the recipe specifies. If you want an even easier filling, roll your tortillas around a generous helping of refried beans, cheddar cheese, or, for more authentically Mexican flavor, queso quesadilla or even queso blanco.

Add the ground beef or chicken to the onion along with the cumin, oregano, salt, and black pepper. Continue to cook, stirring frequently, for 10 minutes or until the beef is cooked through or the chicken has warmed completely.

Add the water carefully to the meat mixture. Bring the water to a boil and continue cooking, stirring frequently, for 5 minutes or until the water has been absorbed into the meat mixture.

Remove the meat from the heat.

The prepared filling can also be refrigerated or frozen for later use. Heat the meat mixture for 10 minutes from room temperature before making the enchiladas.

TO FINISH THE DISH

Preheat the oven to 400 degrees.

Heat the corn oil over medium heat in a deep skillet. Use as much oil as necessary for the tortillas to be completely submerged in the hot oil in your skillet.

Using tongs, carefully dip a single tortilla into the hot oil until the tortilla starts to bubble. Remove the tortilla from the oil with the tongs and dip the tortilla into the prepared enchilada sauce.

Lay the softened tortilla on a plate and spoon on one-twelfth of the seasoned meat mixture. Roll the tortilla over the meat, overlapping the edges of the tortilla. Place the rolled tortilla into a baking dish with the overlapping edges on the bottom. Repeat this procedure with the remaining tortillas and meat.

Once all of the enchiladas have been placed in the baking dish, pour over the remaining enchilada sauce, being sure to cover the enchiladas evenly. Sprinkle the cheese evenly over the enchiladas.

Cook the enchiladas in the preheated oven for 10 minutes or until the cheese is melted and the sauce is bubbling.

Serve the enchiladas garnished with minced onion and cilantro.

For immigrants without large amounts of capital and perhaps without restaurant experience, a taco truck is a good way to get started in the food business in the United States. The investment is much less than that required to open a restaurant, and there are no employees to manage. The owner of a taco truck doesn't have to worry about being accepted by his new community because he takes his food to the people he knows will want it. The food sold is simple but delicious and is often prepared outside the truck without the pressure of waiting customers.

Los Parados is one of the many taco trucks that can be found in North Charleston. In a city like Charleston where tourists flock to the historic downtown district, it is very expensive to open a restaurant in the heart of the city. A taco truck can be an entry point, serving the workers building the suburbs and renovating the many venerable buildings downtown.

Los Parados became one of the most well known taco trucks in the city. Because of its reputation for good food, the owner was able to set it up outside of a Hispanic market and wait for customers to come to him. The truck was so successful that when space opened beside the market, Los Parados became a restaurant. At first, it was a simple restaurant with more kitchen than dining space. There was a small counter area, but most customers still ordered their food to go, just as they had from the truck. With the restaurant anchored next to the market, the truck began moving with the workers again. Soon the restaurant grew, adding table space for patrons to stay and enjoy their meals and expanding the menu to include soups and enchiladas that could not be served easily from the truck.

Julio is the manager at Los Parados. The first thing you learn from Julio is that even before he came to the United States, he just wanted to work. In his native Mexico, he was happy, but employment opportunities were scarce. Jobs didn't come by often, and when they did, they didn't bring much money. So he listened when everyone said that he should go to America, that there were jobs in America, that there was money to be made in America. Finally, he decided to try it.

He came to Charleston in 2004. He had heard it was an easy city for immigrants to settle in because there were enough Spanish-speaking businesses that he wouldn't have to know how to speak English and, best of all, there was a lot of work. For Julio, work turned out to be serving food to other workers, first in the Los Parados taco truck and then in the restaurant that grew from it.

Like all successful restaurants, Los Parados is a labor of love. But Julio is quick to clarify that while he enjoys cooking, he does it for work, not just for love. And the work is not easy. Although the slow time between lunch and dinner means that Julio can pick his children up from school, the restaurant is open seven days a week, and as manager, Julio is there every day. But he knows that's one of the things that he has to do for Los Parados to be successful. For Julio, serving food is a business. Where before he saw the taco trucks as an opportunity, he sees them now as competition for the restaurant. "A lot of the taco trucks don't pay taxes, so they're able to sell food cheaper than we can in the restaurant. They can sell tacos for 99 cents. We can't do that here."

Part of the success of Los Parados comes from the bounty of locally available products. Along the coast, seafood is cheap, and *caldo de camarón*, shrimp soup, has become one of the restaurant's signature dishes. While the soup is remarkably inexpensive, the portion is generous and the shrimp in it are as beautiful as any found in the shrimp and grits served in Charleston's finest restaurants.

In the past five years, Julio has seen a marked increase in the number of taquerias opening on the outskirts of the city. While the trucks travel with the immigrant workers, the restaurants are gaining popularity not only with the local immigrant population but also with Charleston natives. To Julio, it's a welcome change. "When I came here, it was hard to find authentic Mexican food."

Those taquerias are a sign of the growing permanence of the Hispanic community in North Charleston. Along with them have come markets, butcher shops, music and video stores, and Spanish-language churches. Julio is likely to be a part of that permanence. His family is here with him. His children are in school here. And he is on his way to achieving his American dream. ⑤

CALDO DE RES (Mexican-Style Beef Soup)

Active cooking time: 1 hour, 15 minutes | Total cooking time: 3 hours, 15 minutes | Yield: 12 main dish servings

Julio provides his favorite version of the beef soup served all over Mexico. Traditionally, the soup uses very bony cuts of meat. The bones make the broth rich and flavorful.

Julio's version differs from many recipes by adding a blend of nuts, garlic, and peppers. The nuts create a thicker broth, and the chile and garlic flavors are more intense than if they were added to the broth alone.

While guajillo chiles may not be a staple in your pantry, they are worth seeking out. Guajillo chiles are sweet, slightly spicy peppers that are allowed to dry in the field. Chayotes may also be an unfamiliar ingredient, or you may know them as alligator pears or mirlitons. Members of the gourd family, chayotes are firm, slightly sweet vegetables with a single large seed. Guajillo chiles and chayotes are staples in Hispanic markets, but you may also find them in the supermarket. In addition, guajillo chiles can be found in spice stores, and chayotes are usually available in Asian markets.

3 pounds bone-in beef chuck roast

3 guajillo chiles

½ cup walnuts

½ cup almonds

4 cloves garlic, peeled

¼ cup + 1 tablespoon vegetable
    or canola oil, divided

8 cups beef broth or water

¼ teaspoon ground cumin

1 tablespoon salt

1 teaspoon freshly ground black pepper

2 medium red potatoes, chopped
    (about ½ pound)

2 medium carrots, peeled and chopped
    (about 1 cup)

2 chayotes, chopped

6 tomatillos, husked and rinsed

½ medium yellow onion, chopped
    (about ⅓ cup)

2 cups fresh green beans, chopped

4 ears corn, husked and quartered

1 cup green cabbage, shredded
    (about ¼ of a small cabbage)

Cut the meat off the bones. Don't worry about leaving some behind. Trim off and discard any excess fat and cut the separated meat into bite-sized pieces.

Remove the stems from the guajillo chiles and roughly chop them, retaining the seeds. In a food processor, combine the chiles and their seeds with the walnuts, almonds, and garlic. Pulse until a coarse paste forms.

Add 1 tablespoon oil and continue pulsing for 30 more seconds to create a smoother paste.

In a large bowl, toss the cut meat in the chile paste, coating the meat thoroughly.

In a large stockpot, heat ¼ cup oil over medium heat.

Working in batches, cook the coated meat for 4 minutes on each side, making sure not to crowd the pot. Remove the meat and reserve.

Add the bones to the hot oil and allow them to brown for 5 minutes, turning once.

Add the water or beef broth to the pot, being careful of splattering. Return the meat to the pot and bring the liquid to a boil. Reduce the heat to low and simmer, covered, for 2 hours.

Cooked white rice

White onion, diced

Fresh cilantro, chopped

Lime wedges

Hot corn tortillas

Kitchen Passport This hearty beef soup can be flavored in any way you choose. While Julio gave us his favorite vegetables, you could also add tomatoes, black beans, pinto beans, hominy, or any other vegetable you like. The most important aspect of this soup is the balance between the richness of the nuts and the acidity of the tomatillos. That contrast is what gives the soup such a great flavor.

While this soup is meant for beef, lamb or venison would also have great results. Or, instead of the chuck roast used here, try different cuts of beef. If you choose a boneless cut of meat, use beef stock instead of the optional water since the bones add a lot of beef flavor to the soup. If you're not worried about having a large amount of meat in the soup, you could use beef shanks. The bones in the shanks will add even more flavor than the bone in the chuck roast.

Add the cumin, salt, and black pepper to the liquid along with the potatoes, carrots, and chayotes. Cover the pot and simmer for an additional 15 minutes.

While the potatoes, carrots, and chayotes are simmering, heat a heavy skillet with no oil over medium-high heat.

Add the tomatillos to the skillet and cook them, moving them constantly, for 10 minutes or until they show charred spots.

Transfer the tomatillos to a food processor.

Add the onion to the hot skillet. Cook, stirring constantly, for 5 minutes or until the onion begins to turn a dark brown.

Transfer the browned onion to the food processor with the tomatillos and pulse until a sauce forms. You should have about 2 cups of tomatillo sauce.

Add the tomatillo sauce, green beans, corn, and cabbage to the stockpot, stirring to combine. Cover the pot again and simmer for another 30 minutes.

Season to taste with salt and black pepper.

Serve with garnishes for each diner to add as desired.

In both large cities and small towns, Mexican immigrants like Pepe, Armando, and Julio have become an integral part of southern life. In southern cities, Spanish-language billboards and newspapers stand side by side with their English-language counterparts. Tejano music has as much of a place on the FM dial as traditional southern blues. Taquerias are becoming as common as barbecue and fried chicken joints. Spanish is heard almost as often as English in restaurant kitchens ranging from barbecue to soul food to fine dining and everything in between. Even with this integration, however, the politics of immigration are as much an issue in the South as in the rest of the United States.

When the subject of immigration reform comes up, the underlying question is, "What are we going to do about Mexico?" Of course, immigrants, legal and illegal alike, come from more places than just Mexico, but Mexican immigrants do make up the largest and fastest growing group of new immigrants moving into the South. And until U.S. immigration provides a better option, immigrants will continue to arrive here illegally, lured by stories of opportunity and perhaps by the chance to bring a part of the American dream back home with them.

Antonio is an illegal immigrant thinking about going home. He has spent a long two years in Tennessee without his family, trying to make enough money to send to them to help them have a better life. When he was in Oaxaca, he was a cook at a resort. It was a prestigious job but one that didn't pay enough to keep his family comfortable, so he came to the United States where there are more opportunities. The opportunities he hoped for haven't appeared yet, though, and he is constantly afraid that he's going to be sent back home in disgrace.

Antonio doesn't want to be here illegally, but the cost of immigrating legally was more than he could afford. Still, Antonio says his legal status isn't his biggest problem. "No, having papers doesn't matter that much. A lot of people do it. My problem is not speaking much English. That makes it hard."

The challenges can be worth it. "I came here because of the economy, for a chance to earn money," Antonio explains. "I can earn as much here in one day as I would in one week in Mexico."

Antonio has never had formal culinary training. He started by taking a job as a dishwasher at a resort hotel. He asked the women working in the kitchen to teach him to cook; then he practiced those recipes at home until he perfected them. He's a natural chef who trusts in his own sense of taste, adding his touches to classic dishes.

The language barrier has been the main reason that he hasn't found work as a cook in his new hometown. While Spanish is spoken in many kitchens in the city, finding those kitchens can be tricky. After all, as an illegal alien, asking for a job from the wrong person could land him in trouble.

Although Antonio is relatively well paid, working as a butcher now, he is a chef in his heart, and he cooks exquisite Mexican cuisine any chance he gets. The butcher job isn't his ideal, but it has offered him an opportunity to introduce new flavors to his southern customers. He makes beautiful sausages and *machaca*, seasoned beef that he hangs on a pole to air dry. Their spicy aromas fill the market.

Antonio's love of food displays a passion that belies his humble beginnings. He rattles off the French mother sauces the way most people would the days of the week. His eyes light up when he starts talking about the great cuisine of Oaxaca. He lists the seven moles even more passionately. He is always ready with a traditional Mexican recipe using any of the meats he sells.

Antonio chose to settle in Tennessee because he had family there already. His decision was a pragmatic one. "Before leaving Mexico, people decide on the best place to go. My cousin told me this city had decent work and not as strong of an immigrations enforcement presence as in some other cities," he says.

But having extended family in a city isn't the same as going home to your own family every night. The cost of bringing his wife and children here and the impact on his children of such a major cultural shift were a huge consideration for Antonio. In the end, they stayed behind. But as he says now, "That was not a good thing. We were poor, but we were together. We could say, 'I love you.' The distance causes problems."

And that's the main reason he's considering going back to Mexico. If he takes a job in Mexico, he could be with his family again. He would not be scared that a routine traffic stop would lead to disaster. "I am always a little afraid. I have to drive very carefully. I always worry about having an encounter with the law," he says.

At the same time, he has not given up on the American dream; he still sees the same possibilities and opportunities that drew him here in the first place. And now he has friends and a familiar place in this country. Even if he does go back to Mexico, he just may return to the American South one day. ❧

MOLE NEGRO (Oaxacan Black Sauce)

Active cooking time: 1 hour, 30 minutes | Total cooking time: 1 hour, 30 minutes | Yield: 2 quarts of mole

Antonio's recipe for *mole negro* proves how complex a mole really is. The trick is to be sure to toast the ingredients without burning them. Try serving this mole with chicken or turkey and potatoes, or, as Antonio recommends, use it in chicken tamales to add rich smokiness and hints of spicy sweetness that no other sauce can provide.

While the ingredient list may be daunting, these items will be found easily in most Hispanic markets. Do not substitute Italian or Greek oregano for the Mexican oregano in this recipe. Mexican oregano is actually an unrelated herb from the verbena family that is much sweeter and more intense than true oregano.

This mole will keep well in the refrigerator or freezer in a sealed container and can add an exotic flair to your meal whenever the urge strikes.

2 ounces dried mulato chiles (about 4)
3 ounces dried pasilla chiles (about 10)
3 ounces dried ancho chiles (about 4)
2 ounces dried guajillo chiles (about 16)
⅓ cup raisins, packed
1 quart chicken broth
3 cups vegetable oil
1 medium yellow onion, chopped
    (about ⅔ cup)
1 clove garlic, minced (about ½ teaspoon)
½ cup roasted shelled peanuts
⅓ cup sesame seeds
½ cup shelled almonds
8 tablespoons Mexican oregano
6 tablespoons cinnamon stick, crushed
    (about 3 4-inch cinnamon sticks)
4 tablespoons whole allspice berries
3 tablespoons whole cloves
2 ripe Mexican plantains, peeled and
    chopped (about 2 cups)
3 ounces dark chocolate, chopped
1½ cups saltine crackers, crushed

Remove the stems and seeds from the dried mulato, pasilla, ancho, and guajillo chiles and rinse them well under cold running water. Dry the chiles thoroughly. Open a window or turn on a kitchen vent because the toasting chiles will emit fumes that will irritate your throat and eyes.

In a heavy skillet over medium heat, toast each variety of chile separately, on both sides, being careful not to burn them. For the mulato and ancho chiles, toast for about 1 minute per side. Since the pasilla and guajillo chiles are thinner, toast them for about 45 seconds per side.

Remove the chiles from the skillet and chop them to ease blending.

Place the chiles in a large stockpot and add the raisins. Pour over the chicken broth and cook, covered, over low heat, being careful not to bring the stock to a boil. The chile mixture will continue cooking while you complete the next steps.

Heat the vegetable oil in a large heavy skillet over medium heat.

Carefully add the onion and garlic and cook for 25 minutes or until browned.

Strain out the onion and garlic and transfer them to the stockpot with the chile mixture, leaving the oil in the skillet.

Carefully add the peanuts, sesame seeds, almonds, oregano, cinnamon, allspice, and cloves to the oil and cook for 15 minutes or until browned.

Strain out the nuts and spices and add them to the stockpot with the chile mixture.

Add the plantains to the oil and cook for 15 minutes or until browned.

Carefully add the oil and browned plantains to the stockpot with the chile mixture. Add the chocolate and crackers to the stockpot, stirring for 5 minutes or until the chocolate is melted.

Working in batches, transfer the chile mixture to a countertop blender and blend until the mixture becomes a thick, smooth paste. Transfer each batch into a large bowl, stirring to combine all batches. The oil will separate out.

Spoon the mole into storage containers, making certain that you cover the top of the mole in each container with the separated oil. Mole will keep in the refrigerator for approximately 2 months or will keep frozen for up to 1 year.

Kitchen Passport What can you do with mole? Antonio suggests tamales.

Making fresh tamales is a completely different experience from buying any that have been frozen or previously cooked. Antonio wraps tamales of chicken and *mole negro* in banana leaves, and as they steam, the leaves impart just a hint of tropical sweetness to the masa, or dough. When you open them, the sweet aroma of the steam from the leaves makes your mouth water, and the smoky spiciness of the *mole negro* adds a complexity of flavor that has to be tasted to be believed.

While these tamales are delicious made with chicken, any meat can be a great tamale filling. Smoked pork or beef brisket will add a nice smokiness to the tamales. If you don't want meat filling, Mexican cheeses can be nicely paired with peppers or onions. You don't have to use plain masa, either. Add corn for texture or pureed peppers for color and flavor.

Just like savory tamales, the varieties of sweet tamales are limited only by your imagination. Try pineapple or raisins and cinnamon. Add purees of fruit, pumpkin, or sweet potatoes to the masa. Even peanuts and chocolate can be included in the tamales for a wonderful treat. One of the simplest traditional sweet tamales adds nothing to the masa except fresh sweet corn and a touch of sugar.

Moles

"Mole is the single dish that best represents Mexico," as Antonio says. Like Mexico itself, it is a combination of Aztec, Mayan, and Spanish influences. It seems simple on the surface, but if you look closer, you'll find an amazing depth of complexity. But what exactly is mole?

In the simplest sense, mole is a sauce. Think of mole as one of the ultimate condiments. Mole can turn bland turkey or chicken into an exotic treat. It can make plain vegetables an exciting side dish. It can change a taco from something simple to a gourmet meal.

The complex flavors of mole have evolved over centuries. A single mole recipe may contain over thirty ingredients and take days to prepare, but the results are worth all the effort. In a great mole, no single ingredient will overpower the rest; instead, you will be able to taste individual flavors of nuts, chocolate, chiles, herbs, and spices as well as the combination of all of them.

Mole is considered to be the official dish of Oaxaca, the culinary capital of Mexico. Traditionally in Oaxacan cuisine, there are seven different moles: *negro* (black), *amarillo* (yellow), *rojo* (red), *coloradito* (brick red), *verde* (green), *chichilo* (ash), and *mancha manteles* (tablecloth stainer). The levels of complexity vary, and the flavor of each is unique. They're all a combination of chiles and spices. Some varieties add chocolate, nuts, and tomatoes or tomatillos; in others, the chiles are toasted. *Mole chichilo* adds tortillas and pepper seeds cooked down to ash. *Mole negro* has plantains and raisins for sweetness.

To put mole into perspective, it's a lot like barbecue sauce. Different sauces can make the same meat taste completely different. And they're as unique as the people who make them. There's always something special that the cook adds. Mass-produced, store-bought versions can't compare to those made by hand by people who really care about what they're making and who make moles as part of their contribution to the culture of their region.

No matter which mole you choose to make, you'll quickly come to appreciate the nuances of flavor that mole brings to the table.

Cuba, Haiti, and the Dominican Republic
Refugees, Politics, and the Plate

Just over ninety miles south of Key West, Florida, lies Cuba. To the southeast of Cuba lies the island of Hispaniola, home to Haiti and the Dominican Republic. Each of these three nations has undergone its own path of political and social upheaval. During times of unrest, many people in these countries have fled to the United States.

As close as these countries are to one another and as much as their people have in common, U.S. immigration policy is very different for each country, ranging from a simple and straightforward process to a mire of paperwork and legalities that often ends in refugees being turned away.

Of those refugees who manage to clear all the hurdles they face, many decide to make homes in the South. Having gained their freedom, they are able to turn their attention to opportunity. Though they have left their homelands behind, they find that the foodways of the Caribbean are not so foreign to the South, because enslaved Africans brought similar influences to both areas. For some Caribbean immigrants, opportunity means working with food and sharing their culture and memories of home. And they gladly and freely tell their stories.

Tasting the food Rey Regalado serves today in his Atlanta restaurants, you wouldn't dream he had ever been anything other than a chef. But in his native Cuba, he was trained as a mechanical engineer. In the face of Cuba's worsening economic situation, Rey chose to ignore the Cuban government's anti-American propaganda and to try to reach the United States to help his family. The story of his 1991 escape features all of the elements of a great spy thriller—training for a life-threatening swim, trusting no one, and a journey filled with one danger after another.

Rey lived in Santiago, Cuba, just a short distance from the Guantanamo Bay Naval Base. The base is American territory on Cuba's shores and thus represents a shorter path to freedom for some Cubans. Shorter doesn't mean safer, however. The base was surrounded by the western hemisphere's largest minefield until President Bill Clinton

Reynaldo "Rey" Regalado, Atlanta, Georgia

ordered the removal of the mines in 1996. But because the Cuban government still has mines on its side of the base's perimeter, reaching Guantanamo Bay means arriving via the ocean. Rey and his best friend, Miguel, planned to make the five-mile swim to the base, despite challenges from the Cuban Coast Guard and from Mother Nature.

"There are certain days that the current comes from land out to the ocean, so you can be swimming and swimming and never getting any farther. That's when you get tired and people drown," Rey says. "So we were investigating what days. We actually had friends who worked as lifeguards, so those friends were telling me to go this day or this other day.

"I got lucky. I had a friend who saw me training and training every day. When you see somebody training there, people start to think, 'These guys are going to leave,' because that's what everybody does," he says. "So this friend of mine was telling me, 'You're planning to leave. You're planning to leave.' And I said, 'No, no, no,' because you have to keep that a secret."

Rey's friend insisted. "He said, 'I'm gonna come to your house, and we're gonna sit down and talk. I'm gonna bring a bottle of rum, and we're gonna talk,'" Rey continues. "He said, 'Look, I know you're going. You don't have to say anything. But don't do it. Wait, I have an easier plan.'"

Over that bottle of rum, Rey's friend told him he had access to a fishing boat. Rey had access to a car to get to the beach. If Rey would pick up his friend's family, his friend would bring him along on the boat.

Now, bottles of rum stand behind the bar as Rey relates his story during a lull in the lunch rush. His easy smile today belies the tension he experienced then and the dangers he was about to face in order to escape Cuba.

Rey agreed to the plan but not without trepidation. Even though the journey by boat would be physically safer than his and Miguel's planned swim, there was a new danger: with a larger number of people involved in the new arrangement, secrecy was at risk and their odds of capture increased. Being caught by the authorities in an escape attempt meant facing up to fifteen years in prison.

After weeks of waiting, the time to leave came with little warning. Rey began driving to the beach. "I picked his family up, and I was picking people up all the way to get there. I actually got scared when I got there because there were people here and people there. When a large group is leaving, sometimes the authorities see it, and you end up in jail."

Despite his fear, he took the chance. All of the refugees crowded into the bottom of the fishing boat, waiting to cast off to sea, but there was a problem. One of the boat's mates, perhaps suspecting something, had taken one of the boat's fuses with him when he went into town. All of the refugees had to leave the boat and hide in the bushes while the captain called the mate back to the ship. The fuse was replaced, and the captain sent the mate back to town. As soon as the mate was out of sight, everyone loaded into the boat again.

Their problems weren't over, though. Perhaps the mate spoke to the authorities, or perhaps the word got to them another way, but it became obvious that the authorities were suspicious.

"About halfway out, the captain started getting calls from port. 'Carlito, you need to come back. We have problems here in port. We need you to turn around.'" The captain dealt with the situation, however. "Carlito knew what was going on, so he said, 'Okay, I just threw the nets out. Let me pick them up, and I'll be back in an hour.' He didn't do anything. He just pushed the gas and headed straight to Guantanamo Bay."

Seeing Rey in the restaurant now, listening to his warm voice and rueful laugh, it's hard to imagine what he must have felt on that journey, watching everything he had ever known recede as an uncertain future loomed. Still, the Latin beat of the restaurant's music and the smells of pork roasting and tropical spices cooking make it clear that, no matter what possessions he left behind, Rey brought a part of Cuba with him.

There was certainly no fond farewell from Cuba, and, initially at least, there was no warm welcome for the refugees at Guantanamo Bay. "There was a small patrol boat with lights like a police car. They were speaking English to us, 'Who are you? Who are you?' And we didn't know how to speak English," Rey says. A translator was brought out. "We said, 'Hey, we are Cubans,' and they said, 'Okay, come on.' We found out later that they thought we were Haitians. At the time, a lot of Haitians were coming to Guantanamo by boat."

Although Cuban refugees are generally welcome, the U.S. government still carefully screens them. One reason is to ensure that no agents of the Cuban government are able to reach the United States and act as spies. Another more humanitarian reason is to ensure that each refugee has some means of support in the United States, either from family or from a charitable organization. After being processed in Guantanamo Bay, Rey came directly to Atlanta, where he had family. But there was more than relatives waiting for him.

The ninety miles between Cuba and the United States may not be a huge physical distance, but for Rey, the difference in his life that those miles represent is almost unimaginable. "I was fortunate that I had a cousin here in Atlanta. I came here in December of 1991, just before Christmas, which was my first Christmas ever. I was born after the revolution, so I didn't know what Christmas was. It was nice. It was really emotional."

Even though he was formally trained as an engineer, Rey always had a dream to open a restaurant. Coming to the United States meant he would finally have a chance to realize that dream. He spent his first four months in Atlanta learning English, but as soon as he could, he found a job so he could start saving the money it would take to make his dream a reality.

Rey's desire to succeed was exemplified in his first job, delivering donuts. This service became a business as he and Miguel purchased the delivery rights for multiple routes. After that, Rey started a business as a painting contractor. One day, he noticed something that would change everything.

"I was driving to a job and saw they were building apartments with space on the bottom for retail. I said, 'Wow, this might be my opportunity.' I asked if I could put a sandwich shop in, but they said no, they wanted more like clothing stores."

Rey was undeterred. He saw another space nearby and called about it, only to find out it had just been rented. However, the landlord had another restaurant tenant who was looking to break the lease.

"I came out and looked at the space, looked at the traffic. I had my friend Miguel come out and look at it. He said, 'Rey, this is a good place. Take it.' So I started selling my sandwiches, and people were saying, 'Oh, these are so good.'"

The restaurant's popularity became its biggest problem. Customers on their lunch hour couldn't stay because it was too full. Rey worried that he would have to move his business. Luckily, the dry cleaners next door closed. Rey took over that space, more than doubling the number of tables in the restaurant and adding room for a bar. Now, he is expanding the space a second time.

Rey has also branched out to additional locations. The quality of his food and his dedication to his business inspired some of his customers to invest. "A Cuban doctor came in to eat. He liked the place. He talked to another friend of his, and then they both approached me and said, 'Are you interested in expanding the business?'" With the help of his new partners, Rey now has four locations in Atlanta and may soon have more.

All of Rey's success in the United States is tied, ultimately, to his family. His mother lives in Atlanta now. When the restaurant first opened, she made all the sauce for the pork. Rey's father died of cancer before he was able to leave Cuba; still, his presence is strong at Rey's restaurants.

"My father was an awesome cook. He is why I have this. When I was getting ready to open this, I was going to call it El Cubano, but then at that moment, my father was diagnosed with cancer," Rey says. "Right before I opened the place, he passed away. That's when I decided to call the place Papi's, for my daddy. He would have loved this place."

Rey takes nothing for granted. He is aware of how fortunate he is not only to have escaped Cuba but also to have been welcomed by the United States. Having survived a dangerous escape of his own, Rey has also witnessed firsthand the terrible dangers faced by Haitian refugees desperate to reach the United States.

"When we left Cuba, they brought us here in a big army airplane. I remember the plane opened the belly, and we looked down. And they were dumping big food cases for them to eat in the middle of the ocean."

While he hopes that the Haitian refugees he saw from the plane survived their journey, he knows it was unlikely that they would have been given a home if they ever reached land. Like so many other immigrants, Rey acknowledges the inequities of U.S. immigration policy.

"I think it should be equal for everyone. Why does the United States government do it that way? I think it's because Cuba is Communist. Those other countries are not Communist," he says. "It's a political thing that this government has against Cuba. They say it's okay for a Cuban to come here because maybe that's the way they think it's going to weaken the country, which, as you see, has been there for fifty-something years."

Rey's life has changed much since that frightening day on a Cuban beach. He is happy sharing his food and the memories of his father with the community he loves. He has truly made a home for himself in Georgia.

"Sometimes I feel I was born here because I adapted so easily to the American life that I don't feel a difference. A lot of people ask me, 'If Fidel dies, are you going to go back?' I don't think so." ☜

MOROS Y CRISTIANOS (Cuban-Style Black Beans and Rice)

Active cooking time: 30 minutes | Total cooking time: 2 hours, 20 minutes + 8 hours
Yield: 8 main dish servings

If there is one dish that is served at every Cuban restaurant, it has to be black beans. While the beans are commonly served as a side dish or as a soup in the United States, in Cuba they are often cooked with rice to make *Moros y Cristianos*, a dish that can easily be an entire meal.

This is the Cuban version of the staple rice-and-beans dish of the Caribbean. Its name, literally translated as "Moors and Christians," came from early Spanish settlers who brought stories of medieval battles between Spanish Christians and Moroccan invaders who controlled large portions of Spain for hundreds of years. *Moros y Cristianos* is at least one place where those warring peoples, both black and white, are represented at peace.

Rey uses malanga root as the secret ingredient in his black beans. Malanga is a tropical tuber common in the cuisines of both Cuba and Puerto Rico. It adds a nutty, slightly earthy flavor. Malanga is an example of how the South has embraced immigrants. "You find it at the farmers' markets here in Atlanta," Rey says. You can also find malanga in Asian and Latin markets.

This is a simple dish to prepare, but by cooking the rice in the beans, the rice absorbs all of the flavor of the beans and the *sofrito*. By using this method, the rice becomes a truly integral part of the dish instead of just providing an accompaniment for the beans. Once the dish is together, it needs nothing more than time to allow the flavors to develop to their fullest.

Kitchen Passport A variation on the dish uses red kidney beans instead of black beans. Although both versions are universal in Cuba, it is known by different names. In parts of the country, the dish *Moros y Cristianos* is called *congri*, and the version with kidney beans is called *congri oriental*.

The dish also can be made with different ingredients in the *sofrito*. Coriander gives a lemony tartness; green tomatoes add tanginess; more hot peppers provide a spicy kick. Spanish-style chorizo or southern country ham adds depth of flavor to the dish. To make a vegetarian version, replace the chicken broth with an equal amount of vegetable stock or water.

1 pound dried black beans

1 large ripe tomato, seeded and chopped
   (about 1½ cups)

1 green bell pepper, seeded and chopped
   (about 1 cup)

1 fresh cayenne or serrano pepper,
   seeded and chopped

1 large white onion, chopped
   (about 1 cup)

6 cloves garlic, peeled

1 cup malanga root, peeled and chopped
   (about 8 ounces) (optional)

4 leaves culantro or ⅓ cup Italian parsley,
   chopped

1 teaspoon cumin seed

1 teaspoon oregano

2 tablespoons olive oil

4 cups chicken broth

2 cups uncooked white rice

Salt

Freshly ground black pepper

TO SERVE

Fresh cilantro, chopped

Sort the black beans, removing any rocks or dirt. Place the beans in a colander and rinse until the water passing through the beans runs clear. Place the beans in a large bowl and add water to cover the beans by 2 inches. Soak the beans overnight.

Drain the beans and discard the water. Place the beans in a stockpot and add 4 cups of water. Bring the beans to a boil and allow them to cook for 5 minutes.

Remove from the heat and allow to rest, covered, for 1 hour.

Combine the tomato, bell pepper, cayenne pepper, onion, garlic, malanga root (if desired), culantro, cumin, and oregano in a food processor. Process until the mixture is thoroughly blended, but still chunky, to form a *sofrito*.

Heat the oil in a heavy skillet over medium heat. Add the *sofrito* and cook, stirring constantly, for 10 minutes or until the *sofrito* is starting to thicken and most of the liquid has evaporated.

Add 6 cups of water to the stockpot and return the beans to a boil.

Add the *sofrito* and stir the beans frequently for 1 hour or until you see that the beans are breaking open and forming a creamy sauce.

Add the chicken broth and rice and return to a boil.

Reduce the heat to low, cover, and simmer for 20 minutes or until the rice is tender.

Season to taste with salt and black pepper. Garnish with freshly chopped cilantro.

Sofrito

Sofrito is a component in dishes throughout the Caribbean. In Cuba, it's used as a base for soups, beans, meats, and rice dishes. In Haiti and the Dominican Republic, it's used as a sauce. While *sofrito* is always there, it doesn't stand out as a particular taste; rather, it's the unidentifiable flavor that makes Caribbean cuisine so delicious.

Sofrito originated in the Catalan region of Spain and traveled to the Caribbean with the early explorers and settlers. The original basic mixture of garlic and peppers evolved to include local herbs like culantro and some of the spicier peppers available in the region.

Sofrito should have the consistency of a thick sauce. While the original makers used a mortar and pestle to achieve the right consistency, you can use a blender or food processor. The next step that makes *sofrito* special is cooking. *Sofrito* is always sautéed before being used to produce the best flavors.

Since there's no set recipe for *sofrito*, you can be as inventive as you like with it. The only constants are garlic, onion, peppers, and herbs. The peppers can be as mild or as spicy as you wish, and the herbs can be any mixture you desire. Meats like bacon, ham, or sausage might be added, as well as tomatoes or tomatillos.

While you may see canned varieties of *sofrito* in Hispanic markets, it can't compare to *sofrito* made from fresh, seasonal ingredients. Caribbean cooks often make *sofrito* in large batches and freeze cup-sized portions for later use. No matter how you decide to make yours, *sofrito* can be a simple and inexpensive way to add Caribbean flavor to your kitchen.

Elizardo Sanz, Norcross, Georgia

The first thing you see when you walk into Palomilla's Cuban Grill House is a smile. Every guest is greeted personally by either Elizardo Sanz or his wife, Aracelli. For them, Palomilla's is a second home where their customers become their friends. When Elizardo is out of the kitchen, he often presides behind the restaurant's small bar, making cocktails and delicious Cuban coffees for his patrons. He especially enjoys introducing the strong, sweet, espresso-like coffee to people who have never had it. Watching him work in his suburban restaurant, he seems a natural restaurateur. But for all his enjoyment of his business now, working with food was not his original plan, and it is difficult to picture this quiet, unassuming man making a terrifying escape from Cuba.

In Cuba, Elizardo had a college degree and a better-than-average job. Still, the economic conditions were so bad that he felt he had no other choice but to flee to the United States. "If you are in Cuba, you have to be really desperate to do something like that because Cuba is an island, and there is no way to get out of there without a passport," Elizardo

Aracelli and Elizardo Sanz at Palomilla's Cuban Grill House.

says. "The only way to get a passport is through the government, and the government doesn't give passports to anybody if you don't have a really good reason."

It was obvious that he would not be granted a passport, so he began to plan his escape. In 1994, Elizardo and four friends made their first attempt to cross the ninety miles of ocean between Cuba and Florida on a raft they made. "It was a simple raft, four aluminum tubes one way, four the other way, and two inner tubes tied together. That was that. That was my ship."

Once they had assembled their raft, they chose their time to leave and slipped away into the sea. But their journey was cut short. "You have to be really careful to get out because the police boats are checking all the time. The first time, they grabbed us. They had us in jail for two days waiting for the trial. But two months later, we escaped. The second time we made it."

The escape was grueling. "We spent four days on the sea. The raft was sinking. We had water up to the neck. It was a really, really desperate position," Elizardo says. "We put kerosene in the water to keep sharks away. I got burned from my chest down. I lost the skin. I was bleeding."

For the five men clinging to their raft and to hope, help came not a moment too soon. "There is an organization in Miami, Brothers to the Rescue. They fly every day. It's something they do after work. They fly for free trying to find Cubans, and they found us, fortunately for us."

Brothers to the Rescue contacted another plane and had its crew drop an inflatable raft for the men. They also contacted the U.S. Coast Guard and provided the coordinates where the exhausted refugees could be picked up.

After being rescued by the Coast Guard and processed in Key West, Florida, Elizardo started his new life in the United States. He had no family to help him get started, but he did have friends who offered him a place to stay and a job in their chain of restaurants in Miami. Although he didn't know it at the time, the skills he learned working for them for the next seven years would be useful later.

After employment in restaurants, he wanted a change, so he went back to college and made a career in satellites and computers. It was on a business trip to Atlanta that his life changed again.

"When I got here, I got fascinated with Atlanta. I fell in love immediately with Atlanta, and the first time I came here, I bought my house. I told my wife, 'I bought a house.' She responded, 'Are you crazy? What are you doing?' They finished the house in January. The next month, we moved up here."

Elizardo planned to continue working with computers, but the more time he spent in Atlanta, the more he felt a pull to do something else. "I started looking for a business here. And at the same time, we were looking for Cuban food. We found about two places, and the food, it wasn't so good. So I talked to my wife. We have really good experience because my wife has been working in the business about sixteen or seventeen years. So I said, 'Let's go. Let's open a restaurant.' So we immediately started working on the project. We bought this place and started working."

Elizardo had restaurant experience from his time in Miami, but his training as a cook began in Cuba. "We had a little farm. Before Fidel, we had a big farm. But Fidel came and took it. We kept a little of it, and sometimes my mom moved to the farm for six months at a time," he says. "I stayed at home because I had to go to school and to the university, and I started cooking for myself. I was practicing all the time, and finally I learned how to do it pretty good."

Elizardo is proud of his restaurant and the food he serves. "A lot of people come here and say, 'What is your best item?' I tell them, 'The whole menu!' When you ask American people about Cuban food, it's really weird. They don't know about it. They try it at least one time, and almost everybody loves it."

Elizardo's restaurant is located in a strip mall in a quiet Atlanta suburb without a large Cuban population. "Somebody asked me, 'Why are you going to put a Cuban place here? There are no Cubans.' My reason is it's not for Cubans—it's for Americans. We're in America. If the Cubans come, welcome. But I'm cooking for Americans."

Elizardo is not just cooking for Americans; he is becoming one. Like Rey Regalado, he feels that he belongs to the United States at least as much as he does to Cuba. "I have big, big respect for this country. Right now, I say I am half Cuban and half American. And sometimes, I think I am 51 percent American and 49 Cuban," he says. "I have been here for fourteen years. That's more than enough for me to feel like that. If I have to fight for this country, I can go immediately, with no doubt."

Elizardo doesn't have a firm opinion about U.S. immigration policy. However, he does believe that Americans' negative image of immigrants lies in a perceived lack of a work ethic. "Immigration is a really tough thing. I see it this way. I try to work, and I try to be a good citizen every time. Not everybody does the same thing, but I try to do that," he says. "I respect the American people's opinion when they sometimes hate us, the Latins, because sometimes we help our image a lot, but sometimes not really."

The customers who fill his restaurant like Elizardo and respect him for his own work ethic, which shows in the quality of his food. He is proud of the labor that creates his food, but he is also proud of the tie that it maintains with his homeland.

Elizardo keeps a book in the kitchen of his restaurant, *Cucina al Minuto* by Nitza Villapol, sometimes called the "Cuban Julia Child." As he says, "She was really famous. I try to follow all her recipes. That's what I do. Probably that's the success of my food. I try to be close to the original recipes for everything."

The book represents so much to Elizardo. It is originally from Cuba and reached its new home as a gift from his sister. It's well loved with favorite passages marked and obviously read over and over. It has traveled far, but it has ended up where it belongs—in a kitchen where the dreams it carries come to life, bringing the flavors of Cuba to a new land. ◈

ARROZ CON POLLO (Cuban-Style Chicken and Rice)

Active cooking time: 1 hour | Total cooking time: 1 hour, 35 minutes + 4 hours | Yield: 4 main dish servings

Arroz con pollo is the Cuban descendant of *jollof* rice (page 249), an African dish that made its way to the Caribbean during the days of the slave trade. While this recipe is a cousin to Cajun jambalaya, it has some unique elements.

Sour orange is a distinctly Cuban flavor. The sour orange trees of Cuba are descendants of Seville orange trees that arrived on the island with Spanish settlers and flourished. Many Cuban immigrants raise their own sour orange trees, some from seeds they smuggled from Cuba.

While you may be able to find bottled sour orange juice, or *naranja agria*, in some Hispanic markets, most sources agree that it doesn't compare to fresh juice. A common substitution for sour orange juice is a combination of orange juice with lemon or lime juice.

1 chicken, quartered
½ cup orange juice
½ cup lime juice
1 teaspoon dried oregano
1 teaspoon ground cumin
2 cloves garlic, crushed
¼ cup annatto oil or olive oil
1 large yellow onion, diced
    (about 1 cup)
1 large Ají pepper, Cubanelle
    pepper, or green bell pepper,
    chopped

Place the chicken in a large container with a lid. Pour over the orange and lime juices with the oregano, cumin, and crushed garlic. You can replace both the orange and lime juices with the juice of sour oranges if it is available. Seal the container and allow the chicken to marinate in the refrigerator for 4 hours or overnight.

Heat the oil in a large skillet over medium-high heat.

Carefully add the chicken and fry for about 5 minutes per side or until brown.

3 cloves garlic, minced (about
   1½ teaspoons)
1 small tomato, seeded and diced
   (about ⅔ cup)
2 teaspoons salt
½ teaspoon freshly ground black pepper
1 bay leaf
1½ cups beer
1 cup chicken broth
¼ teaspoon saffron strands, crushed
½ teaspoon annatto seeds
1 pound Valencia or Arborio rice, rinsed
1 cup fresh or frozen green peas

Kitchen Passport You can
make this dish spicier, if you prefer.
Replace the mild Ají, Cubanelle,
or green bell pepper with a spicier
pepper like a serrano, jalapeño,
or even habanero. The Valencia
or Arborio rice gives the sauce a
creamier consistency, but any rice
would be delicious. The saffron
adds color and flavor but can be
omitted if the saffron costs more
than you want to spend.

Since this dish is a descendant
of the *jollof* rice of Africa, you
can also substitute other meats
and vegetables for the traditional
chicken and peas of Cuba. Fish or
shrimp would be good choices,
as would be turkey or pork. The
only thing to keep in mind for
substitutes for the peas is that
there should not be much cooking
time once the vegetable has been
added. Frozen or fresh corn, green
beans, or cut carrots would work
well.

Remove the chicken from the skillet and
reserve, draining all but 2 tablespoons of the
fat from the skillet.

Add the onion, Ají, Cubanelle, or green
bell pepper, and garlic to the skillet and cook
for about 5 minutes or until the onion is translucent.

Add the tomato, salt, and black pepper
and continue cooking for 1 minute.

Return the chicken to the skillet and continue cooking for 2 minutes.

Carefully add the bay leaf, beer, chicken
broth, and saffron to the skillet. Bring the
mixture to a boil.

Reduce the heat to low, cover, and allow
the mixture to simmer for 30 minutes.

Remove ¼ cup of the cooking liquid
from the chicken mixture. In a small saucepan, pour the ¼ cup cooking liquid over the
annatto seeds. Simmer over medium-low
heat for 5 minutes before straining the liquid
back into the chicken mixture. Discard the
annatto seeds.

Return the chicken mixture to a boil.

Stir in the rice, reduce heat to low, cover,
and simmer for 25 minutes.

Remove the bay leaf and stir in the green
peas. Allow the arroz con pollo to cook for
another 5 minutes.

Jean Bonnet,
Smyrna, Georgia

Jean Bonnet's tiny one-table restaurant, Chez Carmelle, is a testament to his belief in opportunity. One wall features photos of the largest Catholic cathedral in Port-au-Prince, the capital of Haiti, and the Palais National, the seat of the national government, both among the many buildings that were damaged in the 2010 earthquake. Between these two photos, a poster proudly proclaims the history of Haiti as the first free black republic in the New World. A closer examination of the poster reveals the irony of that claim, as it includes illustrations of seven military juntas and the infamous dictator François Duvalier and his son, Jean-Claude "Baby Doc" Duvalier, among Haiti's leaders.

The opposite wall represents Jean's new home, the United States. President Barack Obama smiles from a large poster between pictures of John F. Kennedy and Martin Luther King Jr., all men who represent freedom to Jean.

Jean came to the United States when he was twenty-one. "My mom came to the U.S. first with my brother. They applied for my visa, for my residence. I came to search for a better future, a better life."

Jean has big dreams, dreams of seeing his restaurant turn into only the first of many, dreams of seeing his children inheriting a restaurant empire. "Whenever people became successful in life, became millionaires, they always started somewhere. Even the families that have millions, some generation before had to start somewhere."

Walking into Jean's restaurant, it's easy to imagine that empire. The smells of onion, garlic, and hot peppers are mouth-watering, and the bakery case is filled with both American and Haitian pastries. Dense traditional coco bread nestles beside light-as-air cinnamon rolls. Haitian meat patties add their fragrance along with fruit-filled Danish pastries. With such options, success should be a given.

Jean believes that success in one generation should be a stepping-stone for the next generation. "When they say 'family values,' it means go over your dad's head. And your children will go over yours." Jean's children have a lot of work cut out for them if they want to go farther than their father on the path to success.

From the very beginning, education was of great importance to Jean. He went to college at New York University, then he worked there as an accountant. After his children were born, he and his wife, Marie, began to think about where the children would go to school.

"A friend introduced me to Georgia. He was a professor at NYU and was from Macon, Georgia. He used to pass me newspapers from Georgia," Jean recalls. "He says, 'You know what? Maybe I'll take you on a trip to Macon.' So I went one weekend and said, 'This is kind of nice.'

Jean and Marie Bonnet at Chez Carmelle.

I went back to New York and talked to my wife. I said, 'I don't want to raise my kids in New York.'"

Jean expanded his own education, taking classes to be a certified nursing assistant to help increase his chances of finding work. He returned to Georgia—this time visiting a friend in Powder Springs, near Atlanta—and decided to pack everything and move.

Later, the simple act of reading a newspaper would change Jean's life again. "I was reading the newspaper and I see Publix grocery stores as one of the ten best places to work. So I went to Publix and gave them my résumé. They said, 'We don't have a job for you.' The lady told me I needed to go to the corporate office."

The corporate office had nothing for an accountant, so Jean stuck with his job working nights at a nursing home. After two months, he decided to try Publix again. Although there was still no job opening for an accountant, there was one in a bakery in one of the stores. Even though it wasn't what he had planned, he decided to take the job.

In this new job, his drive to learn led to success. "There was a program to teach me how to do donuts, mixing, cakes, stuff like that. And I said, 'That's pretty interesting.' And there's a program—all the library books and everything—to be in the management part," Jean says. "After two or three months, I went to the big manager and said, 'I'm interested. What do I have to do to be part of the management team?' So every lunchtime, I got the books and studied."

His hard work paid off as he was promoted to assistant manager and later to bakery manager. One key thing that stuck with him was the great variety of items that a single bag of flour can yield—and the profits to be made from that flour.

Jean also remembers the employee orientation video."When they give you the video to watch, it features George Jenkins the owner of Publix that makes billions of dollars and has stores everywhere. What was he? He was a bagger for a little grocery store. And I said, 'If that man can do it, maybe one day I can do it myself.'"

And one day he did. "I decided it was time to have a little something of my own. My goal is to give good service and good food and make it better and better. My wife is a good cook. I told her if she cooks, I will do the pastry."

Jean and Marie serve as more than cooks, however. Their small restaurant is clearly an important hub in the community. A steady stream of customers enters Chez Carmelle, greeting Jean as an old friend and placing to-go orders. Depending on the customer's familiarity, Jean switches rapid-fire between Haitian Creole and English.

Since everything in the restaurant is made to order, Jean has plenty of time to get to know his clientele and talks with them about life both in Georgia and in Haiti while they wait. It's clear that many of those customers come to the restaurant as much to talk to Jean as for the food.

Many of Jean's Haitian customers have their own stories of escaping to the United States. Jean himself was fortunate to have avoided fleeing Haiti as so many did—on rafts and small boats. He came to the United States during the rule of Jean-Claude Duvalier, a period when Haitian immigrants were welcome. Nonetheless, he still has strong opinions about the opportunities that immigrants should have.

"Something Americans don't remember is that Haiti fought for United States' independence. Haiti helped the United States fight for independence in Savannah. A lot of Haitians fought and died for the United States," he says. "They should do more to help the Haitians. They have a lot of political persecution since Duvalier left."

Still, Jean's pride in his new home is undeniable. As he gives a tour of the space next door that will be part of his expanded restaurant, he unlocks the door with a key on a key ring with a picture of President Obama. With his belief in hard work and education and his drive to succeed, this space may be only the first expansion of his restaurant empire. 🐚

QUEUE DE BOEUF (Haitian-Style Oxtail)

One of the first listings on the menu at Chez Carmelle is *queue de boeuf*. Translated literally, it means "tail of beef," or oxtail. Oxtail is not a typical cut of meat used in American cooking, although it is gaining in popularity. Restaurants love to use oxtails to make rich, flavorful beef stock or to stuff dishes like ravioli with their shredded meat.

In Haitian cuisine, however, oxtails are an everyday food. They are not seen as a luxury item. Rather, they are remnants of the days of slavery on the island. Just as in the South, the cuts of meat given to the enslaved workers on the sugarcane plantations of Haiti were parts that the wealthier people didn't want. And just as in the South, the Haitian people turned those cuts into delicacies.

Haitian cuisine melds flavors from Spanish, French, and African cuisine with the tropical flavors of the island. Because of its heritage of French and Creole cooking styles, Haitian dishes use herbs extensively. You will notice that this recipe calls for a base of parsley, garlic, and green onions to marinate the oxtails. This base is known as *epis* and is used not only as a marinade but also as a soup base and as a condiment to be added at the table.

This recipe starts by having you prepare a fiery orange habanero sauce. In Haiti, spicy sauces are used to season everyday dishes. Spoon just a little onto the finished oxtails to add a spiciness that blends with the sweetness of the tomato in the dish. While oxtails are not the meatiest cuts, you will find that the meat is meltingly tender after cooking and has a very rich flavor.

For the hot sauce

Active cooking time: 30 minutes | Total cooking time: 30 minutes | Yield: 1 pint

8 ripe habanero peppers

½ small yellow onion, chopped
  (about ¼ cup)

1 carrot, peeled and chopped
  (about ½ cup)

⅓ cup white vinegar

1 tablespoon sugar

Juice of 2 limes (about ¼ cup)

Kitchen Passport While this recipe was developed to take a tough cut of meat and turn it into velvet, there's no reason you couldn't use it to prepare a delicious chuck roast or pork butt. You could also try using different herbs in the *epis*. Cilantro would add a more lemony flavor; shallots, a nice bite; tarragon, a more traditionally French element.

The hot sauce is also a good place for variation. If you like spicier food, try leaving some of the seeds in the peppers. If you find the sauce to be too sweet, use only half of the carrot.

Although not required, it is best to wear gloves when working with habanero peppers. If you choose to work with them without wearing gloves, be sure to wash your hands thoroughly after handling them. Be very careful not to touch your face or eyes while working with the peppers.

Remove the stems and slice the peppers in half from top to bottom. Scrape out the seeds and discard them.

Prepare the hot sauce by combining the peppers, onion, carrot, vinegar, sugar, and lime juice in a food processor. Pulse until the mixture is smooth.

If desired, you can strain the mixture through 3 layers of cheesecloth to extract the liquid from the solids and present a sauce with thinner consistency.

For the oxtail

Active cooking time: 1 hour | Total cooking time: 7 hours + 8 hours | Yield: 4 main dish servings

4 pounds oxtail or beef short ribs

FOR THE MARINADE

1 large white onion, roughly
    chopped
4 cloves garlic, peeled
2 bunches green onions
1 bunch Italian parsley
2 teaspoons white vinegar

FOR THE DISH

1 (15-ounce) can tomato sauce
2 tablespoons vegetable
    or canola oil
1 large white onion, sliced thin
1 (6-ounce) can tomato paste
Salt

TO SERVE

Cooked white rice
Habanero hot sauce

Soak the oxtail in warm water for 30 minutes to soften the fat. Clean the oxtail carefully, removing and discarding any excess fat or tendons. If you are using short ribs instead of oxtail, you do not have to soak the meat, but you will need to trim off any excess fat.

In a food processor or blender, pulse the onion, garlic, green onions, parsley, and vinegar until lique-fied. Pour the mixture, known as *epis*, over the ox-tail in a large bowl. Cover and refrigerate for at least 8 hours or overnight.

Preheat the oven to 300 degrees.

Place the oxtail in a large Dutch oven. Pour over a can of tomato sauce and add just enough water to cover the meat. Bring to a boil over medium heat.

Cover the pot and transfer it to the oven. Cook for 6 hours.

Skim off any grease that rises to the surface after the meat has cooked.

You can refrigerate the oxtail at this point and continue preparing the dish the next day. Bring the oxtail to a boil before continuing the recipe.

Strain out the oxtail and reserve. Reserve the liquid separately.

Heat the oil in a large skillet over medium heat. Add the sliced onion and cook, stirring constantly, for 5 to 8 minutes, or until the onion is tender.

Add the tomato paste and stir to coat the onion. Add the oxtail and stir to combine. Cook, stirring often, for 15 minutes or until the oxtail has darkened and the meat is starting to pull away from the bones.

Add 2 cups of the reserved liquid to the meat and increase the heat to medium-high. Cook for 5 minutes, stirring constantly, until the sauce has reduced by half.

Season to taste with salt.

Serve with cooked white rice and habanero hot sauce for each diner to add as desired.

Cristobal Morel's Punta Cana Restaurant is in a former Wendy's in Charlotte, North Carolina. While the bones of its former life are still noticeable, the face of the restaurant is completely different. Where the walk-up counter was, there is now a pass-through from the kitchen where the cooks volley orders in a rapid patter of Spanish. Where customers once came in for quick and familiar mass-market fast food, they now sit down to take their time enjoying exotic tropical flavors unique to the area.

"The Punta Cana name comes from the main tourist point in the Dominican Republic. I found out when I came here that USAir has a flight from Charlotte to Punta Cana every Wednesday. Now you have two flights daily to Punta Cana from Charlotte," Cristobal says. "I have traveled home several times, and most of the time, I was the only Dominican. So I felt that now people would know this name. When people go to the airport, they drive through here, so that gives me some benefits."

Anyone returning from or dreaming of the tropical paradise of Punta Cana would be satisfied by Cristobal's restaurant—the bar has a thatched roof, the drinks are cold, and the music is a lively Latin blend. The atmosphere is ideal, but the food is the real key for Cristobal.

"I love Mexican food, but I try to bring something different—what the people don't find often around the corner. I come in here for one goal, to be Dominican. I don't want to mix one thing with the other. I try to give my customers the best we can from the Dominican Republic."

Cristobal's menu is filled with exotic and delicious dishes from his home country. At lunch, he features many of those same dishes for as small a price as he can, hoping to build repeat business and dinner business.

"Our ingredients are kind of expensive. That's why we cannot have a cheaper lunch. We don't make money off of that," he says. "My goal with this lunch is to let people taste Dominican food. Then maybe they'll say, 'Let me bring my husband or my family back at nighttime to eat the food.'"

Because Dominican food is new to Charlotte, Cristobal does have some issues with customer expectations. Some people aren't comfortable sitting down to eat without having familiar dishes on the menu. "You see the lunch being kind of slow? Maybe you see people come in and then leave because they're looking for a Mexican restaurant?" he asks.

Those expectations are not limited to his customers. Even in the bureaucracy of local government, there is confusion when it comes to Hispanic cuisine. "When I got my license, instead of saying 'Hispanic' or 'Dominican,' they said 'Mexican-style' because it's a concept they have, that everybody Hispanic is Mexican."

Cristobal encountered the same issue at his previous job. He originally came from the Dominican Republic to New York, where he spent twenty-one years working for a grocery chain. "When I started grocering in New York, the biggest economic group was the Puerto Ricans. The customers would think I was Puerto Rican."

Working as a grocer, Cristobal learned skills that have helped him as a restaurateur. He learned to offer bargains, like his lunch menu, to get people in the door. He also learned how to take care of his customers and his business. "I believe I am my own competition. In the grocery business, I said, 'Put your eyes inside—take care of your own business.' When you keep your eyes on someone else, you slip up."

The grocery chain Cristobal worked for sent him to Charlotte in 2005 to oversee the opening of a new store. He loved the South immediately. "In New York, there is stress in the air. You don't have that here."

His wife was not so easily won over. "The first time we came here, we ended up driving a lot in an industrial area, and my wife asked me, 'You want to leave Long Island for this?' After two or three more visits, she started to notice little things like flowers along the highway, and she started to like it."

Cristobal saw opportunity in Charlotte. While there were Dominicans in the community, there weren't many restaurants offering authentic Dominican cuisine. When he found the location where he would establish Punta Cana, he knew it would be the right place for him to create the food he missed and to introduce it to other people.

Although Cristobal is happy in Charlotte, he sometimes thinks wistfully of the Dominican Republic and of his family members still there. "Sometimes I wish I could go back with my family. My wife and I, yes, but my children were born here. They're American. They're not going anywhere," he laughs.

Because he remembers his home as the Dominican Republic under dictator Rafael Trujillo, Cristobal's view of Caribbean politics is different from most Americans'. For one thing, he is pragmatic and accepts the evolution of government policy. "I believe the United States changes a lot on the political matters according to the days."

This pragmatism also extends to his opinion of Cuba's Fidel Castro. Although far from admiring Castro, Cristobal does appreciate how the Communist leader has changed with the times to stay in power. "Fidel Castro is very intelligent, let me tell you. I compare him with Trujillo, who was one of the dictators in my country for thirty-one years. The difference—Trujillo was so tight. Fidel Castro, I believe, he changed with the times and tides like the United States did," he says. "Before, he didn't accept anyone talking English in Cuba. He didn't accept American money in Cuba. He wore, all the time, military clothes. After that, you can see the currents of money from the United States. He wore ties. He changed a lot."

Cristobal does not underestimate the problems of Cubans under their government, but he has not forgotten the desperate times or the atrocities that occurred when he was young and still living in the Dominican Republic, including the Trujillo-ordered murder of the Mirabal sisters, leaders of the anti-Trujillo movement. "He even had the gall to kill the three sisters, and that made his own people bring him down."

With Trujillo gone, the economic and political situation in the Dominican Republic has improved, and new opportunities have appeared for the Dominican people. Those opportunities, however, are in stark contrast to those of their Haitian neighbors on the other side of the island. Their shared border and disparate economic opportunities cause Haitian immigration into the Dominican Republic to mimic situations sometimes seen in the United States.

"In my country, I compare it to the Mexicans in the United States now with the situation with immigration. Who are the people who do most of the labor? They do the labor. The hard labor in my country is done by Haitians—the construction, the sugarcane."

Cristobal understands the desire to seek a better life, to seek freedom and opportunity. He believes in Cubans' right to claim asylum in the United States, but he also believes there should be greater equity among nationalities.

"I think it's a privilege for Cubans when they come to the United States. They've got the rights of citizens then. I believe everybody from the Caribbean deserves the same treatment. We come here to try to get a better life—to work hard and get some money to go back. Sometimes, like in my case, you say, 'No, I'm not going to go back there. I'm going to stay here.' And it's already what, thirty years? Over thirty years, and we're still here."

Cristobal is still here—here enjoying the freedom and opportunity that he wishes for everyone. In his restaurant, he offers the warmth and hospitality that he would see everyone receive. He is living his American dream, bringing his home to America, one plate at a time. 🍽

MOFONGO (Mashed Plantains with Garlic)

Active cooking time: 1 hour, 10 minutes | Total cooking time: 1 hour, 25 minutes | Yield: 4 main dish servings

Mofongo is a common dish on both home and restaurant tables throughout the Caribbean, albeit with slight variations in texture and flavor. At one time or another, all of the island nations have claimed to be the originators of the dish, but its actual origins are much farther away than the Caribbean.

Enslaved West Africans brought the tradition of *fufu* to the Spanish colonies in the Caribbean. Even today, in West and Central Africa, *fufu* is a staple food, a porridge-like dish made by pounding boiled root vegetables like yams or cassava in a mortar and pestle until the desired consistency is attained. New techniques evolved in the Caribbean, and the primary ingredient became the readily available plantains.

Mofongo is made with the starchier green plantains instead of ripe plantains, which are sweeter and less starchy. The green plantains are also used in one of the indigenous snack foods of the region, the crisp, flattened, fried plantain chips known as tostones. While it would be easy to think that tostones are simply fried plantains, an extra step makes all the difference in their flavor and texture. That step is also important to the making of *mofongo*. After an initial frying, the plantain slices are flattened with a specially made wooden press, much like a small tortilla press, known as a *tostonera*. Then the flattened slices are returned to the hot oil for a second frying that adds crispness and produces a softer interior.

Another important tool in the traditional making of *mofongo* is a wooden mortar and pestle known as a pilón, a tool often passed down through families. In Puerto Rico, the pilón is often used as the serving dish for the finished *mofongo*. Any mortar and pestle can be used, but the main difference is that the pilón is taller than it is wide, shaped more like a large coffee cup than the wider bowl of most mortar and pestle sets.

This recipe is for the Dominican version of *mofongo*. While the basic ingredients and techniques are the same throughout the region, the Dominican version is served as a side dish with meat, seafood, or vegetables. The pork cracklings give a rich texture and mouthfeel to the dish, while the starchy smoothness of the plantains makes *mofongo* an easy comfort food.

4 unripe (green) plantains, peeled and
    sliced into ½-inch thick pieces
12 cloves garlic, peeled
1 cup + 1 teaspoon corn oil
    or vegetable oil, divided
1 cup pork cracklings (*chicharrones*)
    or 6 slices thick-cut bacon, cut into
    ¼-inch pieces
1 tablespoon salt

Soak the plantain slices in a bowl of water with a pinch of salt for 15 minutes.

Drain the slices and pat dry with paper towels.

Using a mortar and pestle or food processor, crush the garlic to a fine paste.

In a large, deep skillet, heat 1 teaspoon oil over medium heat.

Cook the garlic paste, stirring constantly, for about 3 minutes or until the garlic is beginning to brown.

Remove the garlic from the skillet and reserve.

If you are using bacon, cook the bacon in the skillet until the fat has rendered out and the bacon is crisp. Remove the bacon from the pan, leaving the fat behind to add extra flavor to the plantains.

Add 1 cup oil to the skillet and increase the heat to medium-high.

Working in batches, add plantain slices to the oil and cook them for 4 to 5 minutes, stirring often, until the plantain slices are a rich, buttery yellow.

Remove the plantain slices from the skillet and flatten them by covering them with a plate and pressing down or by using a *tostonera*.

Return the flattened plantains to the oil and cook for another 2 minutes or until the plantains are a dark gold and begin to look slightly translucent. Drain on a paper-towel-lined plate.

In a pilón or large, deep bowl, combine the hot plantain slices with the reserved garlic, salt, and pork cracklings or bacon.

Using a pestle or muddler, or even the handle of a meat mallet or wooden spoon, mash the contents together until they are just combined, keeping recognizable chunks of the plantains and pork cracklings. Alternatively, you can combine the ingredients in a food processor, pulsing to combine. Do not overwork the mixture or it will be gummy.

Shape into a mound and serve with soup, meat, seafood, or vegetables.

Kurds A People without a Country

Kurdistan, a region of mountains and plateaus, home of Mount Ararat and the headwaters of the Tigris and Euphrates Rivers, cannot be found on a world map. Since the end of World War I, the Kurdish people have become citizens of Turkey, Iran, Iraq, and Syria. They have fought for recognition as a distinct people and sometimes for their very survival, having faced everything from discrimination to outright genocide.

Kurdish refugees first came to the United States in 1976 after a failed revolution in Iraqi Kurdistan. Iranian Kurds soon joined them after a failed autonomy movement there. In the late 1980s, the Kurds of northern Iraq were targeted in a systematic genocidal campaign led by dictator Saddam Hussein in retaliation for the Kurds' support of Iran during the Iran-Iraq War. A series of eight campaigns known as Al Anfar, or "The Spoils of War," left the region emotionally and economically devastated. Sons, brothers, husbands, and fathers vanished without a trace, and few families and communities were left unscathed.

During the Persian Gulf War, a Kurdish resistance movement gained strength in northern Iraq. But after the war, Iraqi forces turned their attention to ending that resistance. Nearly half a million Kurds fled to Turkey. Another 200,000 escaped Iraq in 1996, when their lives were threatened because they had worked with organizations receiving financial support from Western nations.

Today, the largest population of Kurds in the United States is in Nashville, Tennessee. Nashville may seem an unlikely place to find such a community, but in truth, Nashville is one of many southern cities that not only welcome but also encourage immigrants to make homes there. Thriving shops, markets, bakeries, and restaurants as well as the first Kurdish mosque in the United States are all found in a section of Nashville sometimes called Little Kurdistan.

Hamid Hassan,
Nashville, Tennessee

Hamid Hassan is a child of Little Kurdistan. Although he was born in northern Iraq, he came to Nashville from a refugee camp in Turkey when he was only eight years old. Hamid doesn't remember a lot about the Iraq he left behind, a place that no longer truly exists. The village that his parents fled was destroyed, and many people from the region have immigrated to other lands. "Everything was demolished, everything just . . . What stuff we had was gone, and the people, too." What he does remember clearly is arriving in Nashville. "I came here on July 14, 1993," he says, instantly recalling the exact date.

Hamid learned English easily, a skill that was much more difficult for his parents. He also didn't have the deep connections to Iraq that made the transition harder for them. "For me, it was easier than for my parents because my parents still have their parents, brothers and sisters over there. Still right now, it's hard for my parents. They are older, and so it's hard for them to learn the language." For Hamid, being an immigrant is a distant memory. "I feel like I'm from here now because it's been sixteen years. I grew up in Nashville, in this country."

One of the deepest connections to Kurdistan for Hamid has been the food his mother prepares. "My mother is a good chef. Even now, when we get together at her house, she cooks for us." While there are many Kurdish-owned restaurants in the area, including Hamid's own House of Kabob, few of them offer traditional Kurdish home cooking. (Despite the name of his restaurant, Hamid used the spelling "kebabs" in writing out the recipe given below.)

The food Hamid serves in his restaurant is more a result of his experiences than it is true Kurdish cuisine. "Some stuff we use in this restaurant, I tell my mom about it, and she's never heard of it before. We use a lot of Persian food, and that's a little different from Kurdish original food. Some stuff they use, we don't use in Kurdish. But we come as Kurdish, and we are making a version of Kurdish, and Persian, and Turkish food, because we lived in Turkey for many years. So we are pretty much a combination of everything."

But there are differences that make Kurdish cuisine unique. Fresh herbs and vegetables are key to Kurdish meals. One of the signature dishes is *yapragh*, or the Kurdish version of the dolma, stuffed grape leaves, popular in most regions of the Middle East. Hamid describes it as one of his favorite dishes. "The Kurdish, most of the time, they bring a tomato. They take the inside out of the tomato and they put rice in the tomato, and in eggplant they do that, and green pepper. They also bring grape leaves so that they have a combination of stuff. But the Persians, they just use a grape leaf. But we, the Kurdish people, use all

Hamid Hassan at House of Kabob.

these different kinds of things. We put rice in there and fill it up with rice and meat."

After working at House of Kabob for two years, Hamid had the opportunity to buy it. It seemed a natural fit. "I like cooking; I like to play with food. I like anything I can touch. I can put some things together and make something out of it."

But Hamid admits that he isn't the best cook in the family. He depends on his older brother to be in charge of the kitchen. "I've got a bigger brother. He is really the main chef. I usually am in the front, taking care of customer stuff. My big brother is like a genius with anything he can touch; it doesn't even have to be cooking—anything. I phoned him and asked, 'Won't you come help us?' We made him a partner because we knew he would succeed if he came over, if he helped."

Hamid's experiences outside his own kitchen exhibit not only his willingness to try new things but also his family's efforts to be a part of Nashville outside of Little Kurdistan. "I had put together a schedule for me and my family. We go once a week to Mexican, Chinese, or Persian restaurants. We try all different kinds of American food. It's good experience to use all these foods. You find something you never had in your life and something you like."

Hamid returned to Kurdistan for the first time in 2007. For him, it was less like going home and more like making a visit to distant relatives. While he enjoyed the experience of the trip, the memories he carries from childhood are really what Kurdistan means to him. His earliest food memory is extraordinarily vivid. "Flat bread with some fresh yogurt. We used to have a farm; we used to have cows and sheep. My mom would go and get the milk and bring it and cook it and put it somewhere. They'd make the yogurt out of the milk. I'd wake up in the morning, and I would have the sheep milk yogurt and the fresh bread they call *tanoor* and a glass of hot tea. That was the first food memory, and it'll never go away." ⑧

CHICKEN KEBAB

Active cooking time: 30 minutes | Total cooking time: 1 hour, 30 minutes | Yield: 6 main dish servings

Shish kebabs have been a staple food in the Middle East for centuries. Literally meaning "meat roasted on skewers," shish kebabs originated as a way to cook meat quickly over an open fire. The meat was often marinated to mask the flavor if the meat was gamy or less than fresh. For nomadic herdsmen and soldiers in the field, shish kebabs were a way to have a hot meal without having any of the accoutrements of a kitchen.

Over the centuries, shish kebabs became more complex. Marinades were concocted to add flavors rather than to mask flaws in the meat itself. Vegetables were added for appearance as much as for flavor, and the kebabs began to be prepared in kitchens over specially designed grills.

As Arabic influence grew during the Middle Ages, shish kebabs found their way into European cuisine to the west and Asian cuisine to the east. In France, they are known as brochettes and in Portugal as *espetadas*. The *satays* of Thailand and the yakitori of Japan can also be traced back to Arabic shish kebabs.

Hamid's chicken kebabs are a delicious variation. The meat is marinated in rich flavors, picking up the savoriness of soy sauce, the bright zing of lemon juice, the floral hint of saffron, and the heartiness of beef. The skewers will cook quickly, so have the rest of the meal ready before starting them. You can add vegetables to the skewers of chicken or make skewers of only vegetables.

While bamboo skewers are easy to find in most supermarkets and are perfectly acceptable to use for these kebabs, you might consider looking at the metal skewers available at most Middle Eastern markets. Here, you will be able to choose skewers of different widths, lengths, and weights. These skewers are designed for both function and beauty and will allow you to make a great presentation of the meal at your table.

6 tablespoons olive oil

1 teaspoon ground saffron

1 tablespoon soy sauce

3 tablespoons lemon juice

2 packages instant dry beef broth
    or 1 tablespoon beef soup base
    concentrate

½ teaspoon cinnamon

1 teaspoon salt

½ teaspoon freshly ground black pepper

6 boneless chicken thighs

SPECIAL EQUIPMENT

Griddle or grill pan
Skewers

In a large mixing bowl, combine the oil, saffron, soy sauce, lemon juice, beef broth, cinnamon, salt, and black pepper. Whisk until the mixture is thoroughly combined and smooth.

Cut the chicken into bite-sized pieces large enough to be cooked on skewers.

Transfer the chicken to the mixing bowl with the seasoning mixture and stir, making sure to coat each piece with the seasoning mixture. Cover the bowl and refrigerate for at least one hour.

Heat a griddle or grill pan over medium heat. Coat the pan with a light layer of oil.

Carefully push the chicken onto the skewers. Leave at least a finger's width of space between each piece of chicken to ensure even cooking.

Lay the skewers of chicken on the griddle or grill pan. Allow the meat to cook without turning for 5 to 7 minutes or until the meat will pull away from the pan without sticking.

Turn the skewer over and cook for another 5 to 7 minutes.

Serve with a green salad, rice, and cooked vegetables.

Mahir Ahmad,
Nashville, Tennessee

It's a very busy Sunday in the markets of Little Kurdistan. The weekend shoppers are out in force and regular visitors come from other parts of Nashville, but more unfamiliar faces than usual are part of the crowd. This is a very special Sunday not only in Little Kurdistan but in Iraq as well. This is Election Day.

Like many residents of Little Kurdistan, Mahir Ahmad holds dual citizenship in both the United States and Iraq. By keeping dual citizenship, Mahir and the other residents of Little Kurdistan are able to affect the future policy of the country they left behind. However, unlike the absentee ballots cast by Americans abroad, Iraqi voters in the United States must cast their ballots in person in the Iraqi elections. Only nine locations were set up in the United States, one in Nashville.

While this location was good for the local Kurdish population, others had to travel from very far away. Mahir met many of them as he waited in line at the polls. "I had some people from eighteen hours' drive away. Some people came from Jacksonville, Florida; St. Louis, Missouri; even New York."

Standing in his store, Mahir's boyish smile is especially bright today. His pride is as obvious as the ink on his finger that marks him as a voter. "I think it's great. We came here and worked for your country, but we lived there, and we're supporting our country, too."

Mahir feels certain that some of them will eventually return to the Iraq they are helping to build today. "It's so beautiful there. Everything is so safe. I think in a couple of years, a lot of people will be going back. Maybe."

And yet there are others who have everything they want in Nash-

ville. "When people come to visit, they are like, 'We're in Kurdistan.'
You have the mosque right next door. You have the grocery stores. You
have everything, a big Kurdish community here. See, the people living
here in Nashville, they don't miss Kurdistan like the people from other
states because here they see family, and it's still like back home."

For Mahir, that home is a distant memory. He was eight years old
when his family fled from Iraq to a refugee camp in Turkey. In August
1993, when Mahir was eleven, his family came to Nashville. He started
school right away and adapted promptly to life in his new hometown.
"I learned English quick because in the place we lived, we didn't have
any Kurdish families around us, so I picked it up easy."

Today, Mahir manages Mazi Market, just a couple of buildings over
from the market he started working for as a teenager. "I used to work
for Azadi Market, and my dad used to have this kind of store back

home. So when we came here, I worked with them. Since I had experience and my dad had experience back home, we decided to open this grocery store."

A third grocery store is just across the street from Mazi Market. It might seem strange that the markets are all so near to each other, but this proximity helps the Kurdish community feel closer to home. "If you go back home, all the grocery stores are on one street; fabric is on one street; gold is on one street; meat is on one street."

In Little Kurdistan, the butcher shops are a part of the markets. "The meat is local. We process our meat in Hopkins, Kentucky. And our chicken is from Alabama." These local connections allow the markets to offer the freshest halal meats. Mahir imports many of his dry and canned goods from Iraq, which makes his shoppers feel at home because they are able to find familiar brands.

While it would be easy to assume that Mahir and his family would have immediately looked for the foods they were used to having in Iraq and Turkey, one of their first meals in America was surprisingly unlike anything they had tried before: "We went to Krystal," a fast-food hamburger chain popular across the South. "When we came here, we had neighbors across the street from us. They were like, maybe, eighty years old. They supported us, took us to the doctor, and stuff like this. So after the first time we went to the doctor, we went to Krystal. I didn't know. I asked my mom, 'Do you think we should eat this or not?' And Krystal is my favorite burger now." 🍴

DOWJIC (Kurdish-Style Chicken and Rice Soup)

Active cooking time: 1 hour, 10 minutes | Total cooking time: 3 hours, 10 minutes
Yield: 4 to 6 main dish servings

Mahir describes Kurdish cuisine in simple terms. "It's rice and soup and chicken. Probably any house you go to, they eat one of those meals a day. If they don't eat it, they have to eat it the next day. Bread, rice and soup, and chicken."

This soup combines the tang of lemon and yogurt with the richness of chicken and rice soup to create a simple comfort food that is absolutely luxurious. Fresh basil adds a sweetness that contrasts perfectly with the tart creaminess of the soup.

2 pounds chicken thighs

2 medium carrots, roughly chopped

2 ribs celery, roughly chopped

1 medium yellow onion, quartered

2 cloves garlic, crushed

1 tablespoon whole white peppercorns

1 bay leaf

1 4-inch cinnamon stick

½ cup white rice

2 teaspoons salt

½ cup freshly squeezed lemon juice
(from about 2 lemons)

3 eggs

1 cup yogurt

¼ cup fresh basil, diced

Freshly ground pepper, preferably white

Kitchen Passport While the vegetables are removed from the broth in this version of *dowjic*, you can easily reincorporate them with the chicken, if desired. Alternatively, leave out the chicken entirely for a lighter version of the soup. Basil is the traditional herb used to flavor the soup, but thyme, marjoram, or tarragon also make a delicious version.

Cover the chicken thighs, carrots, celery, onion, and garlic with a gallon of water in a large stockpot. Add the peppercorns, bay leaf, and cinnamon stick and bring the mixture to a boil over medium-high heat.

Cover the pot, reduce the heat to low, and continue simmering for 2 hours or until the chicken meat is falling from the bones.

Strain the broth and reserve. Discard the vegetables, spices, chicken skin, and bones.

Allow the chicken to cool enough to handle; shred the meat finely and reserve.

Bring 8 cups of the reserved broth to a boil in a stockpot over medium-high heat. Any remaining broth can be frozen for later use.

Add the rice, salt, and lemon juice to the boiling broth. Continue boiling, stirring constantly, for about 15 minutes or until the rice is tender.

Reduce the heat to low.

In a medium mixing bowl, stir the eggs and yogurt until thoroughly combined and smooth. Very slowly, add 1 cup of the hot chicken broth to the bowl, stirring constantly to combine without scrambling the eggs.

Slowly, stirring constantly, add the thinned yogurt mixture to the stockpot with the rest of the soup mixture. Adding the yogurt mixture slowly will make a smoother soup.

Add the reserved shredded chicken and the basil to the soup mixture, stirring to combine. Continue simmering over low heat for 10 minutes or until the chicken has heated.

Add salt and pepper to taste.

Yogurt

Yogurt has been a staple food in many cultures, including that of the Kurds, for over 5,000 years. The first yogurt was made in Bulgaria where it was most likely accidentally fermented by wild bacteria. Once the technique was understood, it quickly spread south to the Middle East. In fact, the earliest writings mentioning yogurt place it in the Middle East, where it was a common food for the nomadic Turks.

Yogurt was first industrially produced in the early twentieth century by a Jewish entrepreneur who named his company "Danone," the company we know today as Dannon. Yogurt didn't achieve popularity in the United States, however, until 1950, when Gayelord Hauser labeled it a wonder food in his book *Look Younger, Live Longer.*

Yogurt is rich in protein, calcium, and B vitamins. It is also used medicinally as a home remedy, particularly for gastrointestinal conditions.

Americans typically are most familiar with unstrained yogurts. Many varieties contain pectin to produce a thicker texture with less time and expense.

Strained yogurts, like Greek yogurt, are made by straining out the whey, traditionally through a muslin cloth. Filtering out the whey makes the yogurt creamier, richer, and milder in flavor. One of the most common varieties of strained yogurt in the Middle East is *labneh*, yogurt that is strained until it has the same texture as soft cream cheese. It's often used as a spread on bread or sandwiches.

Yogurt can be enjoyed as a beverage. In the United States, many markets sell fruit-flavored liquid yogurt, or kefir. In the Middle East and the Balkans, plain yogurt is often mixed with water and sometimes salt, then served cold.

Yogurt is also a valuable cooking ingredient. Strained yogurt is a great substitute for sour cream in most recipes. Because the bacteria in yogurt change the lactose in milk to lactic acid, yogurt is a great marinade for tenderizing meat. The lactic acid also acts a preservative, meaning that yogurt will have a longer shelf life than regular milk.

The aroma of baking bread fills Tara International Market. In a small kitchen on one side of the store, women are baking *tanoor*, the flatbread common throughout the Middle East but a particular favorite in Kurdish households. If you close your eyes, the laughing voices of the women speaking Kurdish, the aroma, and the sounds of dough being slapped from hand to hand will make you think that you are nowhere close to Tennessee.

Rauf Ary, Nashville, Tennessee

And yet, this scene is taking place in the heart of Tennessee, in Nashville's Little Kurdistan. It's fascinating to watch the women bake the bread as their mothers did before them and back through countless generations. The bread oven at Tara International Market is a traditional Kurdish oven, a metal cylinder insulated with clay or cement with heat rising from a gas burner in the bottom. Instead of baking on sheet pans, the bread is slapped in a deceptively simple maneuver to the side of the oven where it sticks, baking for only a couple of minutes before being lifted off and flung aside to cool.

Rauf Ary's customers seem to know the schedule for bread baking. The bags of flatbread are bought as quickly as the women in the kitchen can pack them. These customers also know Rauf well, chatting with him in a constant flow of Arabic as they discuss their needs and have him cut their meat to order. As one customer helps him bag up a whole lamb that has been cut into soup meat, two English words break out from their conversation: "very tender."

Rauf never planned to be a market owner in the United States. He grew up in Halabja and Assulemaniyah, where he survived the chemical attacks against the Kurdish people in 1988. He graduated from college in Iraq with a degree in electrical engineering, but he didn't get to use his degree. Rauf explains that as a Kurdish citizen of Iraq, his political choices were stark. "The political situation in Iraq was pretty bad. Saddam was a dictator, so we only had two choices. You had to go beside him, or you had to be against him. So I'm one of those people who chose to be against him. I fought nine years against his armies."

After the Kurdish resistance failed, leaving Iraq was never a question; Rauf knew that he and his family would not be safe if they remained. In 1991, they fled to Saudi Arabia, where they stayed for two years and two days before coming to Nashville as refugees on March 3, 1993. He was thirty years old.

At first, Rauf worked in a packaging company for minimum wage, but he was glad to be in the United States. "At least, here the people have free will. How I'm thinking, how I'm dreaming—no one comes to tell me why I'm thinking this, why I'm dreaming this."

Rauf Ary at Tara
International Market.

Soon he was able to find work using his degree. He became an electrician at a large electrical company and stayed there for almost eight years. He was working for the company on a project at Vanderbilt University Hospital on September 11, 2001—the only Muslim employed by the company at the time.

The fear and paranoia during the days after 9/11 created an untenable situation for Rauf. "They were thinking I did that. Everybody came to me saying, 'Osama bin Laden, Osama bin Laden!' A supervisor came to me and asked if I know Osama bin Laden. I told him, 'Don't ask me that question. Because if you know the history of Osama bin Laden's life, you will have to go to the White House and ask the president who Osama bin Laden is.'"

The tension over his religion and ethnicity led him to take an enormous chance. Although he had no other job lined up, Rauf asked to be laid off. The company complied, and he began spending his days at home with his family. But he knew that situation couldn't last long since there was no money coming in to support them.

The owner of Tara International Market was a friend and had mentioned to Rauf that he wanted to sell the market. In October 2001, Rauf made a deal with him. "I only had $100, but I had good credit. I paid him $10,000 with my credit card and for the rest of it, I told him I would give him $5,000 every three months. So that was a story, wasn't it? I started with $100."

As a market owner, Rauf has come to see a side of Little Kurdistan that is invisible to outsiders. While he is not pessimistic about the community's future, he sees problems that have arisen from an unexpected source. "I feel sorry for the Kurdish community here. Most of the people here come from village areas in Kurdistan. When they come over here, they try to get more money and more things. They forget about the kids and their families. So the kids are alone and right now they're lost," he says.

"We have a lot of good people, and we feel sorry when someone asks about the Kurdish gangs. I think if you are far from your parents, it doesn't matter where you come from. When the parents leave the kids to grow up by themselves, well, kids are kids . . . Now their parents are learning to come here and be Kurdish and stay Kurdish."

SELIM BA GOSHT (Kurdish Lamb Stew)

Active cooking time: 1 hour | Total cooking time: 3 hours | Yield: 6 to 8 main dish servings

Simple stews are one of the primary dishes served in Kurdish homes. Tough cuts of meat become tender over the hours they cook, and stews like this one turn a small amount of vegetables into a satisfying meal. The one common factor in these stews is the delicate tomato sauce that adds flavor without requiring much seasoning. The acid in the tomato also helps to tenderize the meat as it cooks.

A special aspect of the presentation of this soup is the herbs. Instead of being cooked into the stew or used as a garnish, they are set out on the table for each diner to add as desired to create the unique blend of flavors that he or she enjoys most.

Rauf recommends that you use bone-in meat to make this stew. The bones add rich, meaty flavor to the stew that meat alone can't. If you use a boneless cut of meat, you might consider using broth in the stew instead of water to enhance the flavor of the dish.

2 tablespoons olive oil

2 pounds lamb shoulder steak
    or lamb stew meat

1 large turnip, peeled and diced

1 small bulb fennel, diced with tops
    reserved

1 medium yellow onion, diced
    (about ⅔ cup)

1 shallot, diced (about ⅔ cup)

1 teaspoon salt

½ teaspoon freshly ground black pepper

1 teaspoon ground cumin

1 (28-ounce) can diced tomatoes

1 (6-ounce) can tomato paste

TO SERVE

Cooked white rice

Fresh basil, chopped

Fresh thyme leaves

Fennel fronds, diced

Green onions, chopped

Heat the oil in a large Dutch oven or stockpot over medium heat.

Add the lamb and cook for 5 to 8 minutes.

Turn the lamb and cook for another 5 to 8 minutes or until the lamb has browned. Transfer the lamb to a plate and reserve.

Add the turnip, fennel, onion, shallot, salt, and black pepper to the pot and cook, stirring occasionally, for 20 minutes or until the vegetables are tender.

Add the cumin, diced tomatoes, and tomato paste to the vegetables, stirring to combine. Return the lamb to the mixture. Add water to cover the meat.

Increase the heat to medium-high and allow the mixture to come to a boil.

Reduce the heat to low and cook, uncovered, for 2 hours or until the meat is tender and falling from the bones.

Serve over cooked white rice with herbs for each diner to add as desired.

Kitchen Passport A stew like this is amazingly versatile. The meat used in the stew can be any variety you like. The vegetables can be either your favorites or whatever vegetables are in season and available to you. Try changing the seasoning to alter the flavor entirely. Other common Kurdish variations use potatoes, eggplant, or okra as the primary vegetables.

Part II
Living the American Dream

My parents moved here, and they are the
ones that started to put the U.S. in my
mind. . . . Finally, because of them asking
so much, one summer we said, "Okay,
let's take the kids to Disney World, and
we will visit them." Then I guess we liked
it so much that we chose to stay.
—Efren Ormaza, Ecuadoran restaurateur,
Chattanooga, Tennessee

Central and South America Family

Family is an important part of everyday life in Central and South America. There, as in so many other countries across the globe, family goes far beyond social connections or business relationships. Extended family represents a refuge in times of trouble or upheaval, with family members often pitching in to help when someone is in need.

Leaving behind a safety net like that is not a casual undertaking. Everywhere in the world, when a person leaves home, family relationships change. For immigrants, leaving family members is often the most difficult aspect of deciding to move away. Still, the United States offers opportunities that are often too great to ignore.

Fortunately, many immigrants from Central and South America are able to stay in close contact with their extended families in their home countries. Some are even able to include them in their businesses. Family members left behind become sources of support, of recipes, and even of products that immigrants serve to their new communities. These connections maintain the bonds of family.

Manuel "Manny" Ochoa-Galvez has a personality almost too great for his restaurant, La Macarena Pupuseria, to contain. His background is perfect for life in a tourist town like New Orleans. "I put myself through school being a travel agent," he says. He talks to his guests about places in Europe and Africa as easily as he talks about the city that has been his home for his entire adult life. Manny is also very proud of the food in his restaurant, recommending entrées and condiments, even sending out special appetizers not on the menu just because he wants to share them.

The restaurant is a family business inspired by his mother's desire to sell her food. "My mother was interested in opening a restaurant. She did not have a lot of the financial resources, but she had a lot of equipment from a previous restaurant. I was able to help her fulfill the dream of selling her food, her wares, to the people."

Things have not always been easy. Like most of the residents of New Orleans, the Ochoas were severely affected by Hurricane Katrina. They

Manuel
Ochoa-Galvez,
New Orleans,
Louisiana

4

Manny Ochoa-Galvez at La Macarena Pupuseria.

have since rebuilt and resumed their normal lives. That they could rebound from such devastation is not a great surprise, because for the Ochoa family, Katrina was only the latest challenge.

Manny was born in San Salvador, the capital of El Salvador. His parents took jobs in New Orleans, leaving Manny and his siblings with family in their home country. In 1976, they brought their children to the United States, when Manny was eleven years old. "The civil war was just beginning to brew. My mother got us out of there just in time because, of course, the war heightened in the '80s. It was very traumatic having to leave the grandparents and the extended family behind."

Still, the Ochoas have maintained ties with their home country and the members of their family who stayed there. Those relatives in El Salvador are an important part of the authenticity of the food they serve in New Orleans today. "My grandmother is very gifted. She was left orphaned very early on, and she was raised by a lady who taught her how to cook. She still does things the old-fashioned way, using the old tools and preparations."

The restaurant depends on more than just the example Manny's grandmother sets. "To this day, she is our agent, if you will, in El Salvador. The *horchata*, for instance, the spices—she prepares that for us. She goes through the process of picking the ingredients, drying the ingredients, cleansing them, roasting them, and then taking them to the mill and packing them. So it's a labor of love."

Manny's restaurant is a bright celebration of those things that mean the most to him. Tables outside allow diners to enjoy beautiful days in New Orleans. Tables inside are scattered on multiple levels. All are set with Salvadoran hot sauces to complement the food. Artwork by New Orleans artists adorns the tropically painted walls.

One wall, however, is devoted to a montage of images from El Salvador. This wall illustrates Manny's philosophy for the restaurant. "One of the things that my mother made very clear is that we are not in the business of serving fusion. We are going to keep the food as real and authentic as it is. She does not believe in messing with something great. And this has been the same tradition with my grandmother. Everything has been pure."

Manny's grandmother's influence on the food he loves stretches past the restaurant and back into his childhood. "Being the Catholic family we were, they used to drag me around. My mother came here and left us in the care of my grandmother. My grandmother, being a church lady, dragged me around to novenas, and at the novenas, they served tamales and homemade chicken sandwiches."

Those sandwiches were the beginning of something special for Manny. "There's nothing like a homemade Salvadoran chicken sandwich, because they go to great lengths to make a chicken sandwich. To this day, I never have had another one like it. So I used to go a lot to the funerals to see the dead people and to eat. They would do the rosary three times, and they had elaborate altars, but, boy, you knew after doing all that you were going to have the best meal."

Manny smiles as he reflects on those early days. He also knows just how profoundly they affected him. "That's how they got me praying and believing in a higher power. It was amazing. I have that connection—love, comfort, food, and God." 🅐

SALVADORAN ENCHILADAS

Active cooking time: 50 minutes | Total cooking time: 50 minutes | Yield: 6 enchiladas

When Americans think of enchiladas, we normally think of the Tex-Mex version of rolled, stuffed tortillas smothered in sauce and cheese. Salvadoran enchiladas are a completely different experience. If you want something to compare them to, the closest dish would be the Mexican tostada, but the Salvadoran enchilada is unique.

The term "enchilada" refers to different dishes in different Central American countries. In Nicaragua, an enchilada more closely resembles the fried or baked meat pie that most of us would recognize as an empanada. Perhaps this difference in definitions shouldn't be that surprising, since "enchilada" is a Spanish word meaning "coated in chile pepper." Obviously, different cultures adapted that meaning to different dishes over time. For a Salvadoran enchilada, a crispy tortilla is topped with lightly spiced meat and fresh vegetables and cheese for a lighter, more portable treat.

For Manny, these enchiladas exemplify the uniqueness of Salvadoran cuisine. It's a surprisingly simple dish with a wealth of flavor. His guests are always surprised by these enchiladas, usually expecting something closer to the Tex-Mex version. But they always enjoy it and often order it again when they return to La Macarena.

You will notice that the pepper used in Manny's recipe is paprika, a sweet rather than spicy pepper. The blending of flavors and textures is delicious. The crisp tortilla gives way to the lightly spiced beef. The freshness of the lettuce, the juiciness of the tomato, the tang of cilantro, the creaminess of the egg, and the nuttiness ofthe cheese bring it all together.

½ cup corn or peanut oil

6 corn tortillas

2 tablespoons olive oil

1 medium white onion, diced
 (about ⅔ cup)

1 green bell pepper, seeded
 and diced (about 1 cup)

2 cloves garlic, minced
 (about 1 teaspoon)

½ teaspoon paprika

½ teaspoon salt

½ pound ground beef

3 cups lettuce, shredded

12 slices tomato

6 slices boiled egg

¾ cup fresh cilantro, chopped

6 tablespoons Pecorino Romano
 cheese, grated

TO SERVE

Hot sauce or salsa

Heat the corn or peanut oil over medium heat in a deep skillet.

Carefully lower a tortilla into the hot oil and fry it for 2 minutes or until it is light brown and crisp. Transfer the tortilla to a paper-towel-lined plate to drain. Repeat with the remaining 5 tortillas.

Heat the olive oil over medium heat in a large skillet.

Add the onion, bell pepper, garlic, paprika, and salt. Cook, stirring constantly, for 5 to 8 minutes or until the onion is translucent.

Add the ground beef and cook, stirring constantly, for 8 to 10 minutes or until the meat has browned. Drain off and discard any excess grease.

To assemble, spread a thick layer of the beef mixture on each cooked tortilla. Top the beef with ½ cup lettuce, 2 slices of tomato, a slice of boiled egg, 2 tablespoons cilantro, and 1 tablespoon Pecorino Romano cheese.

Serve with hot sauce or salsa for each diner to add as desired.

Kitchen Passport Such a simple recipe makes variation easy. Try ground pork or shredded turkey or chicken instead of the beef used here. Shrimp or fish would also be delicious. For vegetarians, refried beans would be a great substitute. If you want the meat mixture to be spicier, use a hotter pepper like ground chipotle or cayenne instead of paprika. You could also replace the green bell pepper with jalapeño or serrano chiles.

The toppings also offer room for variation. Sprinkle on freshly chopped onion or pepper, include avocado, add a dash of lime juice, or use a creamier cheese like queso fresco or even Monterey Jack.

For Edgar Caro, opportunity and family were the two forces that drew him to immigrate to the United States from Colombia. He had visited the country on vacations and always liked it. When it was time for him to go to college to study graphic design, he decided that he was ready to join his grandmother and aunt in New Orleans.

After college, he could have gone anywhere, but by then, New Orleans had won his heart. "At the beginning, I chose New Orleans just because I have family here. I decided to come over just to check it out, but once I got here, and I started getting to know a little bit more of the city, I started loving it and decided to stay. I like living here with the different cultures, and the food is amazing here. It's one of the biggest inspirations for me, just being in a city like this, full of so many things."

He never planned to become a chef, but just as his heart had led him to make his home in New Orleans, it led him to food. "I haven't been in my country in ten years. I wanted to eat the food that I grew up eating. I would go to Latin restaurants over here, and it wasn't the same because they're Honduran or Mexican. They don't serve a lot of things that were in my culture," Edgar says. "I decided I wanted to maybe cook a little bit more of my real food. My grandma cooked it here, and when I started living alone, I wanted to cook for myself and for my friends. I was calling my grandma and getting her recipes, and I started loving it more and more and more."

Learning to cook didn't always go smoothly. "At the beginning, the recipes weren't coming out the right way. It was all trial and error." But one big change kept him going. "When I got married, that's when I started saying, 'Hey, let's not go out to eat, let's just cook more at the house.'" Seeing that his American wife loved the Colombian food he grew up with inspired him to keep learning and to keep cooking.

His first experience in professional cooking came about as a business venture with his uncle in the New Orleans suburb of Kenner. "When he saw what I was cooking, he said, 'Okay, we have to do something about this.' So we did it." Unfortunately, their visions for the restaurant moved apart. As Edgar says, "Family businesses don't always go well." So he decided to move on and open Baru Bistro in New Orleans.

That may sound on the surface like a simple transition, but it was the start of a period of very hard work. "The passion was always there, so it drove me to just do it. It didn't matter how many problems I had to go through; I knew I was going to make it anyway. It was hard, but once again, I had so much passion for what we were doing." Gesturing to the restaurant, Edgar continues, "We did all this—me, my partner, and my wife. We did everything from scratch, but it was really good.

Edgar Caro outside Baru Bistro.

It has rewarded me in a way I never expected to be rewarded. It's very fulfilling."

Although his aunt and grandmother haven't worked directly in the restaurant with Edgar, their support and encouragement have been invaluable to his success. "When it comes to support, one of the most important people would be my grandma. She's really proud of me, the same as my aunt," he says. "They don't have to help with the restaurant. For me, it's just great for them to just come here and eat the food and not complain, because my grandma is the type of person that will tell you, 'It's too salty. It's too this.' So now I've got it at the point where

I know what she likes, and I make it for her and she enjoys it. But my family is a big support for me just when they come back and eat the food."

Even with the support of family, a restaurant succeeds only if the customers are happy. As Edgar puts it, "It all depends on the people that come and try your food. If they enjoy it, they'll want to come back." He was frustrated when he felt that his food was not well received in his first restaurant. "We tried to make people understand that it's not about how cheap it is, that you have to understand the quality of food that certain restaurants get, the quality of the techniques that people do, and everything else that goes into the restaurant. People didn't realize that."

His location on Magazine Street in New Orleans has allowed Edgar to introduce the concept of high-quality Latin cuisine. "Here, people appreciate what we are trying to do—make Latin cuisine better, make Latin cuisine look the way it should look, because we have the same good techniques that French cuisine has or Italian cuisine has. I want people to be happy with what they eat and want them to understand what I'm trying to do and appreciate it."

Although his restaurant in New Orleans has been successful beyond his dreams, Edgar hopes to do more. His passion for his food comes through loud and clear when he talks about the richness of cuisine in his homeland. Colombia is a small country, but the food varies incredibly from region to region.

"There are as many different cultures as there are different ingredients in every single region we have. From the coast, you get beautiful fish and seafood. Then you go inside to the mountains, and you have really good beef and different starches. We have hundreds of kinds of potatoes, just like Peru. We have influence from the Spanish, we have influence from the Africans, and we have influence from the Indians that started it," he says. "One of my main goals is to create a restaurant where I can showcase every single region of my country. I think it's a good country full of different flavors."

MAZORCA (Colombian-Style Corn Salad)

Active cooking time: 1 hour, 10 minutes | Total cooking time: 1 hour, 25 minutes
Yield: 4 main dish servings or 8 side dish servings

Mazorca is one of the most popular dishes on Edgar's menu at Baru Bistro. That's no surprise because the combination of corn, cheese, potato, and tangy dressing is perfection. Literally translated, *mazorca* means "ear of corn." Corn is one of the staple ingredients of Colombian cuisine and is used in many forms in dishes all over the country.

Along the coast of Colombia, *mazorca desgranada* is a common fast food with as many variations as there are people who prepare it. The dish there is less refined than the version Edgar serves, but the combination of flavors is the same.

Mazorca may be categorized as a salad, but in reality, it's comfort food. The corn absorbs the richness of the chicken broth before developing a toasty, nutty flavor from being seared in a skillet. The cheese melts into a creamy glue to bind the dish together. The potatoes layered on top add crunchiness, and the cilantro, green onions, and dressing add a tanginess that cuts through the richness of the potatoes and corn beneath them.

FOR THE DRESSING

1 cup ketchup

1½ cups mayonnaise

4 cloves garlic, minced (about 2 teaspoons)

¼ cup water

⅓ cup lime juice (juice of 3 limes)

Salt

Freshly ground black pepper

TO PREPARE THE DRESSING

In a large bowl, whisk together the ketchup, mayonnaise, and garlic. Add the water and lime juice and whisk until smooth.

Season to taste with salt and black pepper. Cover the dressing until ready to use.

The dressing may be made in advance and refrigerated, but it should be brought to room temperature before serving.

FOR THE POTATOES

2 medium baking potatoes, peeled (about 1½ pounds)

Peanut or soy oil

Salt

TO PREPARE THE POTATOES

Using a mandoline or food processor with a julienne blade, slice the potatoes into thin matchsticks. As you are slicing, drop the sticks immediately into a bowl of cold water to prevent discoloration.

Using a large pot or deep-fat fryer, bring at least 3 inches of oil to 375 degrees.

Working in batches, dry the potato sticks thoroughly and carefully add them to the hot oil. Stir the potatoes gently in the oil for 3 to 4 minutes or until the potato sticks are golden and crispy.

TO FINISH

2 quarts chicken broth

4 ears yellow corn, shucked

3 tablespoons unsalted butter

¼ cup salao cheese or Cotija cheese, crumbled

TO SERVE

Cilantro

Green onions, chopped (green parts only)

Kitchen Passport While Edgar makes his version of *mazorca* without meat, the dish often includes meat when served in Colombia. Consider adding shredded beef, chicken, or seafood. Try adding hot pepper to the dressing for spiciness. Avocado also would be a good addition. While the matchstick potatoes used here are wonderful, the quicker versions served in Colombia use crumbled potato chips instead.

For a vegetarian version, replace the chicken broth in which the corn is cooked with an equal amount of water. For an even more flavorful option, reserve corn cobs from other dishes and simmer them for 2 to 3 hours with enough water to cover them by 2 inches. Strain the liquid through a fine mesh sieve to eliminate any solids. The resulting corn stock has a sweet, rich flavor that can enhance any dish.

Transfer the potato sticks to a paper-towel-lined plate to drain; sprinkle with salt to taste.

Allow the oil to reheat to 375 degrees before preparing the next batch.

Cover the potato sticks with an aluminum foil tent to keep them warm while you prepare the corn.

TO FINISH THE DISH

In a large saucepan, bring the chicken broth to a boil.

Add the ears of corn. Cook for 10 minutes or until the corn is tender.

Remove the corn from the broth and allow them to cool enough to handle before cutting the kernels from the cobs. Discard the cobs; the broth can be reserved for another use.

Heat a heavy skillet, preferably cast iron, over medium-high heat.

Add the corn kernels and the butter. Keep the kernels moving in the skillet for 10 minutes or until you notice dark spots appearing on the sides of kernels.

Transfer the corn to a large bowl and stir in the cheese while the corn is hot. Divide the corn and cheese mixture into servings and place into shallow bowls. Top the corn with the dressing and potato sticks.

Garnish with cilantro and chopped green onions.

Potatoes

Potatoes may seem to be such a simple ingredient that they need no further explanation. They're one of the base vegetables used in kitchens all over the world. From Irish stew to the *frites* of Belgium to the tortillas of Spain to the latkes of Eastern Europe, potatoes have strong ties to every variety of European cuisine. Europeans carried potatoes with them when they traveled to the east, introducing potatoes to Indian cuisine and Thai curries and even to the palace of the emperor of China. They also carried the potato westward, bringing it to North America as they settled the continent.

Although Europeans were responsible for the spread of the potato, it is not native to Europe. In fact, potatoes were an unknown vegetable in Europe until early explorers brought them back from the New World. The first potatoes to take root in Europe were probably not part of a planned introduction of the humble tuber. Instead, they were most likely planted in the small garden patches of returning sailors who had some left in their food stores from their voyage home.

So where did potatoes come from? Most scholars and scientists agree that the potato originated in southern Peru, where they were first domesticated between 3000 and 2000 BCE. They were a staple food in the Inca empire; the Incas even learned to preserve them by leaving them out to essentially freeze-dry in the upper elevations of the Andes. Because potatoes are the only vegetable to supply most of the vitamins needed for human survival, they were a primary source of nutrition. Potatoes were even placed in Incan tombs to provide food in the afterlife.

While it's hard for us today to imagine that anyone would be afraid to eat a potato, its acceptance in Europe was slow. They were thought to be poisonous by many and for centuries were relegated to being the food of only the extremely poor. It was not until the late eighteenth century that they were adopted as a common food by the majority of the population. Even then, it was fashion as much as a change in dining habits that encouraged farmers to plant them. Marie Antoinette caused a surge in the plant's popularity when she wore potato flowers in some of her extravagant hairstyles.

The early fear of poison was actually not ungrounded. Potatoes are members of the nightshade family, and the leaves and stems are poisonous if consumed. Some varieties of raw potatoes contain enough toxins to cause illness, but most of these toxins are eliminated when the potatoes are cooked.

There are now over 4,000 varieties of potato, with skin and flesh of every shade from white to startling blue, red, or purple. They require very little land to produce a large crop, and they thrive in most environments. They are still a staple crop for the people of the Andes and can be found in native dishes all over South America.

Elena Pereira,
Richmond,
Virginia

Elena Pereira owns Pao de Brazil, a small Brazilian bakery and restaurant in Richmond, Virginia. The aromas of flavorful black beans and meat hit your nose when you first walk into the restaurant. Behind the counter are exquisite baked goods and desserts—rice and corn puddings, mango and passion fruit mousse, pastries, and breads like Elena's delicious coconut bread.

At first glance, the space is unassuming. But closer inspection reveals it to be, essentially, an outpost of Brazil. A soccer match plays on one television while a variety program entertains on another, both in Portuguese.

Elena was born in Caratinga, Brazil, about 300 miles north of Rio de Janeiro, but she came to the United States following the suggestion of family members. "My brother was here, and he invited me to come and see if I like or not. I came and I liked the place, and I decided to stay. He is a musician, and he came to study in the university. He was at that time in Brownsville, Texas, and I was with him for four months. But at that time my son was here, too, and he chose to live in Maryland. Then I came to live in Maryland because he was there."

Elena had a dream of opening a restaurant, but things weren't working out for her where she was. Then a visit to a friend led her to move again—this time to Richmond. "I was thinking to open something like this. I looked around Maryland, but Maryland is very expensive. I have a friend living here. She has been living here for thirty years. I decided to come and see, and then I decided to come and open the business here."

Elena's family has come along to support her in her restaurant. Her daughter now works in Richmond at a company that imports goods from Brazil. Her son-in-law works at her restaurant when he is not working at his regular job.

Being in the United States has brought opportunities for Elena and her family here, but it is difficult being away from her relatives in Brazil. "I still have family there. I haven't gone there for seven years because my paperwork from immigration said I can't go out until then. I lost my mother two years ago and I couldn't go. Sad, but it's life."

Despite her separation and loss, Elena is determined to live life to its fullest. She does that through her family here and through her cooking. "I think it's very important when you do something that you like—and it's love, because you put love into everything—I think that's very important. I love cooking—all my life, since I was thirteen years old."

Elena's restaurant exemplifies her pride in Brazil. She plans to use the restaurant to educate her new community about Brazil by staging events where she can promote the culture and the incredible variety of flavors from her homeland. She intends to have local Brazilian immigrants play music while her patrons enjoy her food.

These are big dreams, dreams that Elena knows she would not be able to achieve alone. But she also knows that she will have help. She came here to be with family, and now she knows that her family will be a part of her success. ☙

FEIJOADA (Brazilian-Style Black Bean Stew)

Active cooking time: 1 hour, 45 minutes | Total cooking time: 4 hours, 30 minutes + 8 hours
Yield: 8 to 10 main dish servings

Feijoada is a dish at once familiar and foreign to the southern palate. Smoked pork simmered slowly in beans is a flavor that most southerners grew up with. But when you add in the beef, sausage, and seasonings of *feijoada*, a simple bean stew becomes something more.

According to Elena, if you were going to eat only one meal in Brazil, that meal should be *feijoada*. "The *feijoada* is not only beans. It's beef and sausage and a lot of kinds of meat inside the beans. It's very good. Everybody likes to try this."

There are as many theories on the origin of *feijoada* as there are recipes for it. Some sources say that *feijoada* was the natural descendant of European dishes like French cassoulet that were brought to Brazil by early explorers. Other sources say that it was developed by colonial plantation slaves who used leftover meat trimmings and other easily available and inexpensive ingredients to form the dish. Still others say that it was the result of a melding of cultures—beans from enslaved Africans, sausage from the Portuguese settlers, and *farofa*, or manioc flour, from the indigenous peoples.

While *feijoada* is a heavy dish most often eaten on weekends or holidays, beans and rice are common meals in Brazil. Elena tells us, "We always eat rice and beans everyday there, but we have a lot of kinds." The Portuguese word for beans is *feijoa*, the root of *feijoada*.

What really makes *feijoada* into a special meal are all of the accompaniments traditionally served with it. Recipes for some of them are included below, but you can also serve fried plantains, various hot sauces, fresh orange slices, or boiled yucca.

1 pound dry black beans

1 smoked ham hock

2 bay leaves

1 teaspoon oregano

½ teaspoon cumin seed

1 beef tongue (optional)

½ pound smoked bacon or pork jowl

1 large yellow onion, diced (about 1 cup)

½ pound pork spareribs, separated

½ pound pork butt, cubed

½ pound beef chuck roast, cubed

½ pound Brazilian linguica or Mexican chorizo, sliced and skins removed

¼ pound chunk of Brazilian *carne seca* (dried beef) or pastrami, cubed

4 cloves garlic, minced (about 2 teaspoons)

3 cloves garlic, peeled

½ teaspoon salt

1 dried red chile, diced

1 fresh orange, halved

Salt

Freshly ground black pepper

Sort the black beans, removing any rocks or dirt. Place the beans in a colander and rinse until the water passing through them runs clear. Place the beans in a large bowl and add water to cover them by 2 inches. Soak the beans overnight.

Drain and rinse the beans and then transfer them to a stockpot. Add enough water to cover the beans by 2 inches. Add the smoked ham hock, bay leaves, oregano, and cumin seed to the beans.

Cook, covered, over medium-low heat for 2 to 3 hours or until the beans are tender enough to mash easily.

While the beans are cooking, prepare the tongue if you will be using it. Add the tongue to a pot of cold water and bring to a boil over medium heat. Cook for 20 minutes and remove from the water.

Allow the tongue to cool enough to handle before peeling the skin and fat from it in strips with a sharp paring knife. Discard the fat and skin and dice the tongue into small pieces.

Cook the bacon or pork jowl in a large, deep skillet over medium heat for about 5 minutes or until the fat begins to render.

Add the onion and cook, stirring constantly, for 5 minutes or until translucent.

Add the pork ribs and cook for 2 minutes.

Add the pork butt and beef chuck and cook for 5 more minutes.

Add the beef tongue, linguica or chorizo, *carne seca* or pastrami, and minced garlic, spreading evenly over the top of the meat mixture. Reduce the heat to medium-low, cover, and cook for 30 minutes.

Stir the meat mixture and continue cooking for another 30 minutes.

After the beans have cooked until they are tender, strain ¾ cup beans from the pot. Mash the beans until they form a paste.

In a mortar and pestle or food processor,

mash 3 cloves of garlic with ½ teaspoon of salt and the dried red chile. Add the resulting paste to the mashed black beans.

Remove the smoked ham hock from the beans and discard it.

Transfer the meats into the stockpot of beans, leaving any liquids behind in the skillet.

Add the mashed black bean mixture to the skillet along with any meat juices and increase the heat to high. Stirring constantly, cook for 5 minutes or until the juices have reduced by half and the mixture is thickened.

Add the mixture to the stockpot of beans and meat along with the orange halves. Cover and reduce heat to low. Continue cooking for 2 hours.

Before serving, remove and discard the orange halves, bay leaves, and rib pieces.

Season to taste with salt and black pepper.

Serve with the traditional accompaniments at the table for each diner to add as desired.

MOLHO DE VINAGRETE (Vinaigrette Salsa)

Active cooking time: 15 minutes | Total cooking time: 2 hours, 15 minutes | Yield: 3 cups

This salsa is one of the traditional accompaniments for *feijoada*. It adds a sour kick that complements the richness of the meats and beans. Any fresh pepper can be used, depending on your heat preference. This salsa can also be blended smooth if desired.

½ cup olive oil
1 cup white vinegar
1 teaspoon salt
1 cup Italian parsley, chopped (about 1½ ounces)
4 large fresh tomatoes, seeded and chopped (about 6 cups)
1 large yellow onion, diced (about 1 cup)
2 fresh serrano or Anaheim chiles, diced (optional)

In a large nonreactive bowl, stir together all of the above ingredients, tossing to combine. Allow to rest for at least 2 hours before serving.

Molho de vinagrete can be served either cold or at room temperature and will keep for up to 2 weeks in the refrigerator. Diners should spoon the *molho de vinagrete* over the *feijoada* as desired.

ARROZ BRASILEIRO (Brazilian-Style Rice)

Active cooking time: 30 minutes | Total cooking time: 50 minutes | Yield: 8 to 10 side dish servings

While it is perfectly acceptable to serve simple white rice alongside *feijoada*, *arroz Brasileiro* is simple to make and is a wonderful accompaniment that is delicious even by itself. The initial sauté of the rice makes for a creamier texture, and the garlic and onion give nice flavor without being overpowering.

4 tablespoons canola or
    vegetable oil
1 large yellow onion, diced
    (about 1 cup)
3 cloves garlic, minced
    (about 1½ teaspoons)
3 cups white long grain rice
1 teaspoon salt
2 medium tomatoes, seeded
    and chopped (about 2 cups)
    (optional)
4 cups boiling water
1 bay leaf

Heat the oil in a large pot over medium-high heat.

Add the onion and garlic and cook, stirring constantly, for 10 minutes or until the onion and garlic are golden brown.

Add the rice and keep stirring for another 3 minutes. The rice will be shiny and translucent.

Stir in the salt and tomatoes and then carefully pour in the boiling water. Because you are combining hot water with hot oil, the mixture will likely splatter.

Add the bay leaf. Return the mixture to a boil. Keep at a boil, stirring constantly, for 5 to 7 minutes, or until most of the water has evaporated.

Cover the pot and reduce the heat to low. Allow the rice to cook at a simmer for 20 minutes.

Fluff the rice before serving alongside the *feijoada*.

FAROFA (Toasted Manioc Flour)

Active cooking time: 30 minutes | Total cooking time: 30 minutes | Yield: 1½ cups

Manioc or cassava is a tuber not often seen in markets in the South. While you should use the Brazilian-style manioc flour if it's available in your area, you may have better luck finding cassava flour in an Asian market. Cassava flour may be a finer grind, so you will need to be very careful when toasting the flour to prevent burning. When sprinkled over *feijoada*, *farofa* adds a nutty flavor and slightly thickens the stew.

2 tablespoons unsalted butter

1 medium yellow onion, diced
(about ⅔ cup)

1 cup manioc or cassava flour

1 teaspoon salt

½ teaspoon freshly ground
black pepper

Melt the butter in a large skillet over medium-high heat.

Add the onion and cook, stirring constantly, for 10 minutes or until the onion is golden brown.

Add the manioc flour all at once, stirring to combine with the onion and butter. Stir in the salt and black pepper. Continue cooking over medium-high heat, stirring constantly, for 5 minutes or until the flour has turned slightly brown and smells nutty.

Serve the *farofa* in a bowl at the table for diners to add as a thickener for the *feijoada*.

Leftover *farofa* will keep covered in the refrigerator for up to 1 month.

COUVE REFOGADA (Sautéed Collard Greens)

Active cooking time: 35 minutes | Total cooking time: 35 minutes | Yield: 8 to 10 side dish servings

Collard greens are a southern staple, but the Brazilian preparation is a bit different. The thinner you can shred your greens, the better for this dish. A quick sauté is all the greens need to provide a touch of color to the plate with *feijoada*.

2 bunches collard greens, washed

2 tablespoons canola or vegetable oil

3 cloves garlic, minced (about
1½ teaspoons)

2 teaspoons salt

Clean the collard greens thoroughly.

To prepare the greens, remove and discard the center stem. Stack 3 leaves one on top of the other as evenly as possible. Roll the leaves into a tight cigar shape. Cut the leaves across the width of the cigar shape in slices no wider than ¼-inch. Repeat until all of the greens have been cut.

Heat the oil in a large, heavy skillet over medium heat.

Add the garlic and cook, stirring constantly for 2 minutes.

Add the cut greens and sprinkle them with salt. Cook the greens, stirring constantly for 3 minutes or until they are just tender.

Serve the greens alongside the *feijoada*.

On the southern bank of the Tennessee River in Chattanooga, in the main section of downtown, the Tennessee Aquarium features a display about the rivers of the world. One of those rivers is the Amazon, which has some of its headwaters in Ecuador. Across the Tennessee River, in Chattanooga's hip North Shore neighborhood, a couple from Ecuador is bringing the flavors of the world to town through their restaurant, Terra Nostra Tapas and Wine Bar.

Tapas are a specialty of Spain where the small portions allow diners to try multiple dishes instead of a single large entrée. They also give chefs freedom to experiment with flavors and to offer a larger variety of dishes on their menus.

The eclecticism of tapas is perfectly captured in Terra Nostra's decor. The walls are painted in bright colors and are decorated with unique metal art by a local artist. A flock of exotic animals flies across one wall while a herd of wild horses stampedes from the ceiling of the main dining room. It is in this setting that Efren and Gema Ormaza create unique dishes for their patrons.

Although Ecuador is a Hispanic country, it might seem strange that Efren and Gema have a restaurant focusing on a specialty from faraway Spain. For them, however, it is only natural. "We have traditional food in Ecuador, but being a very small country, we've had a lot of influence from Europe. We also have a great amount of restaurants from France, Germany, and Italy," Gema says.

In fact, Efren's earliest food memory is tied to a European specialty. "I used to enjoy so much the getting together of the family. We used to all go to this Italian traditional restaurant on the outside of Quito. And I had the most delicious pizzas ever."

From an early age, Efren's family made cooking, as well as eating, an important part of his life. "I always had an ability to cook. I am the oldest of forty cousins, and I used to be in charge of all the kiddos, so going through my grandmother's kitchen, there was always pasta and tomatoes and stuff. So cooking pasta and tomato sauce was my first experience of cooking."

When it was time for Efren to go to college, he chose culinary school. It was there that he met Gema, his partner in every aspect of life. They were happy in Ecuador and had no plans to leave, but Efren's family had different ideas.

Efren's sister received a scholarship to Covenant College in Chattanooga, so she came to the United States. While she was in college, she met her future husband and made Chattanooga her permanent home. Soon after, Efren's parents decided to move to Chattanooga to be closer

to their daughter. Their next goal was getting Efren and Gema to join them.

"My parents moved here, and they are the ones that started to put the U.S. in my mind. I was still fine in Ecuador. I was a culinary teacher at the university," Efren says. "Finally, because of them asking so much, one summer we said, 'Okay, let's take the kids to Disney World, and we will visit them.' Then I guess we liked it so much that we chose to stay."

After moving to Chattanooga, the Ormazas worked in restaurants around town for several years until they decided to open a place of their own. Launching the restaurant was hard work, but by supporting each other, they did it. For many couples, the real challenge would have been working together every day. For Efren and Gema, though, the interplay only energizes them.

"Well, we met in the culinary institute, and since then we have been working together all of our lives, so we don't know another way," Gema says. "Sometimes we have differences, but usually one of us will decide for the best reason. But I trust him with all the ideas and the sauces and things like that. He lets me also be myself."

In the restaurant, Efren is the chef and Gema is the pastry chef. At home, Gema does most of the cooking, but even that contributes to their work at the restaurant. "She is trying to come up with new things all the time. We try little bits so we can improve the restaurant at the same time," Efren says. "She also keeps up with the garden, so we get some vegetables and fruit really fresh."

Their customers are very happy with the Ormazas and their dedication to making the best food they can. The restaurant is filled with people sharing the flavors of the dishes with one another. Tapas tend to encourage sharing by their nature, and the dishes prepared by the Ormazas are indeed too delicious to keep to oneself.

One audience, however, demands a special menu. When Gema talks about their favorite meal to eat at home as a family, she says, "My kids now are very American kids, so macaroni and cheese."

"Their favorites are ribs," Efren adds.

The Ormazas are happy in their new home, but they haven't forgotten Ecuador. They work hard to give back to the country that gave them their start. "We put together a charity trip every year. Like this past January, Gema went with the doctors. They saw over 2,000 people. And it's everything you need for free. And we bring specialists—there was a heart specialist, a stomach specialist," Efren says.

So the Ormazas are successful and innovative chefs, restaurateurs, involved parents, patrons of the arts, and dedicated charity workers. It's hard to imagine them having time for any other interests, and yet Gema finds time to garden and Efren has a hobby of his own: racing cars. While food is his passion, he knows exactly what he would be doing if he hadn't found a career in the kitchen. "I would probably be driving professionally, race cars. Or I could be a mechanic."

Luckily for Chattanooga, Efren is a chef. With Gema beside him, they've watched the culinary scene in the city grow and change over the past fifteen years. They have been a part of that change, first working in other kitchens and now in one of their own. Their innovative flavors have encouraged patrons to try more, to expand their ideas of what and how they want to eat. But perhaps the most beautiful part of it all is that they've done it together. ⬧

LOCRO DE PAPAS (Ecuadoran-Style Potato Soup)

Active cooking time: 1 hour, 35 minutes | Total cooking time: 1 hour, 55 minutes

Yield: 8 to 10 main dish servings

While the cuisine of Ecuador is heavily influenced by the cuisine of Europe, that influence is felt most in urban parts of the country. For the majority of the population, the traditional foods that have fed the people for eons are still the most common foods to be found on their tables. Those foods include corn, quinoa, and, of course, potatoes.

The potato originated in Peru and quickly spread to neighboring countries in South America. The hardy and prolific plants became a mainstay for the indigenous population and later for European settlers who came to the region. Now, they are a food of economy. As Efren says,

"Ecuador is a poor country, so people have to eat what they have—mainly potatoes. Killing a cow or something like that is a luxury, but for everyday eating, 75 percent of the population will eat soups, basically based on potato."

This version of that soup shows an African influence—the addition of peanuts. Ecuadoran food is not spicy, so you will notice that there are no hot peppers in this soup. Instead, it is savory, rich, and filling, made creamy by the addition of the blended peanuts. It's a perfect example of how simple ingredients that are readily available can be transformed into something wonderfully special.

2 tablespoons vegetable oil

1 large white onion, diced (about 1 cup)

2 cloves garlic, minced (about 1 teaspoon)

½ cup fresh parsley, chopped

1 tablespoon ground cumin

12 medium red potatoes, peeled and chopped (about 3 pounds)

1 tablespoon salt

¼ teaspoon freshly ground black pepper

6 cups water

1 cup roasted peanuts

1 cup milk

TO SERVE

Green onions, chopped (green parts only)

Heat the oil in a large pot over medium heat.

Add the onion, garlic, parsley, and cumin and cook, stirring constantly, for 5 to 8 minutes or until the onion is tender.

Add the potatoes, salt, and black pepper and continue cooking for 15 minutes.

Add 1 cup water to the potatoes and let the water come to a boil before adding the next cup. Continue until all 6 cups have been added.

Allow the water to come back to a boil and cook for 15 minutes or until the potatoes are soft.

Using a large spoon, mash at least half of the potatoes against the side of the pot and stir them back in to create a thicker, creamier soup.

Reduce the heat to low.

In a blender, puree the peanuts and milk until the mixture is smooth.

Add the mixture to the soup and cook over low heat for an additional 5 minutes.

Season to taste with salt and black pepper.

Garnish with chopped green onions.

Karla and Vivian Montano, Norfolk, Virginia

An American sailor, Tufts University, and a dislike of nylons led Bolivian sisters Karla and Vivian Montano to Norfolk, Virginia, where they now own Luna Maya, a chic restaurant offering the most authentic Mexican and Bolivian food in town.

Karla fell in love with a U.S. Navy officer who was stationed in Bolivia. After they were married, she moved with him to the United States and earned her degree from Tufts University in Boston. Vivian followed her sister to the United States to attend college, also at Tufts. After college, Karla and her husband settled with the navy in Norfolk, while Vivian worked in the financial industry in New York.

After settling into Norfolk, Karla began to wonder what she should do. Opening a restaurant had not been part of her plan. "We didn't grow up in a restaurant background. We both went to college in Boston and had our degrees in economics and international relations, so this was something that I didn't really envision."

Advice from their mother made the bold decision possible. "My parents had always owned their own business back home, and that's something my mom always said. 'When you own your own business, you get to decide what you want to do. You can open and close whenever you want to. It can be whatever you want it to be.' I guess growing up, that had always stuck to my mind," Karla says.

"At first I was considering working either for a bank or some financial institution in this area. But the thought of dressing up in a business suit everyday and putting on the high heels and nylons—I thought, you know, it doesn't seem very appealing to me."

But if Karla wasn't going to work for someone else, she still had to decide what to do. "I thought, 'What do I know how to do?' We grew up in a tradition where all of our meals were home-cooked; we always

Karla and Vivian Montano at Luna Maya.

knew how to cook. And so I thought, well, in this area there weren't that many ethnic restaurants. And I thought, well, why not?"

Vivian agrees that the time was right. "There was one Mexican restaurant in this entire area thirteen years ago. It wasn't really Mexican—it was more Tex-Mex—but people liked it, and they were doing fantastic," she says. "And we said, 'Hmm, should we do a Bolivian restaurant or should we do a Mexican restaurant?' And we thought nobody knows where Bolivia even is, so we thought it would probably make more business sense to open a Mexican restaurant."

Karla and Vivian's restaurant is an elegant example of the modern Mexican restaurant. The colors of the walls are bright and the decor of the restaurant is sleek and modern with touches of traditional Hispanic art creating a great atmosphere for dining. Dishes come out beautifully plated, because, as Karla says, "You eat first through your eyes."

For those unfamiliar with Bolivian cuisine, it might be tempting to think that it was easy for Vivian and Karla to open a Mexican restaurant. As Vivian recalls, "That was a huge learning curve for us because we had not used these ingredients before, but a lot of the methods and the ingredients were a little bit similar to our own food. We were familiar with making those long, multi-hour sauces and all that."

Success came quickly for them, but Vivian is still surprised by the reactions of some of their guests. "I think they immediately noticed us. So we kind of became a destination—people would come from Richmond, or people would come from Williamsburg. And what was interesting to me is that people keep coming in to this day and they say, 'Your restaurant is not Mexican.' And I tell them, 'It's actually more Mexican.'"

Looking back, Karla wonders what she would have done if she knew what she was getting into. "Maybe had I known better, if I knew then what I know now, I don't know if I would have opened the restaurant. I wouldn't have attempted it if my sister hadn't decided to help me out. Because she was in a transition period, and she said, 'Well, I'll go over there and help you get it started.' And the rest is history."

Vivian was Karla's early support, but before Karla made her decision and called her sister for help, she turned to a friend for advice. Vivian recalls her sister's first thoughts about culinary school and the advice the friend gave. "She spoke to a friend who owned a restaurant, Coastal Grill. Tom Colicchio and his partner started this restaurant. The friend, who was just getting started, told her, 'Do not do it. You don't understand. Working for a restaurant is awful. It is horrible hours. You have no life. Forget about your weekends and holidays. Don't go to school. It would be a waste of money. But if you really want to do it, you should work for a restaurant. That will show you.'

"But it led to something else. She asked him, 'How about I work in your kitchen? I'll work for free for a couple of months.' And she did, and she loved it. I can't remember how long she was there. But she really liked it, so she said, 'Hmm, I think I can open a restaurant.' So then she called me."

Vivian was surprised, but in retrospect, Karla thinks that owning a restaurant might have been a natural step for her despite her earlier ambivalence. "I think initially for a lot of immigrants, going into a food-related business just seems natural because we all grew up eating home-cooked meals, and I guess the emphasis really is focused around the table and eating, so I think maybe that is something that really everybody knows how to do."

Fortunately for the Montano sisters, those traditions are strong with their family. In the restaurant's early days, helping hands from the family were useful. "Me and my sister—literally, it was her and me, and the restaurant seated like forty people. I remember every time somebody came to visit us, whether it was my parents or my sister or my cousins, they would always work," Vivian says. "We would be at the restaurant the entire day, so we would put them to work. And my mom would be washing dishes, and my dad would be cleaning the tables. So it was kind of a family effort."

Now the restaurant is successful and well staffed, and, like their mother told them, the Montano sisters can do what they want. Luckily for Norfolk, what they want is to provide traditional Mexican and Bolivian cuisine. "What we try to do is more authentic dishes using authentic ingredients, using all the different types of chile peppers," Vivian says.

Norfolk encourages them to keep introducing more Bolivian specialties and to expand their menu with more authentic Mexican dishes. As Vivian puts it, "When you start getting people familiar with eating ethnic food, they really do like it. That's something that I've found actually very surprising here in the South because you think of southerners as being more traditional, but I think they're very open to trying different things, which has been very nice for us." 🍲

PASTEL DE CHOCLO (Bolivian-Style Corn Pie)

Active cooking time: 1 hour | Total cooking time: 1 hour, 35 minutes | Yield: 8 main dish servings

Pastel de choclo is one of the traditional Bolivian dishes on the menu at Luna Maya. It's a comfort food with a careful balance of sweet and spicy. It's also a seasonal food, best when corn is at its peak sweetness.

The food of Bolivia is not well known in the United States, something the Montano sisters are working to change. In *pastel de choclo*, the heritage of Bolivia comes through in the flavors of the dish. The spices of the chorizo and chicken are legacies of the centuries of Spanish rule, while the sweet corn topping is a nod to the *maiz* of the indigenous peoples.

Pastel de choclo is also commonly found on Chilean menus, but the Montano sisters serve the Bolivian version of the dish. As Karla puts it, "It's kind of letting people know that it's not one and the same. Everybody has their own version."

The meat filling in this dish is flavored by peppers. Because different peppers add different elements of flavor, Karla believes that people should experiment with peppers to find the ones they like. "Everybody feels that peppers are always going to make food spicy. But they're not used only for spice. They're also used to impart some sweetness. Some are nutty; some have a certain level of acidity. So you can really play around with all of them, and they also add color."

The ancho, paprika, and chipotle used here add smokiness, sweetness, and just a touch of heat. They also make the filling a beautiful shade of orange. The corn topping is smooth and sweet, balancing the meat and making the dish more filling. The cheese adds a layer of savory richness that pulls the whole dish together. Serve it as a casserole or in individual dishes for each diner to enjoy.

1 tablespoon + 2 teaspoons olive oil,
   divided
1 pound Mexican pork chorizo,
   skins removed
1 medium white onion, diced
   (about ⅔ cup)
6 cloves garlic, minced
   (about 1 tablespoon)
½ teaspoon thyme
2 teaspoons ground cumin
½ teaspoon ground allspice
⅛ teaspoon ground cloves
1 teaspoon ground chipotle pepper
1 tablespoon ground ancho chile
1 tablespoon sweet paprika
1½ teaspoons salt, divided

Heat 1 tablespoon oil in a large skillet over medium heat.

Crumble the chorizo into the skillet and cook, stirring often, until the chorizo has browned, about 10 minutes.

Strain the chorizo from the skillet and reserve, leaving the oil behind.

Add the white onion, garlic, thyme, cumin, allspice, cloves, chipotle pepper, ancho chile, paprika, and 1 teaspoon salt to the skillet, stirring to combine. Cook, stirring often, for 5 to 8 minutes or until the onion is translucent.

2 pounds boneless, skinless chicken
    breasts, cubed

½ cup chopped cilantro

Juice of 1 lime (about 2 tablespoons)

1 medium yellow onion, roughly chopped

5 cups fresh corn kernels (kernels of
    about 8 ears of corn)

1 cup milk

¼ teaspoon freshly ground black pepper

2 teaspoons sugar

8 ounces queso Chihuahua or queso
    Oaxaca, grated

Kitchen Passport While this version of *pastel de choclo* is based on chicken, beef or pork can also be added or used instead. Other common additions to the dish include minced black olives, raisins, and crumbled boiled egg yolks.

Follow Karla's advice and experiment with different peppers. Try adding yellow Ají peppers to the corn mixture or Spanish-style smoked paprika to the chicken or as a dusting over the top of the finished dish.

Add the chicken to the onion mixture, stirring to combine. Cook, stirring often, for 15 minutes or until the chicken is cooked through.

Remove the skillet from the heat. Add the reserved chorizo, cilantro, and lime juice to the chicken mixture and stir to combine.

Preheat the oven to 350 degrees.

Heat 2 teaspoons oil in a large skillet over medium heat.

Add the yellow onion and cook, stirring frequently, for 5 to 8 minutes or until the onion is translucent.

Remove the skillet from the heat.

Combine the cooked onion with the corn kernels and milk in a food processor. Puree the corn mixture until it is smooth.

Return the skillet to medium heat.

Add the corn mixture to the skillet. Cook, stirring constantly, until the mixture has thickened, about 5 minutes.

Add ½ teaspoon salt and the black pepper, stirring to combine.

Remove the skillet from the heat.

Spread the chicken and chorizo mixture into a smooth layer in a 9-by-13-inch baking dish. Spread the corn mixture over the meat. Sprinkle the sugar over the top. Bake for 30 minutes.

Remove the dish from the oven.

Preheat the broiler.

Spread the cheese over the baked corn mixture. Cook under the broiler for 3 to 5 minutes or until the cheese is melted and beginning to brown.

Vietnam Community

For immigrants, the inclination to gather in communities is natural. A shared language, heritage, experiences, and even cuisine provide comfort in a new land. Vietnamese Americans are one group with an especially strong sense of community.

The journey to the South has been a difficult one for the Vietnamese refugees who have come to call the region home. After being forced from their homes during the Vietnam War, many had no option except to leave their country when the war was over. The mass migrations from Vietnam began in 1975 and continued in waves throughout the 1980s and early 1990s.

After gathering in refugee camps in the Philippines and Thailand, refugees were moved to resettlement camps on army bases across the United States. There they waited for sponsors to help them find jobs and homes in American society. Two of the many places that groups of Vietnamese refugees settled and formed communities were New Orleans, Louisiana, and Louisville, Kentucky, sponsored by the Catholic diocese in each of those cities.

Father Vien Thé Nguyen and Peter Hoang Nguyen, New Orleans, Louisiana

5

There are parts of New Orleans where it is easy to pretend that Hurricane Katrina never happened. The homes are as stately as ever, their gardens just as lush. Businesses are open and thriving. But the farther east in New Orleans you travel, the thinner that illusion becomes. Years after the storm, there are still empty and heavily damaged houses, debris-filled lots, businesses that never reopened—plenty of signs of all the people who didn't come back home.

But if you turn into the Village de l'Est subdivision, you find a community where the storm—although it happened—didn't destroy the lives of the people. Members of this mostly Vietnamese American community were the first to return after Katrina, well before the federal and local government said anyone could come back. They were the first to rebuild their homes and among the first to get electricity restored. For the Vietnamese Americans of New Orleans, the drive to return home was a force greater than any hurricane.

Father Vien Thể
Nguyen at Mary
Queen of Vietnam
Catholic Church.

Father Vien Thé Nguyen, pastor of Mary Queen of Vietnam Catholic Church, is the spiritual leader of the community, celebrating mass with over 6,000 parishioners. He has defended his people fearlessly, facing off against the mayor, the governor, and even the federal government. Immediately after the storm, he traveled throughout the region checking on his parishioners.

"When I was traveling, it wasn't to encourage people to return. It was simply to make connections—for them to know they are still connected. It was a simple fact that they were returning. So there was no encouragement, per se," he says.

"One night as I was driving, I had promised to stop by and visit and have supper with a lady, but I decided to drive straight through, so I called her to say that I couldn't be there," he recalls. "Her question to me was—and this was in September, so this was right after the storm—her question was, 'How can you speed up our return?'" It wasn't a question of if she would return but when—and it couldn't be soon enough.

To facilitate the return, the church, already the center of life in the community, became the center of the recovery effort. Food and supplies were staged there. Volunteers who arrived from all over the country to help with rebuilding water-damaged homes were headquartered there. The church was where returning families went first, as Father Vien was there collecting their names in order to convince the local utility company that power should be restored to the area quickly.

One might think that, given all the difficulties of the last fifty years or more, including over twenty years of war, the Vietnamese people might have surrendered to a sense of rootlessness. Quite the opposite is true, however. Adversity has only strengthened them, as Father Vien explains.

"Vietnamese are really an agricultural people, not just in the sense of an occupation but a mentality. We are tied to the land. We are tied to the community. For us—even though materialistically speaking there is more elsewhere—spiritually, psychologically, it's not more. It's less."

Father Vien is true to the agricultural mentality of which he speaks. For him, a connection to the land means more than just the land on which one's home stands or the land on which his church is built. Born into a farming family, he has an inherent affinity for the soil as a source of life and growth. This shows in the packed bookshelves that line his office walls. Many of the books are the religious and historical texts that one might expect, but with them are also books on beekeeping, wine making, and sustainable agricultural practices.

"I personally just love the agricultural aspect of life. For me to live in the city is a pain," he laughs. If Father Vien can't go to the farm, the farm will just have to come to Father Vien. As the chairman of the Mary Queen of Viet Nam Community Development Corporation (MQVNCDC), Father Vien is leading an effort to start a twenty-acre urban farm in his community, featuring both plants and livestock.

Peter Hoang Nguyen, manager of the urban agriculture program, knows the urban farm is important, because Father Vien is not the only one who longs for that agricultural connection. "When the people first came here back in 1975, they were all moved into a Section 8 housing area. Those are apartments, so they didn't have any land, so whatever strip of grass they could find, they would prep it and grow their own fruits and vegetables."

Given their growing desires, a group of residents ultimately appropriated a plot of unused land. Without any sort of formal decision, the people banded together to clear the land and start planting on it, not only to reestablish their ties to the land but also to raise the produce they had known in Vietnam and couldn't find in New Orleans at the time. When the owner of the property found out, a local priest brokered an arrangement. "They made a deal that the owner would lease it out to them for a dollar a year. They cultivated twenty-plus acres out there between all the community members," Peter says.

A flood in the 1990s wiped out everything that had been done, but it was rebuilt. After Katrina, however, the situation was different. "The same group now is a lot older than when they started out back in the '70s and early '80s, so now those big gardens are not being used. You've got debris everywhere. You've got overgrown weeds," Peter explains.

Katrina did not wash out the desire to be self-sufficient, however. "They're still doing it but at their own homes, much smaller and more condensed. Some of the ones that still want to continue and do it in high volume, they have moved along the lagoon that runs through the community because the water's free. But that water is the runoff from the streets, so we are trying to move them away from that area by creating this urban farm," Peter says.

Although the concepts of organic and sustainable food have only recently begun to move to the forefront of agriculture in the United States, Peter learned the methods early in life. Unlike Father Vien, however, Peter didn't always live on a farm.

"My dad was away in the service, so my mom was mostly the bread-winner in the family. She had a business, and we all helped her out. We had a gas station, and she sold it off a year before the war ended. She purchased a piece of land almost in a swamp area but next to a main road. At the time we were thinking she was nuts, but now looking back, she was pretty smart."

His mother proved to be more than just a smart woman; she was a visionary of sustainable agriculture. "She turned it into a shrimp farm. We also had turkeys. We had like a stilt house with the turkeys on top so their droppings fell down and fed the shrimp. We had to build a levee around the place to keep the water out, and on the levee she planted coconut trees. Before we could really fully enjoy our work, that's when the war ended."

Although the experience was short-lived, it affected Peter greatly, leading him eventually to the role he serves in his community today. Now he himself works with that same sense of connectedness to the environment.

Ironically, the environment is the biggest hurdle for the urban farm now. The U.S. Army Corps of Engineers has designated the land intended for the farm as wetlands. In nature, wetlands are a valuable and diverse ecosystem. In post-Katrina New Orleans, wetlands are also an increasingly protected part of flood control. In spite of the designation, the MQVNCDC will eventually be able to create the farm. However, the group will have to work with the Corps of Engineers and develop the property carefully.

Adding to the frustration of the situation is a nearby landfill. A mile from the urban farm site, the controversial landfill contains household debris from Katrina. The landfill extends far below the water table, and there is no liner. The wastes dumped before the landfill was closed were simply covered over and have the potential to leak into the groundwater and into the surrounding canals. Because the water table in New Orleans is so high, any pollution from the landfill could easily leech into the farm. For Father Vien, this is unacceptable.

"The state's Department of Environmental Quality wants to drain the water from the landfill into the canal, and we are suing them saying no. They have no problem draining that water into it, but when we turn this area into an urban farm, we encounter all kinds of problems."

Still, Father Vien and the MQVNCDC have no intention of giving up. "It can be frustrating, but there's a sense of 'What is the next hurdle?' Let's clear it and move on. It's the doggedness of the mentality that we pursue."

While negotiations with the Corps of Engineers drag on, Peter is moving forward as much as possible. Although the site can't be developed now, markets for its produce can be. One community member leased five acres to the MQVNCDC as a temporary farm. "We can't wait any longer, so we went ahead last month to initiate a program to organize the growers so they can grow for restaurants."

Peter's work is paying off. Chef John Besh, renowned local restaurateur and food personality, has already signed on to buy as much produce from the garden as the community members can raise. "We had our annual Tet festival, and I displayed a conceptual design of the market and urban farm. John Besh happens to be a friend of a priest, and they came by. Besh was all excited," Peter says.

"He said this could be good because he has been buying from out of state, and it's not just high cost, but he has to pay freight, too. So a way for him to save some money is to buy local. And also to promote economic growth, you buy local."

Because Chef Besh owns several restaurants in New Orleans, his produce needs are significant. Peter is excited and a little intimidated as well. He and the urban farm project will make the best of the opportunity, though. "I just got a list from Besh yesterday, and I said, 'Oh my God.' They have a list of seventy-two different items they use weekly. We're not going to be able to provide everything for him, but some of it, so we can get a grower going and making some profit."

The urban farm will be more than just a producing farm, though. Father Vien envisions the farm as a center of activity for the entire community. He plans one pavilion with a farmers' market where the gardeners can sell what they raise and another where food vendors can prepare fresh food for sale to visitors. Every member of the community will have a scenic and peaceful place to go. "There will be pathways where people can walk for exercise. There will be ponds with lotus so that there is both sight and smell."

The most important aspect of the farm, however, looks beyond the present. Father Vien anticipates completing the garden for the community's children. He also possesses his own sense of childlike joy. His eyes gleam as he talks about part of the garden that he is most excited about. "I love chickens because there is such a variety of them, so my dream would be a five-acre area where we want to do livestock, especially chickens, so our children can go and watch them just to see the workings."

Peter also understands the long-term impact of involving the children of the community. "What we're taking care of right now is the gardeners, but what we hope to do is to bring the youth in. Right now, all the youth know is go to school, get good grades, get a degree, and get a job—try to live the American dream."

Peter is supportive of those opportunities afforded the children of the community, but he also knows that the community's future is dependent on the next generation. "We want some of the youth to remain here. We want them to continue with this work. This is our culture. These are our traditions. Somebody has to carry on."

Because these gardens are such an integral part of the community, it's easy to see how important food can be to people who are so connected to the land. The culinary traditions that came with them from Vietnam have remained an important part of the community. But this is a community that is evolving, even in its food. The church is helping Mexican and other Latin American laborers find jobs as the post-Katrina construction boom slows. Father Vien celebrates mass in Spanish as well as in English and Vietnamese. A taco truck parked across the street has become a favorite dining option for the workers at the MQVNCDC office.

This evolution does not detract from the traditions this rich community enjoys. Instead, it adds to it. As the gardeners grow vegetables for the restaurants of New Orleans, they also include the traditional vegetables and fruits that have always had a place on their tables. Their children will be as familiar with salsa as with fish sauce, but thanks to the vision and efforts of Father Vien and Peter, this community will have the opportunity to create a true and lasting relationship between the land and the people who live on it. ⑤

FATHER VIEN'S MEA CULPA CHICKEN

Active cooking time: 30 minutes | Total cooking time: 1 hour | Yield: 4 main dish servings

Even though Father Vien is not a chef by profession, he loves to cook and to introduce family and visitors to the foods he enjoys. While this is not a traditional Vietnamese recipe, it does use flavors and methods ubiquitous in Vietnamese cuisine. This recipe is actually a family collaboration between Father Vien and his sister and brother-in-law. Sharing and working out recipes together is just one way that Father Vien stays close with his family members who don't live in his community in New Orleans.

"I remember visiting my sister in Virginia. She asked her husband to buy steamed chicken from a Chinese restaurant just so we could taste it. So we ate and discussed it. 'How do you make this?'

And then we came up with our own recipe and improved it," he says.

"We now call that chicken the mea culpa chicken here, jokingly, in the sense that Father Luke and Father Joseph just beat their breasts in mourning because they have wasted so many meals that are not as good as this," he laughs.

While steaming a chicken may be a new preparation for you, don't be hesitant to try this recipe. Just the aroma of the steam will make your mouth start watering, and the result will be some of the most tender and juicy chicken that you will ever eat. Father Vien recommends that you eat this dish with your hands, pulling the meat from the bones and dipping each bite into the gingery dipping sauce.

FOR THE CHICKEN

1 head garlic, separated into
    peeled cloves
4 teaspoons salt
2 tablespoons vodka
1 whole fryer chicken, halved

FOR THE DIPPING SAUCE

1 large bulb ginger (about 8 ounces)
4 shallots
4 teaspoons salt
2 cups peanut or soy oil

Using a mortar and pestle or food processor, mash all of the cloves from the head of garlic into a paste with the salt. Once the paste is formed, thin it with the vodka.

Wash the chicken and pat it dry. Rub the garlic paste into the chicken on both sides. Allow the chicken to rest while you prepare the steamer.

Set up a rack in a wok and add water. The water must not touch the chicken. Bring the water to a boil over high heat.

Place the chicken on the rack skin side up. Cover the chicken with a domed lid so that the lid holds in the steam without touching the chicken. Allow the chicken to steam for 20 minutes.

Turn off the heat and allow the chicken to rest, covered, for 5 minutes.

To prepare the dipping sauce, peel the ginger and pulse in a food processor until the ginger is in tiny chunks.

Slice the shallots as thin as possible. Place the shallots in a large heat-proof bowl and coat with salt.

Heat the oil to the point of smoking in a deep skillet.

Carefully add the ginger and stir while cooking for 2 minutes or until the ginger is a dark gold.

Remove the oil from the heat and immediately pour the oil and ginger over the salted shallots. Be careful when adding the hot oil because the oil may splatter. Stir to combine.

Allow the sauce to rest for 5 minutes before serving.

Kitchen Passport Steamed chicken is moist and delicious, and this recipe makes it easy to experiment with some different flavors. Try using a citrus vodka in the garlic paste, or leave out the vodka altogether and replace it with light soy sauce to add color to the chicken skin. You could also replace the salt in the garlic paste with Vietnamese fish sauce. Try adding green onions, lemon zest, or orange zest to the dipping sauce.

And don't lose your second meal from this dish. The water that you used to steam the chicken is full of flavor and is a great start for an Asian-inspired chicken soup. Instead of discarding the chicken bones, add them to a stockpot with half of an onion and a handful of peppercorns. Add the steaming liquid and then add another quart of water. Cover and simmer for 3 hours to extract the most flavor from the bones. Strain out all of the solids and add fresh minced onion, soba or rice noodles, thinly sliced mushrooms, and any shredded leftover chicken. Season to taste.

DUA CAI CHUA (Vietnamese-Style Pickled Mustard Greens)

Active cooking time: 45 minutes | Total cooking time: 2 hours, 15 minutes + 3 days | Yield: 6 cups

When we think of pickling in the South, we normally think of cucumbers or okra, or maybe beets or cabbage. That's because most of our pickling traditions came from long-ago German immigrants. Now, Asian immigrants are bringing a whole new range of pickle ingredients and pickling techniques to the South. These pickled mustard greens are a perfect example.

While this recipe is based on Vietnamese cooking traditions, pickled mustard greens are found on tables across Asia. Like the greens of enslaved Africans in the antebellum South, these greens are an important source of nutrients for impoverished families as well as a traditional condiment in wealthier homes.

This recipe calls for fish sauce. Fish sauce is one of the traditional flavors of Vietnamese cuisine. It was often used as a source of protein to make a meal of rice more nutritious. Father Vien grew up eating food seasoned with fish sauce and immediately noticed a difference when he came to the United States. "The food didn't taste right, because we use fish sauce. Americans use salt. And so we suffered with that."

He remembers eating pickled mustard greens as a child on his family's farm before the war. "One of my earliest food memories is pickled mustard greens. We do our own way of pickling, and the juice is so . . . it's very sour. But you pour that into the rice bowl, kind of soak it like a soup, and then add a little soy sauce to it. That can be a killer. That's real good."

3 pounds mustard greens

9½ tablespoons salt

1 tablespoon sugar

2 tablespoons fish sauce

8 cups water

1 (1-inch) piece fresh ginger, peeled
and grated (about 1 tablespoon)

2 bunches green onions, chopped
(about 2 cups)

4 cloves garlic, minced (about
2 teaspoons)

Kitchen Passport Pickled mustard greens are incredibly versatile. While they're great on their own as a snack, you can also serve them along with soups, noodles, or rice where their salty, sour flavor will be a welcome complement. They can be sautéed and served as a side dish, or they can be incorporated into dumpling fillings. The juice can even provide the acid for a vinaigrette.

Try experimenting with the quantities in the recipe. Replace some of the salt with more fish sauce, add hot pepper flakes, or use a different variety of greens. Add grated carrots and galangal root for different texture and flavor.

Cut the greens into 2-inch squares. Wash them well and spread them out to dry in a single layer, preferably in the sun. If you don't have space for drying in the sun, place the pieces of greens in a single layer on parchment-paper-lined baking sheets. Set the oven at 200 degrees and put the mustard greens in for 45 minutes. When they are ready for the next step, they should be totally dry and appear slightly shrunken.

Combine the salt, sugar, and fish sauce in the water in a large bowl, stirring until both salt and sugar are dissolved. Add the dried mustard greens along with the fresh ginger, green onions, and garlic. Stir to combine well.

Nest a second, slightly smaller bowl into the bowl holding the mixture in order to keep the greens submerged.

Cover the bowls tightly with plastic wrap and leave in a warm place for 3 days.

After 3 days, transfer the greens and liquid to jars and refrigerate.

Unopened jars will keep, refrigerated, for up to 4 months.

Nuoc Mam (Fish Sauce)

CULINARY TOUR GUIDE

If any single flavor is most prevalent in Vietnamese cuisine, it is that of fish sauce. It's a staple ingredient in restaurant and home cooking for both wealthy and poor families. It's used in place of salt in Vietnamese cooking, and while it does impart saltiness, it also adds nuances of its own.

So what is fish sauce? Essentially, it's a sauce made from fermented fish, normally anchovies. Its closest existing Western cousin would be Worcestershire sauce, but Worcestershire's ancestor, the Roman staple *garum*, was actually much closer to the simple recipe of Vietnamese fish sauce. The Asian version of the sauce originally made its way to Europe in the 1600s with Dutch and British sailors who brought it back from China as a sauce called *ketsiap*. That sauce eventually evolved into the ketchup we all know today.

It's theorized that fish sauce was developed accidentally. Small fishing boats couldn't travel far from the shore and consequently ended up catching only the small, bony fish that inhabited the shallow waters.

To preserve the fish, they were packed in wooden boxes and later in barrels with salt and water. After fermentation, they discovered that the liquid produced was flavorful and more satisfying than eating the bony fish. Now we know that the sauce is very rich in protein, a much-needed nutrient in the diets of those early fishermen and their families.

Fish sauce is not strictly a Vietnamese condiment. Variations can be found in almost all Southeast Asian cultures and even in the coastal regions of China and South Korea. While no one knows exactly which culture invented the sauce, natives of any of the countries where it is common will tell you that their homeland developed it first.

You can find fish sauce in any Asian market, most likely multiple brands from multiple countries. You may even be able to find fish sauce in the Asian section of your local supermarket but in more limited variety. *Nuoc mam* is the Vietnamese version of the sauce, but you should try varieties from any of the countries that produce it to find the one that you like best.

Louisville restaurateur Michael Ton is a member of the younger, more mobile generation of Vietnamese Americans. Only six years old when he arrived in the United States in 1975, he has lived in six different states since then. Although Michael's family escaped Vietnam together, they began to separate and spread across the United States soon after arrival.

Today, however, Michael finds himself part of the Vietnamese community in Louisville, a community that began, at least in part, with the arrival of his family. "We came over here as one big family. My dad was overseeing the whole escape. There were about twenty-seven or twenty-eight of us—mostly my mom's side," Michael says. "My mom's side of the family ended up here in Louisville. They were all taken in from the local churches. They were given clothing, all that. People here are very, very nice, and that's the reason why my aunt is still here, because of the people."

Michael was not initially part of the Louisville community because, although he was welcomed to the United States, this welcome came from elsewhere. "At that time, in my immediate family, there were four of us—three boys and one girl—and my mom and dad. We ended up in Baltimore, Maryland," Michael says. "My dad was a high-ranking officer in the South Vietnamese Army, and his best friend was in the U.S. Army, so the friend sponsored my immediate family in Baltimore, where he lived at that time."

From there, Michael's family moved to Texas, where he went to school from the elementary grades through college. While his parents both worked to support the family, Michael and his older brother and sister learned to take care of themselves. And in doing so, Michael's love of cooking was born. "We were left at home by ourselves, so we had to grow up fast. When you're left alone at home, you have to cook, and I always liked cooking."

Michael's first food memory comes from these early experiments. "Wonder Bread—I remember toasting it in one of those little grill things where the door flaps open and putting on Ragu sauce that came out of a jar and sliced Velveeta cheese and then putting it back in there to melt it and call it a pizza."

Because of his aunt, Michael also discovered that he liked restaurants. His aunt owned a successful chain of Chinese eateries, and Michael got his first experience in the restaurant world working for her. He learned both the good and the bad from his aunt. Although her Chinese restaurants were popular in Louisville, she was ahead of her time when she opened a French restaurant in the early 1980s. The people of the city weren't ready for it, and it failed.

"I always enjoyed the restaurant scene, even though it is hard work. I always liked seeing people enjoy themselves. So that kind of got me started," he says. "Seeing my aunt owning restaurants and not knowing much about the back of the house [the restaurant's kitchen], I didn't want to get stuck in a situation where I didn't know what was going on back in the kitchen because someone else was running my business."

Michael already had a degree in business administration and practical experience working in restaurants, but he wanted complete control in an establishment of his own, including in the kitchen. To round out his education, Michael enrolled at the Culinary Institute of America in Hyde Park, New York.

After graduation, Michael worked for large restaurant groups in Boston, Massachusetts, and Raleigh-Durham, North Carolina. With his background and education, Michael was successful, but something was missing. "I did well when I was there, but it just wasn't for me. I always wanted my own place. To own my own hot dog stand or something like that would make me happy."

Ultimately, it was Michael's aunt who led him back to Louisville and back to community. "She ended up here, and she got into the restaurant business, and she's been here ever since, thirty-something years now. She's the one that made that first initial phone call for me to come here. So I ended up coming here and before you know it, we were doing construction on my restaurant."

As work progressed, Michael had his doubts, but eventually they faded. "Doing construction and getting things together, there was always that 1 percent that I was like, 'Aw man, is this gonna work?' When we opened up, probably about two or three months into the project, that 1 percent disappeared. I'm definitely more stressed out owning my own place, but to me, this is a lot more rewarding."

Opening Basa, where he presents his take on traditional Vietnamese cuisine, has been rewarding. Basa was nominated for a James Beard Foundation Award for best new restaurant. He has plans to expand into other ventures like mobile kitchens, still keeping Basa's focus on local ingredients.

Michael doesn't define his success through awards or financial gain—though they are nice. Instead, he is most pleased by his interactions with his community, both the Vietnamese American community and Louisville as a whole. His concerns about opening a restaurant melted away when he saw his customers enjoying his food. "It was like, 'They're embracing it.' In Louisville, they're very welcoming." ⬡

Michael Ton at Basa.

BASA *CHA GIO* (Vietnamese-Style Imperial Rolls)

Active cooking time: 1 hour, 45 minutes | Total cooking time: 2 hours, 35 minutes | Yield: 48 rolls

Cha gio are a traditional Vietnamese dish often served as an appetizer or as a main dish with cellophane noodles. In Michael's version, the mushrooms in the mixture provide a richly dark flavor, while the taro root slices provide lightness.

Michael includes these rolls on Basa's menu as an authentic Vietnamese offering. "Using taro root is very traditional in the imperial roll. Making it most traditional is using rice paper instead of wonton wrappers. One of the things I was afraid of when using rice paper was that it's a little bit chewy. It's crispy, but it's a little chewy."

While it's tempting to eat the imperial rolls as soon as they are cool enough to handle, Michael says that they're best if you eat them the right way. "The traditional way of eating it is to take the imperial roll and put it in the lettuce. Pick the mint and put that in there. You have to have the mint. That kind of goes along with it. Roll it, dip it, eat it like a wrap. That's how you're supposed to eat it."

Peanut or soy oil
1 pound ground pork
½ cup wood ear or shiitake mushrooms, minced (about 2 ounces)
½ pound shrimp, minced
½ cup red onion, minced (about ½ an onion)
4 tablespoons mushroom seasoning
2 cups carrots, shredded (about 3 medium carrots)
2 cups cooked cellophane noodles
48 8-inch rice paper wrappers
½ cup taro root, peeled and sliced thin

TO SERVE
Leafy green lettuce or butter lettuce
Fresh mint
Vietnamese fish sauce
Soy sauce

Using a deep pot or a deep-fat fryer, heat at least 3 inches of oil to 350 degrees.

In a large bowl, combine the ground pork, mushrooms, shrimp, onion, mushroom seasoning, carrots, and cellophane noodles. Using your hands, work the ingredients until they are combined.

Prepare a large, shallow bowl of water. Take a rice paper wrapper and drag it through the water, keeping it submerged for 15 seconds. Lay the soaked wrapper out flat on a plastic or bamboo cutting board. Do not use a glass plate or cutting board as the rice paper will stick to glass.

Place a slice of taro root in the center of the wrapper. Spread a rounded tablespoon of meat filling in a line over the taro slice.

Fold one end of the wrapper from the bottom over one end of the filling. Fold one side over the filling, pulling it tight. Fold the other end over and roll, keeping the rice paper wrapper tight against the filling. Repeat until all of the fillings are used.

Allow the rolls to rest for 15 minutes.

Kitchen Passport The pork in the rolls can be replaced easily with ground chicken, and fish sauce or light soy sauce can substitute for the mushroom seasoning. Add fresh mint or basil to the meat filling. If you don't like the texture of the rice paper wrappers, try spring roll wrappers instead.

Since you'll have hot oil from cooking the imperial rolls, use any leftover taro root to make nutty, slightly earthy chips. Slice the peeled taro root as thinly as possible, using a mandoline if available. Working in batches, lower the slices into the hot oil and cook for 30 seconds to 1 minute or until the chips are a light brown. Transfer the chips to a paper-towel-lined plate and sprinkle lightly with salt for a delicious snack.

Working in batches, carefully lower the rolls into the hot oil. For best results, use wooden utensils to prevent sticking. Do not overcrowd the fryer; the rolls will stick to one another and will not cook properly. Let the rolls cook for 3 to 4 minutes, turning over after 2 minutes. Transfer the rolls to a paper-towel-lined plate to drain and cool.

To serve, place washed leaves of lettuce and mint on a plate. Give individual dishes to each diner to prepare a mixture of fish sauce and soy sauce as desired. Each person should take a leaf of lettuce and place several leaves of mint inside it. Then wrap the lettuce around an imperial roll and dip in the fish sauce and soy sauce mixture.

Bosnia Extended Community

In 1984, the city of Sarajevo, Yugoslavia, hosted the thirteenth Winter Olympics, where the British ice dancing pair Jayne Torvill and Christopher Dean received perfect artistic impression scores from every single judge—the first and only time that has happened. Only ten years later, Sarajevo, the once flawless city, was trapped in the middle of a four-year-long siege that saw over 12,000 killed in the city alone and countless more fleeing the country as war tore their homeland apart.

Many Bosnians escaped to Germany where they began trying to rebuild their lives. But years later, Germany, facing millions of refugees and a declining economy, forced many to leave. Some were repatriated to the newly formed Federation of Bosnia and Herzegovina. Others, feeling that there was nothing left for them in their homeland or that returning would be too risky, chose to move to other countries, including the United States.

Refugees resettling in a new country often bond through shared nationality and heritage. But for many Bosnian refugees, tangible connections are lacking because they did not come to the United States in a mass migration; rather, Bosnian families were brought over singly with the aid of charitable organizations. These groups offered help in finding homes and jobs, but because the organizations were scattered all over the United States, so were the Bosnians. It would have been easy for them in their new homes to become isolated from their former countrymen, but instead they have created a community that has no concern for the distance between them.

Ivana Starcevic, Marietta, Georgia

Alisah Restaurant in Tucson, Arizona, has a message on its website. "In Bosnia we say: 'You can smell good food far away.' In this case, we can smell Bosnian food in different chains of Bosnian restaurants from Tucson, Arizona, all the way to Atlanta, Georgia."

Following the scent leads you to Neretva Market, a small restaurant and Bosnian grocery tucked into a corner of a nondescript strip mall in the Atlanta suburb of Marietta. Neretva Market is distinguished only by a few umbrella-covered tables out front. A group of men, at turns serious and jovial, sit around the tables, drinking small cups of strong coffee.

One man moves in and out of the restaurant portion of the market, bringing coffee and food to the others. This man, Zdenko Starcevic, often joins them, taking part in the camaraderie of shared language and experience.

While Zdenko holds court outside, his daughter Ivana sits at a table inside and talks about how her family came to own the restaurant and market. "The owners before us, they were shutting down, and we knew the owner of the wholesaler where we order our merchandise now. He was suggesting to my mom and dad to get it, and I guess he finally influenced us. Plus, we used to have a restaurant in Germany, so it was just like getting back on track with something we knew."

Ivana was only seven when her family was forced to leave their homeland. "When the war started, we moved to Germany because we had family there. In Germany, you had to extend your visa every three months. After eight years, they quit doing that, so they gave us a choice—to go back home or to fill out paperwork to apply to come to America," she says.

"We applied, we got approved, and that's how we got here. We actually wanted to go to San Diego because my mom's cousin is over there," she says. "But they gave us Georgia," she adds with a laugh.

The Atlanta area has not been a disappointment for the Starcevic family. Their business is successful, and they have many friends both in and out of the local Bosnian community. They also maintain ties to the extended Bosnian community. "We've stayed in touch with family and with friends. I know my mom still keeps in touch with her friends from Bosnia and from Germany."

Because Ivana was younger when she came to the United States, she has had an easier time adjusting to the change. She realizes that others have not been so lucky. "I know a lot of people from my country don't like living here, but I love it. I guess if you're older and you come here, it's harder for you to get used to it. But for me, because I have so many opportunities, school-wise and all of that, it's great."

Ivana has a pragmatic view of life that makes the question of where she lives a moot point. "Even when I went to Germany, my cousins there said, 'Oh, Europe is better. Blah, blah.' When I went over there and then came back to Atlanta, everyone asked if I loved Europe. Of course I did. I had money. I didn't work. I was going around looking at things, buying things. Of course I had fun. But you look at my cousin. He leaves at eleven in the morning and comes back at one at night. It's the same wherever you go. You just have to figure out how to make a living."

Though she is taking time to sit and talk while business is slow, Ivana doesn't shy away from work. In fact, she would like the freedom to do more. "My father and I both cook. He usually doesn't let me do it if he's here. But if he leaves, I do the job. He's always showing me how to do it. It's been almost four years that we have had the store, and he's still telling me every single day what I have to do. I tell him, 'Dad, I'm getting it.'"

Being in the kitchen is more than just a job for Ivana. It is a passion, even more so when she is away from work. "I like to cook. I love to cook, actually. But I like to do it more if I'm not forced to, you know. Of course you like to make your own thing whenever you feel like it, so if we're at home, I always make something. Dad always prepares something, too. I really do like cooking. Just not baking. Don't ask me to bake. Anything but that," she says, smiling.

Having to bake isn't a problem in the restaurant. The menu is short but full of traditional Bosnian dishes, mostly spiced and seasoned meats, including the hand-rolled sausage known as *ćevapi*. As Ivana says, "The most popular dish in the restaurant is the *ćevapi*, although I try to convince people to taste other things. We put combinations on the menu so they can try two things at once, but *ćevapi* is definitely a favorite."

From the men drinking coffee outside to the families who come to shop and dine inside, both the market and restaurant stay busy. Neretva is so successful, perhaps, because it offers a sense of place to people who have had no choice but to flee their homelands. It offers a taste of something familiar in a region that is very different from where they came from. But still, as Ivana so eloquently puts it, "Wherever you go, the food is never the same as it is at home." 🍲

SARMA (Bosnian Cabbage Rolls)

Active cooking time: 45 minutes | Total cooking time: 4 hours + 8 hours | Yield: about 16 large cabbage rolls

When Ivana thinks about the foods she most loves to eat at home, *sarma* is the dish that immediately comes to mind. "It's like sauerkraut filled with ground beef and rice. I've always loved that, but they only make it—I don't know why, but it's like turkey here—for special events and Christmas. I have to wait all the time for Christmas to eat that."

Sarma is a dish rich in history, with roots stretching back to the Ottoman Empire, where it came from the same basic dish that evolved into the grape-leaf dolma of Greek cuisine. It is a traditional holiday food across Eastern Europe, served on Christmas Eve or at weddings.

Sarma is a comfort food with layers of flavor perfect for a cold winter day. The tartness of the sauerkraut cooks into the cabbage-wrapped parcels resting on it. The meat filling is rich, with the ham contributing a note of salty smoke. The sauce adds a layer of sweetness from the tomato, and the feta brings a perfect note of creaminess.

1 large cabbage, whole
1 tablespoon olive oil
½ medium white onion, minced
 (about ⅓ cup)
½ green bell pepper, minced
 (about ½ cup)
1 medium carrot, grated
1 rib celery, minced (about ½ cup)
1 clove garlic, minced (about
 ½ teaspoon)
1 pound ground beef
½ pound ground pork
½ pound smoked ham, minced
1 cup uncooked white rice
1 teaspoon salt
1 teaspoon freshly ground black
 pepper
1 pound sauerkraut
8 ounces feta cheese, crumbled
1 (6-ounce) can tomato paste
2 cups water
2 tablespoons paprika

At least one day before making the *sarma*, remove the tough outer leaves of the cabbage, core it, and rinse it thoroughly. Reserve the outer leaves in the refrigerator. Freeze the rest of the cabbage in a large zip-top storage bag. When you're ready to prepare the dish, thaw the cabbage, and the leaves will be pliable enough to make the cabbage rolls.

Preheat the oven to 350 degrees.

Heat the oil in a large skillet over medium heat.

Add the onion, bell pepper, carrot, and celery. Cook, stirring constantly, for 5 to 8 minutes or until the onion is translucent and the bell pepper is tender.

Add the garlic and continue cooking, stirring constantly, for 2 more minutes.

In a large mixing bowl, combine the ground beef, ground pork, ham, rice, salt, and black pepper. Add the cooked vegetables, mixing with your hands to combine thoroughly.

Drain the sauerkraut and spread it into the bottom of a large Dutch oven or covered casserole dish.

Lay a cabbage leaf out flat on a plate, smoothing as much as possible. Heap 2 tablespoons of the meat mixture in the center of the cabbage leaf. Fold the top of the leaf over the filling, bring the sides together, and roll the leaf as tightly as possible, encasing the filling completely. Repeat until all cabbage leaves are used.

Layer the cabbage rolls on top of the sauerkraut, seam side down. Any excess filling can be rolled into meatballs that can be cooked along with the cabbage rolls.

Sprinkle the feta cheese over the rolls.

Combine the tomato paste in a bowl with the water and paprika and stir well. Pour the sauce over the cabbage rolls.

Cover the rolls with the reserved outer leaves of the cabbage.

Cover the dish and bake for 1 hour.

Reduce the oven temperature to 325 degrees and continue baking for 2 hours more.

Allow the rolls to rest for at least 15 minutes before serving.

Paprika

CULINARY TOUR GUIDE

In American cooking, paprika often doesn't get its due. It has been perceived as a spice that was long on color but short on flavor and has been all too often relegated to the back of the spice rack. Used for years to brighten up the looks of potato salad or deviled eggs, paprika deserves to take its place at the forefront of flavor.

Like the famed seven moles of Oaxaca or the seemingly infinite curries of India, paprika is rich in flavor and history. Christopher Columbus brought the first paprika pepper plant, a variety of bell pepper, to the royal court of Spain from the Antilles. By the late sixteenth century, paprika peppers had reached the Balkans, including Bosnia. In the cooler European climate, the peppers evolved to be milder than Columbus's original gift to Isabella.

Paprika had a great impact on the cuisine of Bosnia, but it was to the north, in Hungary, that the spice truly found a home. There, paprika was originally

In Mobile, 350 miles away from Marietta, Osman Ademovic sits in his restaurant, Osman's, talking about his favorite food, *ćevapčići*, small beef sausages. When we tell him we love them too, he is surprised.

Osman Ademovic, Mobile, Alabama

"Oh, where have you had *ćevapčići*?" he asks.

We tell him about Neretva Market, and he replies, "Oh, yes, I know him."

Osman was born in Banja Luca in the former Yugoslavia. Because he loved to cook, he chose to go to culinary school. It was there that he met his wife. "Yeah, she's a chef too. I'm cooking here; she's cooking at home. I never cook at home," he says.

Although his home now is Mobile, Osman hadn't planned on the move. "I'm a war refugee. It's different. I'm a refugee, not an immigrant. I left the country in 1992, then we went to Germany and stayed there for five and a half years. And then, because Germany had too many refugees, they tried to send them somewhere."

Germany's decision forced Osman and his family to move again. "We didn't have a chance to go back to Bosnia, so we filled out an application to the American embassy to see if they would accept us."

Their application was accepted, but America is a big target. Their ultimate destination was up in the air. "We didn't choose. If you have family, you can tell what part of the country you want to go to, but if you don't, they ask if you have any wishes. My wife said, 'I don't want to go where the snow is. And close to the water.'" So they came to Mobile.

used medicinally as a cure for fevers before becoming an ingredient in the cuisine. In 1937, Hungarian scientist Albert Szent-Györgyi won the Nobel Prize in Medicine for his discovery of vitamin C. Much of his experimentation was done with paprika. Clearly, there is a great deal to be said for traditional medicine.

Today, Hungary grows more than forty types of paprika. The primary varieties found in U.S. markets are sharp (hot), sweet, and smoked (pimentón), a specialty of Spain. Paprika is also grown domestically; California producers raise a variety of sweet paprika.

Paprika requires heat to release its best flavor, but it burns easily. It works best mixed in with stews like Hungarian goulash, slowly cooked sauces like the one used in *sarma* (page 121), casseroles like *pastel de choclo* (page 100), or dishes that cook quickly like *ćevapčići* (page 126).

Osman Ademovic at Osman's.

Coming to the United States presented Osman with the opportunity to learn more about food and with the need to learn something else: English. "When I came here, I started working at the best restaurant in town. I worked there about two years. One of the owners is originally from Sicily. He's an immigrant, too. I knew in Europe how I could get anything I need, any spice—I knew the name. It took about two years for me to learn the English names of those spices," he says.

Like his culinary kinship with the Starcevic family in Marietta, Osman has always felt a sense of extended community. Indeed, it has influenced his entire culinary career, beginning in Europe. "It was the original Yugoslavia before the war and it broke apart. Italy is our neighbor. Greece is our neighbor. Hungary is our neighbor. Austria is our neighbor. That part of Europe, you can find any kind of food you want to, because that's the neighborhood. We even have lots of Turkish dishes because we were under the Turks for years," he says.

"I don't cook food from where I'm from, but still, you can taste a lot of those Bosnian seasonings in how I do vegetables and soups. But lots of my food is German, Italian, or French. When I opened the restaurant, I did not concentrate on serving Bosnian customers because we have only maybe sixty families here. So I tried to bring in American customers," he recalls. "I didn't know anybody. I didn't have any family to support me, or friends. Normally when you open a restaurant, you have friends and they bring friends to support you, but I didn't have that. It was kind of tough."

Osman's experience and hard work have paid off. His restaurant is successful enough that he has been able to open a second location and expand his menu. "Now I can sell anything, because I have a good name in the town. Here in Mobile, they eat ethnic food now. There's no question. Whatever—Vietnamese, Thai, Chinese. But when I had just opened up, I used to have customers walk in, read the menu, then walk out. They were not used to those kinds of foods, especially here in the South. But now, the customers I have, I don't have any problems. They eat pretty much anything." ✑

ĆEVAPČIĆI (Hand-Rolled Bosnian Sausages)

Active cooking time: 1 hour, 25 minutes | Total cooking time: 1 hour, 40 minutes | Yield: 24 sausages

Osman tells us that if there's any single food that no one should leave Bosnia without trying, that food is *ćevapčići*, often simply referred to as *ćevapi*. These hand-rolled sausages are a favorite dish of almost every Bosnian.

The name *ćevapčići* comes from the Arabic word "kebab" with the addition of a Slavic diminutive. While the sausages today are cooked in a skillet or griddle or over a grill, it is easy to see how they could have been cooked on skewers in the past.

While you can vary the mix of meats, the traditional blend of beef, lamb, and pork provides a rich base for the spices. The flavors of paprika and garlic work together to make what is really a very simple preparation into something wonderful.

Serve the *ćevapčići* with warm flat bread, spicy *avjar* (Eastern European vegetable spread), and creamy *kajmak*, a cheese spread (recipe follows).

1 pound ground beef
1 pound ground pork
1 pound ground lamb
1 medium white onion, diced
   (about ⅔ cup)
4 cloves garlic, minced (about
   2 teaspoons)
2 tablespoons fresh flat leaf parsley,
   chopped
½ teaspoon cayenne pepper
4 tablespoons sweet Hungarian
   paprika
Pinch of nutmeg
1 teaspoon salt
2 teaspoons freshly ground black
   pepper
1 egg white

Combine all ingredients except the egg white, blending thoroughly with your hands to evenly mix the meats.

Allow the meat mixture to rest at room temperature for at least 15 minutes or overnight in the refrigerator if possible to intensify the flavors of the spices.

Heat a heavy skillet or griddle over medium heat.

Add the egg white to the meat mixture, working well to combine.

Separate the meat mixture into 2-ounce pieces, roughly the size of a walnut. Shape into fat cigar-shaped rolls.

Working in batches, place the sausage rolls carefully in the skillet or on the griddle, making sure not to crowd the pan.

Turn after 3 to 4 minutes until all sides have seared and the centers are cooked to medium, about 12 minutes total.

KAJMAK (Bosnian-Style Cheese Spread)

Active cooking time: 5 minutes | Total cooking time: 35 minutes | Yield: about 2 cups

The *labneh* used here is a soft yogurt cheese found in the refrigerated section of most Middle Eastern markets. If *labneh* isn't available in your area, substitute plain yogurt.

4 ounces *labneh* or 6 ounces plain yogurt
4 ounces cream cheese
4 ounces butter (1 stick)
4 ounces sour cream

If you are using yogurt instead of *labneh*, allow the yogurt to strain through a fine mesh sieve to thicken the yogurt and remove excess liquid.

Bring the *labneh* or yogurt, cream cheese, butter, and sour cream to room temperature.

In a food processor, blend together the cream cheese and butter until they are smooth and fluffy.

Stir in the *labneh* or yogurt and sour cream.

Kajmak will keep, covered, in the refrigerator for up to 3 days.

Merima Kreso sits in the sunny front room of her restaurant, Kreso's, in historic Bardstown, Kentucky. The restaurant is a truly amazing testament to Merima's creativity. The building was an old movie theater, abandoned for at least thirty years. The Kresos have restored the space beautifully, keeping the art deco floors and crystal chandeliers intact in their intimately elegant dining rooms.

It's only natural that Merima would be drawn to such a grand building for her American restaurant. She owned a spectacular restaurant in Bosnia for twelve years before war forced her and her family to flee to America. "It was located in an old castle, and we had a really beautiful restaurant. It had a nice terrace looking over the river in the city. We had about 400 seats outside and 180 inside. And we had a very traditional Bosnian kitchen in this restaurant," she recalls.

The Kreso family came to Bardstown in 1995 as refugees and immediately felt at home. "The Episcopal church across from our restaurant sponsored us like family and gave us the opportunity to start here. This church helped us, found us an apartment, and gave us some furniture."

The family's strong work ethic wouldn't allow them to accept charity for long, though. "They said you can come here and stay a few years and get help, but my husband and I, we are very hard workers. I never liked to be on help from the government. I never liked to ask what the country needed to give to me. I always like to say what I am going to give to this country," she states. "We came on July 21, and we started working on August 10. We were refugees in this country for only twenty days. The priest asked us what we needed, and my husband and I just said that we needed a job."

For the Kresos, that job was in a local sandwich shop. Merima's natural instincts to prepare good food kicked in immediately. "When I came there and I saw the food, I started to make my food right away. The first thing was goulash. Then I made my own lasagna."

These were foods that she brought with her from Bosnia, foods that she was excited to introduce to her new neighbors, and she shared them at the sandwich shop for eight years. "We have very traditional food in Bosnia. Parts of Bosnia have different kinds of food. The ex-Yugoslavia was a very excellent place for food—from Macedonia to Serbia to Croatia to Bosnia and Herzegovina to Montenegro. We have these old beautiful foods. Everything was homemade."

Her restaurant today is very eclectic. Merima bases her menu not only on dishes that she knows but also on what ingredients she has at hand. "We create the food. I look in my coolers, and whatever I have there fresh, I will make something with it."

Merima Kreso at Kreso's.

That use of fresh ingredients and tradition of making food from scratch come from Merima's Bosnian upbringing. "Most people in Bosnia make lunch and dinner at home. Women go to the market and buy fresh food," she recalls. "That's what I am missing here most, especially in a small town like this one. I would like to go in the market and look at my spinach and look at my onions, look at my meat, the way it was in my country. I don't try to say that's easy, but I think that's much more healthy."

Merima has other concerns about some American foodways. "Here in America, I think food is much more a business, especially the big companies that are producing food. I found chicken salad in the grocery store, and it says it is good for three months. I really don't understand. Who knows what you have in this stuff to keep it good for three months!"

Shopping and eating habits haven't been the only parts of American life that have surprised Merima. She had an interesting experience when they opened their restaurant and started looking for skilled workers. "I have one person who came to apply, and he says, 'I am a line cook.' I say, 'What do you do?' He says, 'I fry chicken.' I don't understand that you have to have one person in a restaurant who is doing just this. We do everything. We're cooking, we're cleaning, we're on the grill. We're on the dishwasher. We're everywhere."

Merima's kitchen was the start of changes in the food of Bardstown. "When we first came here, I don't think there were any ethnic kitchens. I think we were the first to start to change. When I started to make lasagna, I think I was the only person making homemade lasagna in a restaurant here."

Bardstown has changed Merima, too. "From the American kitchen, I like the steaks and I like pies very much. I bake cheesecake that is the very best in the whole area, but I learned to make it here. When I first came here, I started to make pecan pie and derby pie because a lady I worked with gave me the recipe. She taught me this, and I liked it. I still make them."

Her view of American food is that it is always changing as America itself changes. "American food is actually influenced by all the other countries of the whole world. And when I say 'American' food, you have everything here. You have people coming here, like immigrants. You have that adding to the American kitchen."

Because Bardstown isn't a large city, it would be easy for the Kresos as an immigrant family to become isolated. "We were the first Bosnian family in Bardstown. Then there were three or four more families, but they all went to Louisville because they had different needs. They got jobs there."

The Kresos have remained a part of the Bosnian community, though. They do this through contact with their friends from before the war. "The first couple of years we didn't have any connections with our best friends because all of us just needed to go when we left Bosnia. After a couple of years, though, we established our lives here, and we started asking for each other. We now see everybody, and we are so happy that we found so many of our friends."

But as much as they are a part of their extended Bosnian community, they have become an integral part of the Bardstown community. As people walk past the restaurant and see Merima in the window, they smile and wave. When service starts, regular customers begin coming in to say hello and sit down to a favorite meal. It's a result of Merima's theory on how a restaurant can be a part of a community. "Every single day we are here working. We like this. We like to give back to this community. Here we aren't just owners. We aren't just cooks. We are friends to the people, and that makes us different." 🕮

MERIMA'S CHICKEN BREAST STUFFED WITH SPINACH AND FETA

Active cooking time: 45 minutes | Total cooking time: 45 minutes | Yield: 4 main dish servings

This isn't a traditional Bosnian recipe, but it is one of Merima's favorites that she has developed for her restaurant. It uses her philosophy of keeping basic ingredients on hand and taking the time to think about your evening meal in advance.

There are no exotic ingredients here; there's nothing you will need to go to a specialty store to find. The flavor is simple and fresh. "Time and love are the most important things in the kitchen," Merima says. "If you cook at home and have dinner as a family, you'll get your kids in the kitchen and get to know them better. My most beautiful memory is coming home from school and opening the door and smelling whatever my mother was cooking. It let us know that Mom was there and that she cared about us."

By pounding out the chicken into thin patties, the chicken will cook through quicker in the skillet so that the spinach in the middle won't overcook. The filets may look overstuffed to you before you cook them, but the spinach will wilt quickly.

2 large boneless, skinless chicken breasts,
    about 1 pound
1 pound fresh spinach, chopped
8 ounces feta cheese, crumbled
4 tablespoons shredded Parmesan cheese,
    divided
1 tablespoon olive oil
2 cloves garlic, minced (about 1 teaspoon)
¼ cup fresh parsley, minced
1 cup half-and-half

TO SERVE
Buttered egg noodles

> **Kitchen Passport** A milder
> cheese than feta would also be
> delicious in this recipe. Look for
> a soft white cheese that will melt
> quickly. Fresh mozzarella, fontina,
> taleggio, or even brie would work
> well. If the creamy sauce seems
> too heavy to you, substitute
> chicken broth for the half-and-
> half. Allow the broth to reduce
> and add 1 teaspoon cornstarch
> to the liquid if it is not as thick
> as you like. Add salt to taste.

Slice open the chicken breasts as if to butterfly, but cut each into 2 roughly equal pieces.

Spread a sheet of plastic wrap flat on your work surface. Lay one piece of chicken on the plastic wrap and cover loosely with another sheet of plastic wrap. Using a heavy pan bottom or a mallet, pound the chicken breast until it is no more than ½-inch thick at any point. Repeat until all chicken breast pieces have been flattened.

In a large mixing bowl, combine the spinach, feta, and 2 tablespoons Parmesan cheese, stirring to distribute equally. Continue stirring until a loose mixture is formed.

Spread half of a chicken breast with 3 rounded tablespoons of the spinach and feta mixture and fold over the top. Repeat until all chicken breast pieces have been filled.

Heat the oil in a large skillet over medium heat.

Add the garlic and parsley and cook, stirring constantly, for 2 minutes or until the garlic is fragrant.

Add the stuffed chicken breasts and cook, undisturbed, for 3 to 5 minutes or until the chicken is golden brown.

Carefully flip the stuffed chicken breasts and continue cooking for another 3 to 5 minutes or until the second side is golden brown.

Transfer the chicken breasts to a warm plate to rest while you prepare the sauce.

Reduce the heat to medium low.

Add the half-and-half to the skillet, stirring to loosen any bits of chicken from the skillet. Add the remaining 2 tablespoons Parmesan cheese and cook, stirring constantly, until the cheese is melted and the sauce has thickened enough to coat the back of a spoon, about 10 minutes.

Return the stuffed chicken breasts to the skillet with the sauce and allow the chicken to cook in the sauce for 2 minutes.

Flip each chicken breast and cook for another 2 minutes.

Serve over buttered egg noodles.

The Indian Subcontinent
Feeding the Technology Boom

The two primary tenets of the American dream are freedom and opportunity. The burgeoning southern economy has been a boon to Indian information technology (IT) workers. Virtually every business in the South, from banking to manufacturing to transportation, requires IT. Business growth has meant that demand for IT workers has outstripped the supply of qualified American workers. As a result, companies send jobs overseas and bring qualified workers to the United States.

As the number of Indian workers increases, more restaurants, stores, and other businesses open to cater to them. And on occasion, Indian IT workers elect to pursue a different type of opportunity, venturing into the world of food to test their business skills and creativity.

"We got engaged last night!"

Rabiul Hossain,
Atlanta, Georgia

A young blonde woman and her grinning fiancé have just sat down with their plates from the buffet when friends of theirs happen into the restaurant. The friends greet them and the restaurant's manager with equal warmth as they all offer their congratulations to the happy couple.

As the friends talk, Rabiul Hossain, the manager of Panahar Bangladeshi Cuisine, goes back to overseeing the dining room and welcoming customers. Rabiul says that scenes like this are common in the restaurant. "We try to give as much service as possible. We try to be as friendly as possible. We try to make it like it's your home."

Panahar just may be the only Bangladeshi restaurant in the entire state of Georgia, but it is right at home in a shopping center along Atlanta's Buford Highway. To the left of Panahar is an Ethiopian restaurant; to the right, Ecuadoran and Peruvian. The strip mall also features a Mexican grocery, a Chinese buffet, and a Latin ballroom.

That sort of diversity is common among the shopping centers of Buford Highway. While Atlanta has great ethnic restaurants scattered throughout the city, in no other place is ethnic diversity so concentrated. Rabiul enjoys working in the neighborhood and having the op-

7

portunity to sample all that it has to offer. "Buford Highway is great. You can find any kind of food here."

The stores along the highway help the diverse restaurants flourish, quite a change from the days when Rabiul's father first came to the United States. "You go to the international farmers' market, you can find everything. There are Bangladeshi stores—supermarkets where they bring things from Bangladesh—so you can find everything. When my dad moved over here, they barely had anything."

Rabiul's father, Mohammed Khurshid Alam, is one of the owners of Panahar. Khurshid immigrated to the United States from Bangladesh in 1991. Unlike many Indians who enter on H-1B visas as temporary technology workers, Khurshid came on an OP-1 "opportunity" visa.

The two U.S. State Department programs differ significantly. The H-1B program is designed to help American businesses find talented workers. The OP-1 program—known as the green card lottery—is designed simultaneously to control the number of immigrants and to increase diversity among the immigrants who are allowed into the United States.

In 1989, Rabiul's uncle entered himself, his son, and Khurshid into the lottery for the highly prized visas. Six months later, the three men received letters from the U.S. government—Khurshid and his nephew both won a chance to get a visa. Khurshid's brother, who initiated the process, did not.

When Khurshid left Bangladesh, he was a businessman. "He had his own little store, fixing TVs and selling TVs, too," Rabiul says.

In order for a chance at success in the United States, Khurshid had to leave all of that behind and start over. "When he came over here, he didn't speak much English. He needed a job, so from a friend, he got a job in an Indian restaurant. He started as a dishwasher, and after that, he saw the cooking. He became the tandoori chef, then slowly, as he saw the other chefs cooking, he got a little knowledge and became assistant chef, and after a while, he became the main chef."

Khurshid has been the chef at Panahar since it opened. The transition from Indian chef to Bangladeshi chef was not a difficult one for him. "Indian food and Bangladeshi food are similar. Bangladeshi food is less spicy and has less turmeric," Rabiul says. "We don't use curry. Curry is the Indian term, which is a mixture of powders. We don't use that. We have individual spices that we use, so certain dishes have certain spices. So from his knowledge of cooking and his knowledge of the taste of Bangladeshi food, he got it all together."

When the original owner of Panahar experienced financial difficulties, he sold the business to Khurshid. Success was not immediate for

Rabiul Hossain at
Panahar Bangladeshi
Cuisine.

Khurshid, but it came eventually. "There were tough times, but we are doing better now," Rabiul says.

Now that they have found success, Rabiul and his family are able to help others. Sanjay Das Ripon is working as a waiter at Panahar; he gained his green card in the lottery of 2005. He smiles as he talks about what his life is like in the United States. Recognizing that American culture is very different from Bangladeshi culture, Sanjay says, "Whatever you do here, you can do with no problem. One thing that's very important is religious freedom."

With his freedom, Sanjay also plans to pursue opportunity. "I have a plan to study and to possibly have a business someday."

As the day's crowd thins at Panahar, Rabiul watches the newly engaged couple leave and reflects on another group of customers. "I had some folks come in. They live pretty far away—past the airport. So the son wanted to come here for his birthday, and the dad, he didn't want to come. First of all, it's too far. Second of all, it's not burgers. That's what he said. So I talked to them, and I made a list of my favorite dishes for them to try," Rabiul says.

"After he had it, I was walking by the table, and he said, 'Can you come over here, please?' He said, 'Well, you know me. I am a very traditional American person—I eat burgers, pizza, fries . . .' But after having this, it changed everything."

Rabiul is changing things for Americans, but is America changing him? Perhaps just a bit. "We're in the South, so I have a little grill outside. Sometimes when everybody's off, I invite everybody that works over here, some of my friends, my family, to get together and have a little barbecue." 🐐

GOAT *HALIM* (Bangladeshi-Style Goat Stew)

Active cooking time: 50 minutes | Total cooking time: 3 hours, 5 minutes + 3 hours

Yield: 6 to 8 main dish servings

Halim is one of the dishes that Rabiul believes best represents Bangladeshi cuisine. The cracked wheat and lentils used in the dish are staples in the Bangladeshi kitchen, and goat is commonly used in meat dishes throughout the country.

Halim originated in Iran and Afghanistan and traveled east through India along trade routes. This thick stew with its aromatic spices and base of soft grain was originally served as a breakfast dish after cooking overnight on the embers of the day's fire.

In Bangladesh, cooks grind spices fresh everyday to get the most intense flavors. You might consider using a coffee or spice grinder or even a mortar and pestle in your own kitchen to get the same results.

The garnishes given here are as impor-tant as the dish itself. While the stew is wonderful on its own, it doesn't reach its true potential without these traditional additions. The crisp onion, peppers, and radishes add both flavor and texture; the tartness of the cilantro and lime contrast with the creaminess of the stew.

This is a perfect stew for a winter day. The cracked wheat cooks into a creamy base, and the goat is some of the tenderest meat you will ever eat. The spices combine to create wonderful aromas that you won't be able to help smiling about when you open the pot.

If you're not comfortable using goat, or if goat is not available to you, you can use the same amount of lamb. Goat and lamb can commonly be found in Middle Eastern markets.

1 cup cracked wheat (bulgur)

½ cup red lentils

½ cup ghee

½ teaspoon ground cumin

1 large white onion, chopped fine
    (about 1 cup)

1 (2-inch) piece fresh ginger, peeled
    and grated (about 2 tablespoons)

½ teaspoon ground cloves

3 cardamom pods

2 4-inch cinnamon sticks

1 tablespoon salt

2 pounds goat shoulder meat, cubed

1 large turnip, diced

2 medium carrots, diced

1 cup baby spinach, chopped

1 fennel bulb with greens, diced

¼ teaspoon crushed saffron threads

TO GARNISH

Warm naan bread

½ medium yellow onion, sliced thin

1 cup cilantro, chopped

½ cup peppermint leaves, chopped

8 hot green chile peppers, chopped

2 limes, quartered into wedges

8 radishes, sliced

Kitchen Passport The dish can also be made with chicken or beef, or the meat can be left out entirely for a vegetarian version. Potatoes, celery root, and rutabaga would also be delicious. Rice can be substituted for the cracked wheat. Simply prepare the dish as given, omitting the cracked wheat, and serve with steamed rice or rice pilaf. The stew will be thinner but just as flavorful.

In a large bowl, cover the cracked wheat and lentils with water and allow to soak for at least 3 hours.

Drain the water from the bowl and reserve the cracked wheat and lentils.

Preheat the oven to 300 degrees.

In a heavy ovenproof pot, heat the ghee over medium-high heat.

Add the ground cumin and cook until fragrant, about 3 minutes.

Add the onion and cook, stirring constantly, until the onion begins to brown, about 8 minutes.

Add the ginger and continue cooking for 1 minute.

Add the cloves, cardamom pods, cinnamon sticks, and salt. Continue cooking for 2 minutes.

Add the goat meat, stirring to combine. Cook until the goat meat has browned, about 10 minutes.

Add the turnip, carrots, spinach, and fennel. Cook, stirring constantly, for 3 minutes.

Add the saffron and the soaked cracked wheat and lentils, stirring to combine. Add 4 cups of water and cook, stirring often, until the mixture comes to a boil.

Cover the pot and transfer the dish to the oven. Cook for 2 hours.

Allow the *halim* to rest for 15 minutes.

Remove the cinnamon sticks and cardamom pods before serving.

Serve with warm naan bread along with the other garnishes for each diner to add as desired.

Ghee

If there is a single indispensable ingredient in Indian cuisine, that ingredient is ghee. Ghee is similar to clarified, or drawn, butter, butter cooked slowly until the solid milk fat renders out, leaving behind a clear, golden liquid. Ghee is different from clarified butter in that it is cooked longer to give it a richer flavor, and that richness carries over into its role in Indian culture and cuisine as well.

The first documented mention of people making butter comes from the sacred songs of the people of northern India, dating back 4,000 years. For these people, butter was more than a food. They used it for lamp oil, as medicine, and as a skin coating to protect them from the harsh winters of the region.

Through colonization and conquest, butter moved south. It was quickly discovered, however, that butter could not be stored as easily in the warmer climate. Southern Indians were the first to clarify butter and found that the process kept the fat from spoiling. In ancient times, the liquid produced was known as "The Royal Oil."

In the Hindu culture of India, the cow is a sacred animal representing the soul. Butter made from cow's milk is the only animal fat that strict Hindus will eat. Because of ghee's relationship to the cow, it has an important place in Hindu religious ceremonies and in Hindu temples. The lamps that burn in the holiest of Hindu places are wicks burning in bowls of ghee.

In Indian folklore, honey and ghee are the foods of the gods. In fact, in Hindu mythology, Prajápati, Lord of Creatures, created ghee by rubbing or "churning" his hands together. He then poured it into fire to engender his progeny, man.

In Ayurveda, the ancient natural healing system of India, ghee is an important medicinal component. According to Ayurvedic texts, ghee develops strong medicinal qualities as it ages. It is also said to promote learning and increased memory retention.

So how is ghee made? Pure butter is melted and simmered long enough to boil off all of the water and to have the solid milk fat sink to the bottom. The longer it simmers, the stronger the butter flavor will be. After simmering, the solids are discarded and only the golden liquid remains. Because the fats and water that encourage the growth of microorganisms are gone, ghee can be stored at room temperature for months. And, since the milk proteins have all been removed, ghee is a safe food for the lactose intolerant.

In Indian cuisine, ghee is used especially, but not exclusively, for cooking meat. Chefs of many nationalities like to cook with ghee because it cooks at a very high temperature without burning.

If there is any doubt of the importance of ghee in Indian culture, it can be put to rest by reading a 3,500-year-old hymn of the *Rig Veda*:

This is the secret name of Butter:
"Tongue of the gods," "navel of
    immortality."
We will proclaim the name of Butter;
We will sustain it in this sacrifice by
    bowing low.
These waves of Butter flow like gazelles
    before the hunter . . .
Streams of Butter caress the burning
    wood.
Agni, the fire, loves them and is satisfied.

Santhosh Pasula grew up in Hyderabad, in southern India. Growing up with the famous street food of the region and his mother's delicious home cooking, he developed distinct ideas on flavor and on the way food should be enjoyed. However, it wasn't until he came to the United States that he realized how uniquely his background had prepared him to work with food.

Santhosh Pasula,
Charlotte,
North Carolina

Santhosh first came to the United States in 2000 as a software engineer. He originally went to work in California's Silicon Valley, but a job with a bank led him to Charlotte, North Carolina. Charlotte became his home, and it was there that he acted on his newfound passion for cooking.

He cooked before he came to the United States, but he didn't get to do much since his mother loved to cook, too. "When I came here, I had to cook—there was no other way—so that's how I developed a passion for it."

His mother must have seen potential for him to be a great cook because she set him up to succeed before he left home. "When I actually moved from India to here, my mom, she had a book which is written by one of the local chefs, and it's probably like a 300-page book. And when I was coming here, she gave me that book. She had that for about twenty-plus years, then she gave it to me. I still have that book with me."

Santhosh recalls the rich flavors of Indian cuisine and the care his mother put into preparing dishes. Everything she used was fresh, and she taught her son the ways that fresh ingredients can improve the final dish. "In India, you get stuff and make ingredients out of it, like, for example, turmeric powder. I've never seen my mom buy turmeric powder. She buys the root, then she grinds it and makes the powder out of it—same thing with the coriander powder and the chile powder. She buys sun-dried chiles in bulk and then makes it."

At first, cooking was a hobby, a way for him to enjoy the flavors of his past, but his passion for it grew. Finally, he decided he should open a restaurant. "I had to take a break from my job. I actually left my job. I had so much passion that I left my job and took one and a half months off. I put all my savings in."

Santhosh had never owned or worked in a restaurant before, but he did have some experience with the concepts of cooking for large numbers of people before he left India. "Back home whenever there's a wedding or a big ceremony, most of the time they used to call the chefs to the wedding hall. In every wedding hall, most likely they would have a kitchen in the back, and the chefs would come there and cook the food in the kitchen. And they generally cook for 500, 600, sometimes up to 2,000 people. It depends on how many guests you have," he recalls.

"I had some experience as a caterer. If there's a wedding, people go there and gather for a week, ten days, and the caterers take the responsibilities and do it. Most of the time, I was involved in the responsibility of making chefs work, so I was always in the kitchen, making sure things were going right and getting stuff—whatever the chefs asked for. I had pretty good experience as far as large-volume cooking is concerned."

Santhosh enjoyed using his restaurant to introduce the foods of India to Charlotte natives who had never experienced them. While he liked serving authentic dishes, he also enjoyed improvising new dishes to teach people about the flavors of Indian food. "We had a crowd from the University of North Carolina at Charlotte, and they had never been to an Indian restaurant, so they said, 'Do you have a burger?' Then we said, 'We don't have a burger, but we can make a burger, Indian style.' We made a vegetarian patty and a chicken patty mixed with all the spices. So we were able to customize it to some extent."

He was also able to use the lunch buffet as a learning environment for his customers. "I've met a lot of people who never knew what Indian food was. And I always used to tell people we offer a lunch buffet, so go to a buffet. You can try whatever you want, then you can decide. If you go to a buffet, you will have twenty different items, and you can see what you want. And then you'll get an opinion," he says. "When I opened the restaurant, I saw people come in that way and ask me questions about how Indian food is made or what exactly we put in it, and I always used to invite them to come over to lunch. So people are getting acquainted as far as our food is concerned."

Unfortunately, economic woes changed everything for Santhosh. He was forced to close his restaurant and return to working in IT. "It was the bad economy," he says. His wife was already struggling, trying to maintain the restaurant. "I had no problem running it, but she was getting tired. She's a civil engineer. At one point, we decided she could do better in her job, so she went back to her job. I tried to run it by hiring people, but I didn't find reliable people. Even if I found someone, they wanted more, so eventually the business took a nosedive, and I closed."

But his passion for his food is still there. He and his wife provide catering services from their home, and he has not given up the dream of returning to the restaurant business. "This time, if I try again, I will probably get a working partner who can take care of the business, and I'll not be in the driver's seat. I'll probably be as navigator. Better I get all those links connected before I think about giving it to someone to run."

That passion comes through loud and clear when he gives a quick lesson in curry. He smiles as he gives tips that are simple only on the surface. "If you want to make Indian food, I would say you have to learn how to make onion gravy and then how to use tomatoes. Crushed tomato has to be used in such a way that it adds flavor to the gravy. As long as you know this stuff, you can pretty much make curry, any curry."

Santhosh may not be teaching restaurant customers about Indian food anymore, but his passion to share his knowledge still burns. Now he has someone new to teach. He shared his story in a hospital cafeteria, breaking away for just a few minutes from his wife and their newborn child—a child who will surely learn the best of both worlds, the flavors of the South and the flavors of India, a child who may someday be given a book that traveled far to inspire passion for the cuisine of a faraway place. 🕮

BIRYANI (Hyderabad-Style Spiced Rice)

Active cooking time: 1 hour | Total cooking time: 1 hour, 50 minutes + 8 hours | Yield: 6 to 8 main dish servings

When asked if there's a single dish that any visitor to Hyderabad must try, Santhosh immediately answers, "Biryani. Hyderabad is known for biryani. Everyone in Hyderabad loves biryani, and they probably eat biryani once a week."

Biryani most likely originated in Persia, where it is still a common dish throughout the Middle East as both biryani and as pilaf. In fact, the only significant difference between the two dishes is that the rice in biryani is fried in ghee before being boiled. Rice for pilaf is not fried.

Hyderabadi biryani is one of the best-known variations of the dish not only throughout India but throughout the world. There are multiple legends of this version's origin. Some say that Timor the Lame brought the dish from Kazakhstan.

Others say that Mumtaz Mahal, the famous occupant of the Taj Mahal, created it as a complete meal for her husband's soldiers. In truth, biryani most likely originated in the nizam's kitchens as a blending of cuisines from northern Muslim cultures.

Santhosh says, "Biryani is basically the food that was introduced by Nizam Mir Qamar-ud-din Khan. The nizam was the ruler of Hyderabad once upon a time. And his chefs pretty much introduced biryani."

Traditionally, biryani is cooked slowly in an earthenware pot sealed with pastry until the dish is ready to serve. Here, the dish is sealed with aluminum foil before the lid is put on in order to achieve the same effect. Since the rice and meat are both already cooked, the time in the oven is decreased.

The dish that results is both beautiful

and delicious. The biryani will be aromatic from the spices used. The rice grains will be separate, not sticky, and some scattered grains will be made gorgeous and golden by the saffron. The basmati rice gives a slightly nutty flavor; frying the rice before cooking it enhances that flavor and caramelizes the starch coating on the rice to help decrease stickiness. The chiles in the marinade are included for sweetness, not for heat.

2 pounds boneless lamb

1 (1-inch) piece fresh ginger, peeled and grated (about 1 tablespoon)

6 cloves garlic, minced (about 1 tablespoon)

4 green chiles, sliced thin

½ teaspoon saffron

2 tablespoons milk

¼ cup ghee, divided

3 cups basmati rice

1 bay leaf

1 4-inch cinnamon stick, broken into 2 pieces

2 green cardamom pods

1 large yellow onion, sliced thin

¼ teaspoon ground cayenne pepper

¼ teaspoon turmeric powder

½ teaspoon cumin seeds

2 dried red chiles

2 whole cloves

2 black cardamom pods

1 teaspoon salt

½ cup yogurt

½ cup mint leaves, chopped

½ cup cilantro leaves, chopped

¼ cup grated coconut

¼ cup whole cashews

¼ cup sliced almonds

¼ cup golden raisins

2 tablespoons lime juice

Cut the lamb into bite-sized pieces, removing any excess fat.

Using a mortar and pestle or food processor, mash the ginger, garlic, and green chiles into a smooth paste.

Coat the meat with the paste and refrigerate it in a sealed container for at least 8 hours or overnight.

Stir the saffron into the milk in a small bowl. Allow the saffron to soak in the milk while continuing the cooking process.

Preheat the oven to 275 degrees.

In a large saucepan, heat 1 tablespoon ghee over medium-high heat.

Add the rice and stir to coat, cooking for 5 minutes or until the rice becomes slightly translucent.

Add 6 cups of water to the rice. Add the bay leaf, half of the cinnamon stick, and the green cardamom pods.

Bring the rice to a boil and continue to cook, stirring constantly for 10 minutes or until the rice is slightly tender.

Remove the spices and discard them.

Heat 3 tablespoons ghee in a large skillet over medium heat.

Add the onion and cook for 15 minutes or until the slices are crisp and golden brown.

Add the marinated lamb and stir, continuing to cook for 5 to 8 minutes or until the lamb is cooked through.

Remove the meat mixture from the heat.

Using a mortar and pestle or spice grinder, grind together the remaining cinnamon stick, cayenne pepper, turmeric powder, cumin, red chiles, cloves, seeds from the black cardamom pods, and salt. Discard the shells of the cardamom pods.

Stir the spice mixture into the yogurt. Combine the yogurt mixture with the meat, stirring to coat the meat evenly.

In a large Dutch oven, spread ⅓ of the meat mixture on the bottom. Spread ⅓ of the rice mixture over the meat. Repeat this layering process, finishing with a top layer of rice.

Pour the saffron and milk evenly over the layers. Sprinkle the mint, cilantro, coconut, cashews, almonds, raisins, and lime juice over the rice.

Cover the Dutch oven tightly with foil before putting on the lid. Place the dish in the oven and allow it to cook for 45 minutes.

Between assignments, IT consultant Madhavan Sadhasivam spends his time in a booth reading, studying, and searching for job opportunities in the restaurant portion of Saigruha India Mart in Memphis. Although the aromas of delicious and excellently prepared Indian food waft through the restaurant, Madhavan isn't there to eat. Instead, he prefers to cook for himself.

Madhavan came to the United States in 2007, originally working for a company in New Jersey. He later transferred his work visa to a Memphis company and moved to the South. The transition from India to the United States has not been a particularly difficult one because Indian goods are readily available. "If you talk about New Jersey, you get everything, really; it's better than in India. It's an awesome environment for the Indian people."

Moving to the South has not been a hardship, either. "I have seen in Memphis also a lot of Indian groceries and restaurants. I don't think we are lacking for getting anything. We can get anything which we used to get in India."

The market is a perfect example of the availability of ingredients for traditional Indian cooks. Spices line one wall, their aromas mingling with those of the cooking food in the restaurant. Freezers line the opposite wall, filled with frozen vegetables and prepared items like flatbreads, cheese, and meals. In between, jars of exotic condiments vie for shelf space with sweets and other snacks, while coolers hold fresh produce and imported Indian soft drinks.

Like Madhavan, many Indian IT workers look for the ingredients necessary to make traditional Indian food at home. In cities with growing populations of Indian immigrants, markets like Saigruha serve those needs.

Madhavan's love of good food stems from his days at home in India. He grew up in the town of Salem in the state of Tamil Nadu. After graduating from college in his hometown, he began working to further his career, so he looked to the state capital, Chennai. "It's a place where you go for opportunity."

In Chennai, career opportunities abounded, but the culinary options weren't as plentiful. "Comparing Salem and Chennai foods, Chennai is not that good. It was like here, the difference you have between southern food and food in other parts of America. I did not like the taste of Chennai food, and I wanted to eat my own kind of style, so I started cooking."

Madhavan had a head start on cooking. "My mom and sister cook really well. Whenever they used to cook, I used to watch. What are they doing? What are the ingredients they are putting in? I love my mom. So whenever she cooked, I tried to learn."

Although he is on the other side of the world now, Madhavan still has a connection to home cooking, a technological connection. "Now the Internet is huge. I started to download some videos to see how to make things, to correct what I am doing wrong. I started seeing a lot of websites. I started improvising myself. If you go to YouTube, you can find whatever recipe you want. If you want to make a chicken curry, you will see clippings there."

Having a restaurant as an office could easily make a dent in his cooking habits, but now Madhavan has a new reason to cook—the opportunity to pass on what he has learned. "Now I am cooking for my friend. He doesn't know how to cook, so last week I started cooking for him. On weekends I go to his home and cook for him because he wants to eat typical south Tamil Nadu food. And since I know how to cook all those things, I go to his home and cook biryani, whatever he wants. Restaurants are okay, but I am trying to teach him how to cook all this stuff."

Like his love of good food, teaching comes naturally to Madhavan. "Basically, I am my mom's son." 🐚

CHICKEN CURRY

Active cooking time: 1 hour | Total cooking time: 1 hour, 30 minutes | Yield: 4 to 6 main dish servings

Chicken curry is believed to have originated in northern India, in the Punjab region. Curry is a generic term, used to describe both a spice blend and a general category of spiced dishes in Indian cuisine. The name comes from the Tamil word *khari*, which is usually understood to mean "sauce" or "gravy." Curry has spread to every continent, where it has been adapted to include the spices most prevalent in the indigenous cuisine of the region and where new dishes have developed with distinctly different flavors both from the original Indian dish and from each other.

You will notice that there is no curry powder used in Madhavan's recipe for chicken curry. Instead, he uses the spice blend garam masala, a mixture that often includes peppercorns, cloves, bay leaves,

hot peppers, cumin, cinnamon, cardamom, nutmeg, star anise, and coriander. The name of the blend is from Hindi and means "hot mixture." Every brand of garam masala sold in Indian markets will have its own unique formulation of these spices and may even include additional spices.

The curry leaves come from a tree native to India, Sri Lanka, Bangladesh, and the Andaman Islands. The delicate and highly aromatic leaves have been used to flavor dishes for over 2,000 years and are a common ingredient in south Indian cuisine. You can find dried curry leaves at most Indian markets. Be sure to check for fresh or frozen curry leaves as well since the aromatic qualities of the leaves decrease when they are dried.

3 tablespoons ghee

¼ teaspoon brown mustard seeds

8 curry leaves

2 medium yellow onions, minced
(about 1⅓ cup)

4 ripe medium tomatoes, seeded
and chopped (about 4 cups)

4 green chiles, seeded and chopped

2 teaspoons garlic paste

2 teaspoons ginger paste

2 tablespoons garam masala

1 teaspoon ground cumin

2 teaspoons ground coriander

½ teaspoon chili powder

¼ teaspoon freshly ground black pepper

3 pounds boneless, skinless chicken thighs,
cut into 1-inch cubes

TO SERVE

Cilantro leaves, chopped

Cooked white or basmati rice

Kitchen Passport If desired,
add coconut milk to the mixture
after the chicken has cooked
through to make a milder, creamier curry. Stir in 2 cups coconut
milk for sweet flavor. If you prefer
a curry that is mild and creamy but
more tangy, add 2 cups yogurt
after the chicken has cooked. Do
not allow the curry to return to a
boil after adding either coconut
milk or yogurt.

For a vegetarian curry, use potatoes, cauliflower, or any starchy
vegetable in place of the chicken.

Heat the ghee in a large, deep skillet over medium heat.

Add the mustard seeds and cook for 3 to 5
minutes or until the mustard seeds burst open.

Add the curry leaves and onions and cook
for another 3 to 5 minutes or until the onions
are translucent.

Add the tomatoes and green chiles to the
onion mixture and cook for 6 to 8 minutes or
until the chiles are soft.

Mash the onions, tomatoes, and chiles in
the skillet until the mixture has the consistency
of a thick gravy.

Add the garlic and ginger pastes to the
gravy and continue cooking, stirring constantly,
for 3 to 5 minutes or until the mixture is fragrant
with garlic and ginger.

Add the garam masala, cumin, coriander,
chili powder, and black pepper to the gravy
mixture. Cook for another 1 to 2 minutes, stirring constantly.

Add the chicken to the gravy mixture and
stir to combine. Cover the skillet and allow the
chicken to cook for 10 to 12 minutes or until
the chicken has cooked through.

Reduce the heat to low and continue cooking the chicken, covered, for an additional 20
to 30 minutes to allow the flavors to penetrate
the chicken.

Garnish with chopped cilantro leaves and
serve with rice.

Indian buffets across the United States include the ubiquitous dessert *gulab jamun*, balls of powdered milk and flour dough deep-fried then boiled in syrup. With only rare exceptions, these are made with industrially produced powdered milk because very few people invest the time and effort required to follow the traditional methods. This dessert and many others are known in India as *mithai*. "*Mithai* is a Hindi word. Bengali call it *mishti*, and that means 'dessert,' like sweet dessert," says Sudha Moy Dutta, owner of Mithai House of Indian Desserts.

Sudha Moy Dutta, Cary, North Carolina

Sudha grew up in East Bengal surrounded by *gulab jamun* and other *mithai*. "My father was a banker. His uncle formed a bank, and my father and all the cousins worked for him. While they are doing the bank, his uncle was very fond of *mithai*. And in our hometown, where they founded the bank, there is no good *mithai*, but in our ancestors' home, Brahmanbaria, sixty miles from there, in that area *mithai* is very good. It's renowned in Bengal—now in Bangladesh."

Using his pragmatic banker's mind, Sudha's great-uncle came up with a plan. "My father's uncle told him, 'Why don't we put in one *mithai* shop? Then we can have good *mithai*. Bring one chef from there and put one in, because our bank needs a lot of *mithai* for clients.'"

The uncle's decision wasn't purely for his clients, however. It was for his family, too. As a child, Sudha was aware of the *mithai* shop in Bangladesh—it was there "long before I was born," he says—and that meant that "from a young age, I know *mithai*. And we, our family, all eat a lot of dessert, milk *mithai*. We eat a lot. You cannot believe how much we eat."

When Sudha grew up, he did not go into banking or *mithai*. Instead, he came to Durham, North Carolina, because his brother was teaching physics at North Carolina Central University. Sudha enrolled in college and earned his degree before going to work in the telecommunications industry. But *mithai* was not entirely in his past.

When he first came to the United States, Sudha lived with his brother and sister-in-law. "I saw my sister-in-law making different kinds of Indian desserts, and she really didn't know how to make it. One day, I saw she was making *gulab jamun* from powdered milk, and I said, 'What are you making?' She said, 'It's *gulab jamun*.' I said, 'Why are you making it like that?' 'That's the way I learned.'"

Sudha laughs as he retells the story. "Then I said, 'Well, that's not the right way.' She said, 'You know any better way?' I say, 'I know a better way, but I never tried myself. But that's not the way to make *gulab jamun*.' That's the way I got interested, you know, and then at least once or twice a month, I made a different kind of *mithai* and made my friends and family guinea pigs. That's what I did for a long time."

Sudha Moy Dutta
at Mithai House of
Indian Desserts.

Making *mithai* might have remained strictly a hobby for Sudha because, although his family loves the desserts, actually making *mithai* would not have been a career choice for him in India. "People joked all the time, 'You all are doing banking, and you all are selling *mithai*.' That's a big contrast. Selling *mithai* in Bengal, where we are from, is not a prestigious business."

Nonetheless, Sudha loved making *mithai* as much as eating the desserts. When he returned to India in 1982 to be married, he took time for some advanced *mithai* training. "I went to Calcutta, got married, and I went to Bangladesh, to my hometown, Comilla, in the eastern side of Bangladesh, close to the India border. The second day I went to the factory, and I told our main chef—his name is Shumbu—'Shumbu, nobody knows how to make *mithai* over there.' I work with them one week. I stayed around eight or nine days, and on six or seven days, I worked with them. Every day, three hours, four hours, I worked.

"Then I went back to Calcutta. I told her what I did, my newlywed wife, and I don't know what she was thinking at that time. 'My husband is in India; he's making *mithai* over there. What's he gonna do? He's gonna go to America and make *mithai*?'"

Sudha did just that. While he kept his day job, he began to make more *mithai* to share with friends. "I made some *gulab jamun* for my niece's third birthday and gave everybody a surprise. When people ate that *gulab jamun*, they thought I brought them from India or Bangladesh. They didn't believe that I made it."

Soon, Sudha's fame as a *mithai* maker spread, and he began to receive requests for his *mithai* for local events. "They have an international festival, and the Hindu temple puts a stall in the civic center. Seven days before, the priest's wife called me and said, 'Can you give me some *mithai* for the international festival? We can sell it.' I said, 'How many do you need?' 'Give me 400 or 500, as many as you can.' I said, 'When?' She said, 'Next Saturday.' I said, 'You're telling me 500 *mithai* for next Saturday?'"

He still shakes his head at the memory years later, but he was able to provide her with *mithai*. "She said, 'Oh, you keep *mithai* in the freezer all the time.' I said, 'In the freezer I might have 200 or 300, not 500.' Maybe 300 I had."

He had frozen *mithai* to give her because his background as an engineer had encouraged him to experiment with methods of preservation. "*Mithai*, I can freeze it, and it stays good for six months, no taste change. And that kind of practice I started doing to see how long it could stay in an airtight container with the syrup inside."

In 2002, the telecommunications market experienced a downturn, and Sudha's company began layoffs. He decided to take early retirement, and his friends were very helpful with suggestions about how he should spend his free time. "A lot of my friends asked, 'Why not open a *mithai* shop? I said, 'It's a lot of work, and I don't know how much would be good.'"

After giving it a lot of thought, he decided that there could be demand for quality *mithai* in Durham and the surrounding area. "In North Carolina, there was no Indian dessert store, you know. You had to go to New York, Washington, or different cities, big cities."

Sudha opened his first *mithai* shop in Durham near his house. Although the local market for his *mithai* was not large enough initially to support the store, his reputation for making delicious *mithai* using traditional methods spread. He was soon shipping *mithai* to stores in Charlotte, Richmond, and the Washington, D.C., area as well as to individual customers all over the United States.

"Everybody was telling me to move to Cary, because the Indian community there is very big." So in 2006, Sudha closed his Durham shop and opened his current location in Cary. While he is still shipping his *mithai* to his established customers, his local customer base has increased.

But with that larger customer base came questions about cost and quality. "Bengali *mithai* is expensive, and there's a lot of cheap *mithai* in the market. Like this *gulab jamun*, when I make it, my cost is more than double the regular powdered milk *gulab jamun*," he says. "The problem is that a lot of people don't understand the quality, even Indians. Indians know the Bengali *mithai* are very good desserts. But only 20 percent of Indians maybe have some experience eating it. They know of it but never try it. And to them, which one is good, which one is bad doesn't make much difference."

Sudha uses his *mithai* to teach his customers the difference. He also teaches the lessons of *mithai* in his own kitchen to his chef-in-training, a man with no cultural familiarity with *mithai*. "He's Hispanic. He's a Salvadoran. I'm pushing him to grow some taste. I say, 'If you make something, you have to eat it. Otherwise, you cannot make this good,'" he says. "He eats some, but he doesn't like that much even though he's making it. I'm pushing him all the time. I say, 'You need to eat some. Then you know which one is good and which one is bad.' The chef has to taste. That's the bottom line. Otherwise, they cannot make a good product."

While he tries to inspire his cook, Sudha has his own inspiration. "I never desired to do this. This started when I came here. Day by day by day, I'm getting interested. I was never interested in cooking *mithai*, but now I have gotten interested in cooking a lot of other stuff, too. When you make something, and everybody eats it and says, 'Hey, that's good,' that feels good. That's motivation."

That good feeling does more than keep Sudha cooking. It kept him in the South as well. "When somebody back home asks me, 'How is your *mithai* shop doing?' I say, 'Name-wise, I have a very good name, but name-wise is one thing. Money-wise is a different thing.' The only mistake I made—I should have opened this store in one of the big cities. But I tried to open something in the South because . . ."

He pauses to find the words. "Thirty years ago, the South was more conservative. I worked in a factory in a small town. I was the only Indian working. The rest of them were black or white. I was in management, so I used to hear both sides, and I know how conservative things were. But I see a lot of change. And that's why I decided why not open here and introduce Indian desserts to the South." 🐚

RASGULLA (Bengali-Style Milk Sweets)

Active cooking time: 1 hour, 30 minutes | Total cooking time: 2 hours, 45 minutes + 4 hours

Yield: approximately 15 *rasgulla*

It is believed that *rasgulla*, the traditional sweet of Bangladesh, originated there and then spread westward during the seventeenth century. Today, it is a popular dessert in Bangladesh, India, and Pakistan.

Rasgulla is based on a simple cottage cheese known as *chenna*. Added flour helps to lighten the cheese and bind it into balls that are then cooked in syrup until the sugar has permeated the balls to the center.

For those unfamiliar with making cheese at home, Sudha describes the process with a laugh. "It is hard to make, but it is simple to make." The key is attention to temperature and time. If the milk is too hot when the acid is added, the cheese will be firmer, perhaps too firm to make *rasgulla*.

Sudha learned the techniques of both a cheesemaker and a confectioner from the chef at his family's *mithai* factory, including how to control and judge the texture of the cheese. "Shumbu told me, 'Babu'—*babu* means boss in Bengali—'Babu, you have to understand, by touching the cheese you see what *mithai* you can make with it.'" While making cheese may seem intimidating, it's worth the effort. The texture to seek for *rasgulla* is similar to that of ricotta—a soft cheese with very little distinct curd. To make this a quicker dessert, you can substitute 1 cup ricotta for the *chenna*. Follow the remaining recipe steps as you would if making *chenna*.

Either way, the desserts you prepare will be soft, light pillows bursting with sweetness, something truly unique and delicious.

FOR THE *CHENNA*

½ gallon whole milk, non-homogenized if available

¼ cup distilled white vinegar or lemon juice or 1 teaspoon citric acid

FOR THE *RASGULLA*

4 tablespoons all-purpose flour

FOR THE SYRUP

2 cups granulated sugar

1 quart water

1 tablespoon milk

SPECIAL EQUIPMENT

Colander or sieve

Cheesecloth

Candy thermometer

TO PREPARE THE *CHENNA*

Shake the ½ gallon of milk to distribute the cream before pouring into a wok set over your largest burner. Turn the burner to high heat and cook the milk, stirring constantly to prevent any sticking, until the milk reaches a simmer at 170 degrees.

As soon as the milk reaches that temperature, add the vinegar, lemon juice, or citric acid. Continue cooking, stirring constantly until the milk reaches 185 degrees. Adjust the heat as needed to maintain this temperature. Cook for 15 minutes at 185 degrees, stirring occasionally.

Line a colander or sieve with cheesecloth and set it into a large mixing bowl. Pour the curds and whey into the lined colander. Allow the whey to drain for 10 minutes.

Lift out the cheesecloth containing the curds
and tie it above either a bowl or your kitchen
sink. Allow the water to drain for an additional
30 minutes.

TO PREPARE THE *RASGULLA*

Lay the chenna or ricotta out in a thin layer on
a smooth work surface. Scatter over the flour
and, using the heel of your hand, rub the flour
into the curds, forming a soft, loose dough.
Cover the dough with a damp cloth and allow
it to rest for 15 to 20 minutes.

TO PREPARE THE SYRUP

While the dough is resting, dissolve the sugar
in the quart of water in a medium saucepan
over medium-high heat. Add the tablespoon
of milk when the sugar has melted and bring
the mixture to a boil, stirring occasionally. Continue boiling for 5 minutes and then reduce the
heat to low.

TO FINISH THE DISH

Pinch off walnut-sized knobs of dough and
shape them into spheres. Carefully lower
the spheres into the hot syrup. Once all of
the cheese balls have been added, increase
the heat to high and boil the spheres for
20 minutes.

Using a slotted spoon, preferably wooden,
transfer the cooked balls to a plate and allow
them to rest at room temperature for 4 to 5
hours. Reserve the syrup for serving.

Before serving, return the reserved syrup
to a boil and cook for 15 minutes or until the
syrup is reduced by half. Drizzle the syrup over
the *rasgulla*.

Japan and South Korea
Blue Collars and Bluefin

As foreign automobile manufacturers have moved production to the United States, many have located their facilities in the South. Companies from Japan and South Korea have a strong presence here—Toyota, Honda, Nissan, Suzuki, and Hyundai. In addition, smaller companies have regional facilities to produce the parts to support the automobile manufacturers.

While these factories are an economic boon to the South, they also provide the impetus for a culinary boom. As managers and workers come to the United States from their home countries, they create a market for traditionally prepared food from those countries. The restaurants that open primarily to serve those employees also serve their communities, bringing new flavors and culinary traditions to the South.

Sugano grew up along the rural coast of Japan. He spent his days going to school, fishing with his father, working in the family's vegetable garden, and enjoying the simplicity of rural life. But he shared a dream with his father: they both loved to cook and dreamed that someday Sugano would be a professional chef.

*Sugano,
Lexington,
Kentucky*

So when he was seventeen, Sugano went to culinary school. He spent years learning the incredibly varied skills that would make him a great sushi chef. Using only a sharp knife, Sugano can create elegant patterns on paper or on bamboo leaves to decorate plates, lamps, or menus. As beautiful as the designs are, Sugano explains that in Japanese culture, they have a greater purpose than beauty. "Two years I studied for this. There's a lot of cuts for the knife, to cut the bamboo leaf. When the bamboo leaf is cut, you put it in the water or the juice for protection from bacteria. If the bamboo leaf is inside with the food, it's keepable for a week. The cuts for the bamboo leaf they put for decoration keep for longer because older people in Japan may have no refrigeration."

Sugano applies his precise knife skills to his food as well. He is one of the few chefs in the world certified to prepare fugu, better known in America as the highly poisonous blowfish. Serving fugu takes skill,

Sugano at his restaurant.

but it is worth the effort. "I can do it. In Japan, I have a license. Not too many people have a license. In Japan, you have to work in a regular restaurant—working, but doing it also for the experience and taste. After ten years, you can test for the blowfish test. It takes half an hour to clean the fish. It's then sliced for a beautiful presentation. And the bone, and the skin, or the filets, and the fin—everything is used. In Japan, it's very expensive for the blowfish."

As Sugano explains, learning which foods would be available in different seasons and which flavors would be best served in each season was a long process during his training. "I started when I was seventeen years old, but in Japan I cooked for maybe five or seven years for the study. In springtime, what kind of fish come, or what kinds of vegetables are ready? In the summer, you need to know what kinds of shellfish or different fish are used."

It took a lot of time and dedication to learn those skills, but once he could call them his own, the whole world opened to him. Sugano—once a boy from the countryside—could suddenly go anywhere he wanted because he could make beautiful, delicious food that people loved to eat.

He began to travel, spending a few years in one place before moving to another. First, he went to Hawaii. "That was in 1968, in Honolulu. At this time, there was no sushi there. I was twenty-four years old, and I came for the first time to the United States." He returned to Japan and then went to America again before moving to Tokyo, where he cooked at the American embassy. After that, he worked in the great hotels of Tokyo. Next, he began to teach his skills to students in Thailand and China.

Eventually, he found out that Japanese companies were opening in parts of America where there was no Japanese food. He heard that these companies wanted skilled Japanese chefs to come with them to open restaurants or cafeterias so that the Japanese employees in these companies, in an unfamiliar land, could have food with which they were familiar.

His first job of this sort took Sugano to Smyrna, Tennessee, just south of Nashville. "I was requested for the first time when a Nissan factory opened for Smyrna." After Smyrna, he worked for another Japanese company in Nashville. "A lot of Japanese people came for the Kashima Corporation. They were doing the construction for the building and road and bridge. At this time, there were a thousand Japanese people working in Nashville and Murfreesboro, but we had no restaurant, no grocery. So, they requested a contract from me for two years. I did a restaurant in Nashville."

After that, he took a job with a venture company in Bowling Green, Kentucky. Then he was asked to open the first Japanese restaurant in Lexington, Kentucky, where Toyota was opening a new headquarters. "The boss came to Lexington just starting Tachibana Restaurant. He was starting in town before anybody did, so he said, 'Sugano, you help; you will like this.'" After two years in Lexington, Sugano went back to Japan and began to travel in earnest, working with his chefs association.

He cooked along the American Gulf Coast, in Germany, in England, and in Hong Kong. Japan Airlines took him to Chicago to cook for a new restaurant there. And then Lexington called to him once again. "I came over here before the first Iraq war. This time I was in Chicago for two years. Then the Chicago food distributor was having a warehouse opening day party. I went over there, and I met the manager from Tachibana. He said, 'Sugano, please help!' And I came back in 1993 or 1994."

This time he made a home in Lexington. When Toyota moved its headquarters to Cincinnati, Ohio, and asked him to come along, he chose the long commute instead of relocation, which would have disrupted his family. But he was no longer a young man, and the lengthy drive was hard on him. "I could not move up there because my daughter was going to school in Lexington, so every day I was going to Cincinnati. I had a big accident, twice! So I decided it was time for me to be slowing down."

When Sugano completed his commitment to the company, he didn't renew his contract; however, he still wanted to cook. "During this time in Cincinnati, I was named twice the best restaurant, but I came back to Lexington anyway. I was looking for another job, more like a restaurant like this."

"This" is a restaurant all his own. When a friend offered Sugano a small, nondescript location in which to establish his eatery, he took it. And while he didn't change the outside, he turned the inside into a traditional Japanese restaurant. Some of his first customers were Japanese, but many were not. He began to be noticed and was featured in a *Gourmet* magazine piece about Japanese cuisine in Kentucky. "I opened here in 2001, something like that. In two years' time, I was in a very popular food magazine. Very funny, you know, they said it was very sophisticated for Japanese food but the place is unsophisticated," Sugano laughs.

But none of that changed anything for him. He is comfortable with his life in Lexington. He still makes his own soba and udon noodles. He still buys fresh vegetables, like broccoli and green tomatoes, from the carts of Amish farmers. In many ways, it's as if he is still a boy from the rural coast of Japan instead of an older man living on the rural outskirts of a city in the American South. 🍵

SHIROMI SASHIMI (White Fish Sashimi)

Active cooking time: 15 minutes | Total cooking time: 15 minutes | Yield: 4 appetizer servings

The preparation of a sashimi plate is an opportunity for a sushi chef to practice the highest art of his or her trade. Only the best fish is used for sashimi, and each cut should pay special attention to preserving the textural qualities of each variety of fish used. While the fish is the star of the plate, the garnishes are also important. They should be visually pleasing in color and texture to contrast with the fish. For example, grated carrot might be used to garnish a white fish, while white daikon radish might be used to garnish a red or pink-fleshed fish.

Traditionally, sashimi is served as a starter for a meal so that the diner's palate will be at its freshest to enjoy the subtleties of the fish. Sugano easily expresses his ideas on sashimi. "Maybe simple is best. Color is important, but in a lot of things, it is important that it is very simple."

You will note that this recipe does not use soy sauce or wasabi. The combination of pungent garlic juice, tart lemon juice, and crisp sea salt serve to enhance the delicate flavor of white fish, while the richness of soy sauce and the heat of wasabi would overpower it. As it is, this recipe makes a light and delicious combination of fresh flavors and delicate textures.

1 pound fresh white fish, such as halibut
   or sea bass
2 cloves garlic, peeled
1 lemon, halved
1 teaspoon sea salt

Using a very sharp knife, cut the fish into slices on a bias no thicker than ¼ inch and no longer or wider than 3 inches. Lay the slices out on a serving plate or board.

Using a garlic press, crush the garlic cloves one at a time to release juice over each slice of fish. Remove any garlic pieces that fall onto the fish.

Squeeze the juice from half of a lemon over the fish, making sure to discard any seeds.

Sprinkle the sea salt onto each slice of fish, making certain that individual grains of salt are visible.

Serve immediately.

Kitchen Passport This recipe can be adjusted quite easily for parties. If you are making a larger amount of sashimi and not serving it immediately, place the slices in a bowl of ice water to maintain freshness. Pat dry before serving. Also, consider a method other than the garlic press to extract the garlic juice. You can make about ¼ cup garlic juice by pulsing the peeled cloves of a head of garlic in a food processor until they form a creamy paste. Then press the paste through a mesh strainer and filter the resulting liquid through a coffee filter to produce clear garlic juice.

Consider serving sashimi with *ohitashi*, a simple dish of fresh spinach blanched then plunged into an ice bath. Combine 3 tablespoons Japanese soy sauce, 2 tablespoons sesame oil, and 1 teaspoon sugar to make a dressing. Toss the spinach in the dressing and sprinkle on 1 teaspoon sesame seeds. "Japanese food can be easy for American people to like," Sugano says. "Everyone is different. Some people might like olive oil or wasabi. But for me, sesame seeds, soy sauce, and sugar—that's good."

Sushi Rolls

CULINARY TOUR GUIDE

For most sushi beginners, the ubiquitous California roll is the first variety of sushi to be tasted or ordered comfortably in a Japanese restaurant. While it's a great starting point, it's important to know that the California roll was invented in the United States to suit Western tastes. It doesn't exist in Japan.

Other sushi rolls, however, are authentic tastes of Japanese cuisine. These rolls are known as *makizushi*, and they come in as many varieties as the mind can conceive.

Futomaki are perhaps the most common variety. In these rolls, complementary ingredients are rolled inside rice with seaweed, nori, on the outside. The fillings may be raw or cooked, and some varieties are vegetarian.

The California roll with its rice on the outside is a variation on the traditional Japanese *uramaki*. These rolls are layered with rice, then nori, then the filling ingredients before being rolled with the rice as a sticky bed for other toppings like toasted sesame seeds or roe.

Other varieties of *makizushi* replace the nori entirely with thin omelet, soy paper, cucumber, *shiso* leaves, or even parsley. These rolls are made as much for their beauty as for their flavor.

Because of the variety of flavors and the availability of cooked ingredients, *makizushi* are very popular in the West. They're also

Jeung Donoho didn't come to Lexington, Kentucky, because of a Korean company. Quite the opposite: she is in the United States because an American company came to Korea, bringing with it the man who was to become her husband. While it might have been difficult to leave family behind and travel halfway around the world, for Jeung, it was the only thing to do. "I love my husband. That's why I'm married. Coming over here and loving him, I don't mind anything," Jeung laughs.

Jeung and Susane Donoho, Lexington, Kentucky

Jeung's daughter Susane says that her mother's personality made the move easier than it might have been. "My mom has always been the type of person that's been very adventurous; she always wants to do something new, to go somewhere new." But Jeung's husband made it easier, too. "My dad made sure that there were Koreans here in Lexington so that my mom would not be the only one."

That thoughtfulness affected Susane as much as it did Jeung. "For as long as I can remember, even looking back in pictures, there's always been Korean people at the house. We always went to a Korean church. I always laugh because all the children's birthdays were used as excuses for women to get together and cook all day."

Lexington was a good place for Jeung to adapt to the United States and to still feel connected to home. "There is a large population of Koreans

fun to eat, typically served in bite-sized pieces that are easily picked up with chopsticks.

The common ingredient across all types of *makizushi* is sushi rice. This is a short-grained Japanese variety of rice that is mixed with a dressing of rice vinegar, sugar, and salt before being added to the sushi rolls.

The popularity of *makizushi* is not limited to Japan or to the West. In South Korea, *gimbap* is a popular fast food based on *futomaki*. Where only white rice is used in sushi in Japan, short-grain brown rice is commonly used in *gimbap*. The rice in *gimbap* is seasoned with sesame oil instead of the vinegar mixture used in

Japan, and the fillings are always cooked. The flavors are bolder and often spicier than those of Japanese *futomaki*, making them more palatable to the heat-loving Koreans.

To make your own sushi rolls, the only special equipment you must have is a flexible bamboo mat to aid in rolling. While rice is traditional, blends of other grains can also be used or added to the rice. Use combinations of fillings that you like.

The key to successful sushi rolls is patience. Take your time in making the rolls, and don't expect your first ones to be as beautifully perfect as those served in Japanese restaurants. Just keep practicing and enjoy the results of your experiments.

Jeung and Susane Donoho at Arirang Garden.

in Lexington. There's actually two Korean churches that both have a large congregation, and there's a Korean language school as well," Susane says. "If you go into the churches and things like that now, there's twice as many Korean college students as there are Korean elders. The University of Kentucky is actually encouraging Koreans to come here, and they help you find jobs, translating jobs, things like that."

When Jeung decided to open a restaurant in Lexington, she knew that the Korean community would help her business, but so would the Japanese community. "Japanese people love Korean food. They absolutely love Korean barbecue. We have people who travel from an hour away, two hours away, or if people are just passing by, they'll look us up," Susane says.

Of course, just being a Korean restaurant doesn't explain Jeung's success, nor does the presence of a Korean community. In fact, Arirang Garden is in a building that housed another Korean restaurant, one that failed. The location did provide a good start, though. "I remember what seemed to be the most trouble was finding a location. I remember going to so many places with my parents. We were lucky to find a Korean restaurant that had the ventilation system," Susane remembers.

In addition to the dishes that Jeung prepares for the menu, Arirang Garden offers *gogi gui*, Korean barbecue. A refrigerated buffet offers a variety of cuts of meat—some marinated, some not—as well as seafood and vegetables. Customers make their choices and return to their tables where they cook their meal on gas grills built into the tables.

While it sounds like a simple formula, there are many things to consider, from the quality of the ingredients offered to the guests to the wide range of condiments that accompany the meal. Jeung works hard to provide the best possible experience for her customers. "My mother came in and sort of upped the quality and things like that. She's really enjoyed it, and it seems like a lot of the customers have as well," Susane says.

Finding a restaurant that was already equipped surely helped with opening the business, but it is not likely that any challenge is too large for Jeung, especially considering her long career in food. "I think I started to cook early. I like to cook. I like something baking. I like to eat. I like to cook. In elementary school, I cooked the rice. But at the time there was no rice cooker, so we needed to cook the rice on charcoal," Jeung says.

"Charcoal, like a fire?" Susane asks, surprised. "That doesn't sound very easy."

"No rice cooker at that time, so to cook rice is very difficult. So we need to know how much water."

"My mom's always taught me, you don't do water by the cups or anything like that; you do it by the measurement on your hand. You want the water to be at a certain point on your hand when you press down the rice. I still don't get it right. Not every time."

Jeung has no trouble with the rice or any of her other specialties, but she is not one to rest on her laurels. "She was telling me just a few minutes ago that she likes to try new things. She watches Korean TV a lot, and when they have new recipes, she'll immediately jet into the kitchen and try it. And if it's wrong, she'll try and try and try until she can get it right," Susane says.

When Jeung is asked what she would do if she weren't cooking, Susane quickly comments, "Go crazy." Jeung says no, but Susane continues, "She's a workaholic. She's here six days a week. One day she's closed, and even that day she's usually here preparing for the following week."

"When I'm cooking, I'm happy," Jeung laughs.

That spirit is at the heart of Jeung's success. From the moment guests enter the restaurant to the moment they leave, their dining experience is crafted to make a pleasant memory, a memory that will draw them back to have that experience again. Happy cooks make good food, and good food makes happy diners. And those diners become more than guests. As Susane puts it, "We have a lot of people who come in here now who we consider friends and family." 🦪

OI SOBAEGI KIMCHI (Korean-Style Pickled Cucumbers)

Active cooking time: 25 minutes | Total cooking time: 55 minutes | Yield: 4 side dish servings

These spicy cucumbers are a traditional side dish, or *ban chan*, served with Korean barbecue. The acidity of the kimchi cleans the palate between bites of freshly cooked, smoky meats and vegetables. It also makes for a perfect snack on a hot summer afternoon.

While this is a type of kimchi, the flavor is much milder than the cabbage kimchi with which most people are familiar. Unlike that version, this one spends less time in the marinade and doesn't ferment at all.

As Susane describes it, "It's all depen-dent on taste. If you like it saltier, you want more salt. And lots of red pepper."

Jeung uses a Korean variety of ground red pepper. If you can't find Korean red pepper at your local Asian market, Jeung recommends grinding red peppers yourself for the best results.

Served cold, this dish is a great mixture of tartness and heat. And if you don't like cucumbers, you may enjoy them served this way. Like Susane says, "I'm not a big fan of cucumbers, so the longer it marinates, the less it tastes like cucumber. And I love it. It's completely different."

2 to 3 salad cucumbers (about 1 pound)

2 teaspoons white vinegar, 25% acidity
   if available

1 clove garlic, minced (about ½ teaspoon)

1 (1-inch) piece fresh ginger, peeled and
   grated (about 1 ounce)

Pinch of salt

Pinch of sugar

Korean red pepper flakes

Prepare the cucumbers by slicing them in half lengthwise and removing the seeds. Then slice the lengths into crescent-shaped slices no more than ¼-inch thick.

Combine the sliced cucumbers, vinegar, garlic, and ginger in a non-reactive bowl. Add in the salt, sugar, and Korean red pepper flakes to taste. Stir well and allow the mixture to rest in the refrigerator for at least 30 minutes before serving.

Cucumber kimchi will last, covered, in the refrigerator for up to a week. The flavor will intensify the longer it rests.

> **Kitchen Passport** You can find variations of simple, cooling cucumber salads in almost any cuisine that contains spicy food. For a Mexican take on this side dish, peel the cucumbers and slice thin, then replace the vinegar with lime juice and the Korean red pepper with ground chipotle or ancho pepper.

MUL MANDU (Korean-Style Pork Dumplings)

Active cooking time: 1 hour | Total cooking time: 2 hours, 40 minutes | Yield: 36 dumplings

Mandu have been a favorite dish on the Korean peninsula since the seventeenth century. While some attribute their origin to Mongolian conquerors from the fourteenth century, others believe that *mandu* made their way to Korea from the Middle East via the Silk Road. It is impossible now to determine their exact origin, since dumplings are historically a part of the cuisines of the Middle East, Eastern Europe, Russia, China, Mongolia, Korea, and Japan.

Mandu are deceptively simple. Their complexity lies not so much in their in-

gredients as in the techniques of preparing them. Beautiful dumplings take patience and skill. As Susane says, "My mom, she's very picky about her dumplings. She won't even let me help her, because I can't make it look the same as she can."

Jeung confirms this with a laugh. "I don't want nobody touching them."

Susane goes further. "Every one I do, she has to take it apart and redo it, because it's just not as pretty as she can make them."

Jeung learned to cook by taste and sight instead of by measurements, techniques that Susane finds hard to replicate. "My mom's teaching me slowly. I try to watch as much as I can. She's waiting until I'm old enough to respect how to cook everything and respect all the secrets."

Even without a practiced hand to make perfect, beautiful dumplings, this recipe results in a delicious dish. A simple dipping sauce of soy sauce, sesame oil, rice wine vinegar, and fresh ginger is all that you need to have a perfect feast.

2 teaspoons salt

½ small head cabbage

1 pound ground pork

¼ cup green onions, chopped

1 medium white onion, diced (about ⅔ cup)

¼ cucumber, peeled, seeded, and diced (about ¼ cup)

3 cloves garlic, minced (about 1½ teaspoons)

1 (⅓-inch) piece fresh ginger, peeled and grated (about 1 teaspoon)

2 tablespoons soy sauce

½ teaspoon sugar

¼ teaspoon vegetable oil

1 tablespoon cornstarch

36 round *gyoza* or *mandu* wrappers

Bring 4 quarts of water to a boil over high heat.

Add the salt when the water begins to boil. Add the cabbage carefully and cover the pot.

Reduce the heat to medium-low.

Allow the cabbage to cook for 15 to 20 minutes or until soft.

Strain the boiled cabbage in a colander, pressing to extract as much liquid as possible. Wrap the cabbage in a towel and squeeze out any remaining liquid. Chop the cabbage finely once it is cool enough to handle.

In a large mixing bowl, combine the pork, cabbage, green onions, white onion, cucumber, garlic, and ginger.

In a smaller bowl, stir together the soy sauce, sugar, and oil until the sugar has dissolved. Pour the soy sauce mixture over the pork mixture, mixing thoroughly with your hands to distribute the ingredients evenly.

Prepare a baking sheet by sprinkling it with cornstarch so that the dumplings will not stick and tear.

To prepare the dumplings, place a tablespoon of the pork mixture in the center of a wrapper. Dip your fingers in a bowl of water and dampen the edges of the wrapper. Fold the wrapper over the filling, pinching the moistened edges closed to seal the dumpling. Repeat until all of the dumplings have been made.

Prepare a bamboo steamer or vegetable steamer over a pot of boiling water. Either spray the steamer basket with cooking spray or line with a cloth or cabbage leaves to prevent sticking.

Working in batches, steam the dumplings, covered, for 10 minutes.

> Kitchen Passport In South Korea, dumplings are prepared with various fillings. Substitute beef for the pork in this recipe or replace the cooked cabbage with spicy kimchi. Sautéed mushrooms could be used for a vegetarian version. A dash of rice wine vinegar added with the soy sauce will add a bit of tartness. If you can't find round wrappers, *mandu* can be made as triangles using square Chinese wonton wrappers.
>
> Another common use for *mandu* is in soup. Prepare a simple meat or vegetable broth and slowly stir in raw egg to form threads, similar to Chinese egg drop soup. Add steamed *mandu*, sliced green onions, and slivers of fresh ginger right before serving.

Fumiko Demura relaxes in her restaurant, Little Tokyo, before the Saturday dinner rush begins. Fumiko is as elegant and gracious as her restaurant is clean and bright. Her daughter Okiyo, young and smiling and swathed in an oversized leather jacket, joins Fumiko and sometimes translates.

Fumiko and Okiyo Demura, Ridgeland, Mississippi

Fumiko came to the United States in 1982 because her husband, Tomio, took a job as an engineer in a shipyard in Alabama. The shipbuilding industry soon experienced a downturn, however, and Tomio was laid off. As they were considering other job opportunities, a friend suggested that they open a restaurant. "We were thinking about changing jobs, and since Mississippi is very close to Alabama, a couple of friends in Jackson suggested that maybe we do business for a restaurant. So we decided to do that," Fumiko says.

Little Tokyo in the Jackson, Mississippi, suburb of Ridgeland is actually the second of the family's three restaurants. Now the establishment is always filled with loyal customers, but initially, things were very different. In 1987, Tomio and Fumiko opened the original Little Tokyo Japanese Restaurant in downtown Jackson. It was the first Japanese restaurant in Mississippi.

Fumiko was concerned about acceptance of such an exotic cuisine in a smaller city, so she publicized the opening of the restaurant. The grand opening was a success, but business quickly fell off. "At the very beginning, for about six months, we honestly didn't have any customers. After the grand opening, there were just days where we would have only maybe two or maybe one customer that whole entire day," Okiyo says.

While the Jackson area is now host to a Nissan plant, it was not manufacturing or Japanese workers that saved the restaurant in its

Fumiko Demura, Takashi Kimura, and Okiyo Demura at Little Tokyo.

early days. Instead, Little Tokyo's saviors came not from another country but from a whole other world—Hollywood. "*Mississippi Burning* was the first crew that came through. And the director and the cast, I guess because they already had a sense of sushi and they really liked it, they came almost every single day to our restaurant," Fumiko says.

The cachet provided by the film world helped establish a local clientele for Little Tokyo and ensured its future. It was actually not until 1993, five years after the cast and crew of *Mississippi Burning* saved the restaurant, that the Nissan plant opened in nearby Canton, Mississippi. The influx of Japanese workers led to more customers for the restaurant and also to more authentic dishes on the menu. "Before the Nissan plant came, we didn't have too many traditional Japanese foods in our menu. After they came, we started introducing more and more, like types of grilled fish that American people usually would not like and different types of traditional seasonings," Okiyo says.

That is not to say that the dishes at Little Tokyo weren't already authentic. But some changes were made to create dishes geared more toward American tastes. "You know, in Japan, we don't deep-fry things into sushi so much. But here I think the soft shell crab, shrimp, and also crawfish, they like to fry it first and then put it into sushi," Fumiko says.

"What she's saying is that we don't have to make huge changes to a certain dish, but what we might do is fry a little bit more or put some fried things into it or make it taste sweeter because Americans tend to like sweeter things," Okiyo adds.

They've also developed unique sushi rolls that cater to the tastes of Jackson. One of their most popular rolls is a fried catfish roll. The catfish is battered in tempura, and the roll is served with a Japanese take on that favorite condiment of Jackson, Come Back Sauce. (For the uninitiated, Come Back Sauce is a smooth, zesty sauce distantly related to Thousand Island dressing that is served with salads, French fries, and everything in between in Jackson.)

The Demuras used the fried fish to introduce sushi to hesitant diners. "To elaborate just a little more, she started with the roll that had a fried piece of shrimp in it to let southern people start accepting sushi. People had a sort of a phobia toward raw fish, fish in general," Okiyo says. "But now, years later, people have become so accepting of sushi and fish that the very people who were totally against raw fish and fish itself can now tell the difference between 'good' sushi and 'not good' sushi. And it's not just Japanese; there's American people, too," Okiyo continues.

The Demura family respects the art of preparing good sushi. Because the traditional Japanese dishes came later to their restaurant, sushi was the cornerstone of their business for years. The quality of their sushi built their reputation in the Jackson community. Fumiko has taught Okiyo that the simplicity of sushi is an illusion. It's much more complicated than it looks.

"She was saying to me that sushi is often referred to as the finest type of cuisine or food and the reason why is because sushi is so—you think it's simple, it's just a raw piece, a slab, of fish. But if you think about it, in order to serve sushi, it has to be the freshest type of fish that you can serve because it's raw. You don't serve just any raw thing," Okiyo says.

"When it comes to cooked food, you can just serve it and flavor it and do all sorts of things to it to make it taste good. But when it's sushi, you have to just serve it, and it's just there. It's just simple itself. So it just has to be a really good taste in and of itself. So in order to serve sushi, it's very difficult to do it well. Sushi is just amazing because it requires the freshest and the best quality in order to serve it at all."

The Demuras have an interesting direct source for the freshest—and sometimes most unusual—seafood: Kodiak, Alaska. The name Kodiak may bring to mind big brown bears snatching salmon from streams, but they're not the only ones fishing on the island. Fishing boats based in Kodiak bring in king crab, halibut, black cod, and king salmon, including the rare white-fleshed salmon. All of these delicacies end up on the menu at Little Tokyo.

"Kodiak, Alaska, is very good for fish. The water is fine, very nice. Every time I go over there to have a king crab or king salmon, it's great. I want to bring it over here to show the people," Fumiko says. Thanks to her husband and Federal Express, the seafood makes its way to Mississippi.

Because Tomio spends so much time in Kodiak, the Demuras decided to open their third restaurant on the Alaskan island. While Tomio is there overseeing the restaurant and seafood purchasing, Fumiko glides through the dining room in Ridgeland, welcoming guests and ensuring that everything runs smoothly.

The only thing that pulls her away is a customer at the family's grocery store next door to the restaurant. Fumiko unlocks the door and warmly welcomes the familiar customer, who bypasses chopsticks and t-shirts and novelty sushi coffee mugs and heads instead for bonito flakes, creamy Japanese mayonnaise, and *mochi* ice cream treats. More people come in, and Fumiko is gracious and patient as they shop, making certain that they're able to find what they need to prepare Japanese meals in their own homes.

After her customers leave, she locks the store again and returns to the restaurant, which is where she feels she belongs. "Since I have been in the restaurant so long, food and the restaurant is my life. I like people, and I like to help the people to enjoy, and the restaurant does those things." 🎐

LITTLE TOKYO TUNA TARTARE

Active cooking time: 15 minutes | Total cooking time: 45 minutes | Yield: 1 appetizer serving

While it's easy to associate raw fish with Japanese cuisine, the Japanese are not the only people to enjoy raw meat as part of a meal. Legend has it that the Tatar people of Central Asia ate raw meat as they rode their horses because they didn't want to take the time to stop, set up camp, and cook. In truth, however, steak tartare was first served in France, where it took its name from the savory white sauce served alongside it.

In the making of a tartare, the meat is minced and tossed with spices; it then is served either formed into cakes or loose on the plate. While the original preparation uses beef, other meats like venison, bison, pork, or even horse can be found in the restaurants of Europe. Tuna tartare came later, but the beautiful ruby flesh of the fish and its rich flavor made it a natural fit for the technique.

In this recipe, Fumiko combines the technique of tartare with Japanese flavors to create a unique and beautiful presentation. You can control the spiciness of the dish by increasing or decreasing the amount of *rayu* sauce that you toss into the mixture. *Rayu*

is a common Japanese condiment made by steeping dried hot peppers in sesame oil. If you can't find a Japanese version of *rayu* in your local Asian market, look for red chile oil. The preparation will be the same, but the oil used probably won't be sesame.

Another perhaps unfamiliar ingredient used here is ponzu sauce. This condiment is actually more complex than it appears. It is made by steeping *bonito* (dried fish) flakes and seaweed in a combination of rice wine (mirin) and rice vinegar. After straining, *yuzu* juice, a tart citrus juice, is added, often along with soy sauce. If you can't find ponzu sauce, combine equal parts mirin, rice vinegar, and soy sauce with lime juice to taste.

This dish is all about contrasting flavors and textures. The smooth richness of the tuna is enhanced by the spicy, nutty *rayu* sauce. The ponzu adds a note of salty tartness. The tomato adds sweetness and the cucumber a cool crispness, and the avocado melts into luscious fattiness. The wonton skins add a crisp platform, and the wasabi mayonnaise gives the dish a creamy balance.

2 ounces tuna

¼ cup cucumber, seeded (about ¼ of a
    small cucumber)

¼ cup avocado (about ¼ of an avocado)

¼ cup tomato, seeded (about ¼ of a
    medium tomato)

1 tablespoon ponzu sauce

1 teaspoon *rayu* sauce (chile-sesame oil)

1 cup peanut or soy oil

3 3-inch wonton skins

FOR THE WASABI MAYONNAISE

2 teaspoons wasabi powder or 1 teaspoon
    wasabi paste

2 tablespoons mayonnaise

Kitchen Passport While this
dish was designed for tuna, there's
no reason not to experiment with
other types of fish. Salmon or halibut would work beautifully. You
could even use rib-eye steak in
place of the tuna.

Dice the tuna, cucumber, avocado, and tomato into ¼-inch cubes.

Mix all the diced pieces together with the ponzu and *rayu* sauces. Allow the tuna mixture to rest in the refrigerator for 30 minutes.

While the tuna mixture is resting, heat the oil in a small skillet over medium heat.

Carefully lower a wonton skin into the hot oil. Allow the wonton skin to cook for 5 seconds or until the wonton skin has bubbled all over.

Flip the wonton skin over and allow to cook for another 3 seconds. Rest the fried wonton skin on a paper-towel-lined plate to drain. Repeat with the remaining wonton skins.

Prepare the wasabi mayonnaise by stirring together the wasabi powder or paste and mayonnaise until smooth.

Place ⅓ of the tuna mixture onto each wonton skin. Stack them on top of each other, each at a slightly different angle.

To serve, make a design on a plate with wasabi mayonnaise and place the stacked wonton skins on the plate.

Part III
Bringing Tradition to the Table

The meat is good, but the gravy is what is important.
You can ignore the meat, but you have to sop up the gravy.
—Yilma Aklilu, Ethiopian restaurateur, Memphis, Tennessee

China The Secret Menu

Careful observation at many Chinese restaurants reveals an interesting detail: a second stack of menus under the host's stand. Non-Chinese diners typically get the Americanized menu, the one with egg rolls and General Tso's chicken and pretty pictures. This menu lists the dishes invented in America for American tastes, while the pictures reassure timid diners that there's nothing too scary there.

A little bravery and a polite request can get you a look at that other menu, the one filled with Chinese characters but no pictures. This is the "scary" menu, the one with jellyfish and chicken feet, the one with pork belly and ox tongue. This is the menu that allows Chinese chefs to keep their regional food traditions alive and to introduce you to the flavors of a culture that might not be as familiar as you think.

In general, Americans know little of Chinese regional food traditions. As Chinese immigrants have opened restaurants over the years, they have stuck with menus that have had success in the United States, not with menus that necessarily represent their culinary heritage. China and the United States are very similar in one way. A person from Minnesota and a person from Mississippi may both be Americans, but it would be a mistake to assume that they share the same culinary traditions. Chinese regional cuisines are just as varied.

Like American cuisine, Chinese cuisine in America is constantly evolving. While some chefs serve dishes that have been common in China for centuries, others marry Chinese techniques and flavors with American regional ingredients to create new dishes that are no less authentically Chinese than their creators.

Da He Yang sits quietly at a table in his restaurant, Tasty China, keeping a close eye on everything that happens, listening and smiling at his guests' responses to their meals. He is a calm presence, and his pride in his first restaurant is impossible to miss. It is also impossible not to return his brilliant smile.

At his restaurant, Da He has become the curator of what many diners regard as a shrine to authentic Chinese cuisine. Although he was not a restaurateur in China and did not become one as soon as he im-

Da He Yang, Marietta, Georgia

9

Da He Yang at
Tasty China.

migrated to the United States in 1992, it was always a dream for him. After spending fourteen years in North Carolina, he moved to Marietta, Georgia, and made his dream a reality.

The menu at Tasty China is a playground for the taste buds. The majority of the dishes are in the style of Szechuan province, but the menu is peppered with dishes from other regions of China as well as with American Chinese creations. This fits in with Da He's philosophy about food in America. "America and China are different cultures, but one idea is the same. American people have a different culture than Chinese, but we're all human. If I like the food, other people will have to have some liking for it, too."

Looking closer at the menu at Tasty China, you will see some dishes based on ingredients familiar to many southern palates. Tongue, oxtail, pig feet, and pork intestines (better known in the South as chitlins) are the main ingredients in many authentic Chinese dishes. Like impoverished southerners who learned to make something delicious from the parts that other people would throw away, the Chinese learned to use every bit of an animal to avoid waste. In skilled hands, these parts become not only edible but true delicacies.

As an American, Da He has always been a southerner. His first home after immigrating to the United States was in North Carolina, where he worked at a Baptist church. The pastor of the church became a mentor for him, and Da He made other friends whom he has remained close to even after he moved to Marietta. "North Carolina will always be a home for me," he says.

But despite the warmth of the community he found in North Carolina, Da He's first restaurant experiences there were discouraging. "Other Chinese people told me that American people only like sweet and sour." But he knew that if people tasted authentic Chinese food, they would love it. "I can't say that I am a complete success, but I think my idea has been proved. People come here wanting to learn how Chinese people really cook. American people like to try these foods."

All cooks thrive on encouragement, and Da He is no exception. He positively glows with pride as he relates the story of a woman whose daughter called from Boston saying she missed his food. "People talking about liking the food and wanting it when they are not here makes me feel stronger in my idea, that doing something correct to Chinese cooking culture is good. Some people come in and say, 'You do this and I like it,' and that makes me feel good."

Da He is as much a teacher as he is a restaurateur. He hopes to educate the people who come into his restaurant about the unique cuisines of China. As an educator, one thing he emphasizes is the simplicity of Chinese cuisine. Authentic dishes don't mix too many flavors, focusing instead on enhancing one single flavor. But the variety of spices and preparations make the possibility for any single ingredient almost endless.

Still, Da He is frustrated by the way people order only foods with which they are most familiar. His eggplant dishes are bestsellers on the menu, but he feels that eggplant's popularity with his guests overshadows other items he offers. "We make a whole lot of vegetables. I even have hot and numbing mushroom. In my menu, I have winter melon, hot and numbing winter melon. But not too many people order it just because people understand eggplant, so they do not want something else. I think day by day over more time, maybe people will get tired of eggplant. Maybe then another thing will show up better."

Marietta is a town on the outskirts of Atlanta. But even in the larger city, getting fresh, quality ingredients can be a challenge for Da He. "Sometimes we order something from a special restaurant supply company from California. But if it's raining or snowing, maybe this week no more stuff will come."

Da He keeps some American Chinese dishes on his menu. "I cook it still doing it right, the Chinese way. Now we've got to leave it, like we cannot take it out. If we take it out, customers will say, 'Oh, I need this.'"

He has dreams to offer more authentic Chinese flavors to his Marietta customers by introducing a new kind of restaurant. "In this room, you would have Szechuan. Another room has another restaurant. If you like hot, spicy food, you eat in this room. You don't, you eat in another room. But all of it is Chinese culture; they would even look like Chinese rooms in America."

Tasty China's neighbors provide some of Da He's best encouragement: a Mediterranean grocer on one side of the restaurant and a Latin club and grill on the other side. "I think that I am doing this the right way. My neighbors come in and say, 'Yes. You do this. I like it.'" ⑤

HÚI GŪO RÒU (Twice-Cooked Pork with Garlic)

Active cooking time: 1 hour | Total cooking time: 2 hours, 40 minutes | Yield: 6 main dish servings

Húi gūo ròu literally translates as "meat that has been returned to the pot," and that's exactly what this dish is. The pork belly used here is first boiled with a spicy sauce, then it's sliced thin and cooked to crispness in a hot wok.

Da He likes to serve this dish to guests in his home, and it's easy to see why. Pork belly is nothing more than uncured bacon, and this preparation draws out the rich fattiness of the meat, the same fattiness that makes bacon so delicious. It's also an easy dish to prepare in advance. The meat can be refrigerated for up to three days after it has been cooked the first time, so the short time of the second cooking allows for the dish to be brought to the table quickly.

The flavors of this dish are uniquely Szechuan. The spiciness of the chile oil balances the tanginess of the bean sauce and the saltiness of the soy sauce. The garlic adds a note of pungency, and the ginger adds brightness. The richness of the pork contrasts perfectly with the crispness of the bok choy.

16 cloves garlic, peeled
4 tablespoons red chile oil
4 tablespoons light soy sauce
4 tablespoons chile bean sauce
2 pounds pork belly
1 tablespoon salt
2 large bok choy or 8 baby bok choy
2 tablespoons peanut or soy oil
1 (2-inch) piece fresh ginger, peeled and grated (about 2 tablespoons)

Using a mortar and pestle or food processor, blend the garlic, red chile oil, light soy sauce, and chile bean sauce into a paste. Divide the paste in half, reserving half for later use.

Rub the pork belly with half the garlic paste and place the pork in a large pot. Add the salt and then enough water to cover the pork by 1 inch.

Bring the water to a boil over medium-high heat.

Cooked white rice

> Kitchen Passport Consider
> adding 1 teaspoon crushed Szech-
> uan peppercorns when you make
> the sauce with the ginger and
> garlic paste. These peppercorns
> introduce an interesting change to
> the dish. Szechuan peppercorns
> produce a sensation of tingling
> numbness that can offset the fire
> of the hot peppers so common in
> Szechuan cuisine.

Reduce the heat to low and simmer the pork belly, covered, for 1 hour.

Drain the pork and discard the liquid. Allow the pork to rest on a cooling rack for 15 minutes or until the pork is cool enough to handle and is not dripping any water from the rack.

Wrap the pork tightly in plastic wrap and refrigerate for at least 30 minutes.

While the pork is resting, prepare the bok choy by separating into individual leaves and washing thoroughly. If you are using large bok choy, slice out the ribs and cut them into 1-inch pieces. Cut the leaves into 2-inch-wide ribbons.

Unwrap the pork and cut it into thin slices, no thicker than ¼ inch.

Ensure that all of your ingredients are close at hand before continuing. The high heat of wok cooking does not allow time for preparations during the actual cooking process.

Heat the peanut or soy oil in a wok over high heat.

When the oil begins to smoke, add no more than 8 pieces of pork to the oil and cook for 1 minute on each side or until the pork is golden brown. Transfer the pork to a plate and continue working in small batches until all the pork has been fried.

Add the ginger to the wok and cook for 15 seconds or until the ginger's fragrance has become stronger.

Add the reserved garlic paste to the wok and stir into the oil, cooking for 1 minute.

Return all of the pork slices to the wok and stir them to coat with the sauce. Remove the pork from the wok, leaving most of the sauce behind. Cover the pork and keep warm until serving.

If you are using a large bok choy, add the sliced ribs to the sauce in the wok. Allow the ribs to cook, stirring often, for 2 minutes or until the ribs are slightly tender but still crisp. Add the leaves and cook for 1 minute or until the leaves have wilted and are soft. If you are using baby bok choy, cook the whole leaves with ribs for 2 minutes.

Serve with cooked rice.

The Wok

It's hard to imagine Chinese cooking without the wok, but most scholars today agree that the wok probably originated in India and made its way into Chinese kitchens thousands of years ago via trade. It's an indispensable kitchen item, perfect for sautéing, stir frying, steaming, and deep frying.

True woks are made of metal alloys that can withstand extremely high heat without deforming. Its shape allows for high concentration of heat at its bottom with lower heat along its sloping sides. While pots with a similar shape can be found in other cultures, such pots are not made to cook over high heat the way a wok is.

That high heat cooking may have developed because of the scarcity of fuel in many parts of Central Asia. Being able to cook something quickly in a pot would have been very important. Because of its shape and durability, a wok could be set directly on hot coals to heat rapidly.

Today, your choice of a wok will depend on your preference and your stove.

If you have an electric or induction stove, you will need a flat-bottomed wok. If you have a gas stove, you can choose either a flat-bottomed wok or a rounded-bottom wok with a ring to hold it over the flame.

You will also have a choice of metals. A stainless steel wok is beautiful and functional and requires the least maintenance. Cast iron is heavy and offers you less temperature control because it absorbs heat. A cast iron wok will also require seasoning. A carbon steel wok is the most traditional type and offers the best temperature control with quick heating and cooling, but, like cast iron, it will require seasoning. Think twice before purchasing a non-stick wok. The high heat required for true wok cooking may damage the coating.

No matter which type of wok you choose, you will come to love having one in your kitchen. And don't limit it to Chinese dishes. Use a wok to prepare Indian curries, to sauté fresh vegetables, or to cook almost any dish where high heat is needed.

There is a trick to ordering your meal at Mr. Chen's Chinese Cooking: don't. Instead, put yourself in the hands of Wu Lung Chen, Mrs. Chen. While the servers are the friendly and efficient face of the restaurant, Mrs. Chen is the soul of the dining room. Petite and elegant in a colorful Chinese dress, she loves nothing more than a customer who is willing to try the traditional dishes she recommends.

Xia Chun Chen, Wu Lung Chen, and Shu Feng Chen, Birmingham, Alabama

Behind the scenes, Xia Chun Chen, Mr. Chen, is in the kitchen cooking those dishes. Far from being merely a cook, however, Mr. Chen is a trained chef with forty years of experience. His exquisite dishes and Mrs. Chen's hospitality have made their restaurant a must-visit destination in Birmingham.

Mr. Chen and Shu Feng "Sherry" Chen take a break together to talk about Mr. Chen's life in food. He carries on a lively conversation with Sherry, who translates. Occasionally, Mr. Chen emphasizes his point with brief pronouncements in English.

Mr. Chen was born in rural Taiwan. As a young man, he was drawn to food as a career. "He just loved to cook," Sherry says. "First, he wanted to try. He went to a big restaurant, wanting to become the trainee, you know, just wanting to learn. And then later on he found he really loved it."

Following his first experience, Mr. Chen chose to go to culinary school. "He got training, very serious training, in Taiwan. It's not like most chefs, you know, where it's only like three or five years. It's very traditional, step by step. He got very serious, detailed training. It's like the French chefs," Sherry says.

After school, Mr. Chen worked in Taiwan, and eventually his reputation led to an opportunity in the United States. "Because he's a very good chef in Taiwan, his friend wanted him to come here to open a restaurant."

Life in America meant making adjustments, including in his cooking. "When he first got here, he didn't know how to cook Chinese food in the American way, because it's all changed. He started learning and training in American Chinese food. He learned it in about a week, and then later on, he decided it was not the right way to cook the food."

Mr. Chen's dedication to authentic Chinese food has paid off. "A lot of American people come here and say, 'I want to try real Chinese food.' That's their goal, why they come into this restaurant. Because you know, now a lot of Chinese restaurants have been opened. When you come to the first one, then a second one, a third one, and a fourth one, then you have found which one is the best."

Some compromises have been made, though, for the sake of American tastes. "He keeps his rules in making Chinese food but changes

Sherry Chen, Wu Lung Chen, and Xia Chun Chen
at Mr. Chen's Chinese Cooking.

a little bit, like our favorite dishes here. If he makes something Kung Pao, he doesn't add MSG. Instead of MSG, he swapped that one with a little bit of sugar to match the tastes here. He changes a little bit, but basically focuses on real Chinese food."

One place where American Chinese dishes have appeared is the lunch menu, because these dishes can be made to suit customers' demands for a fast meal. Traditional Chinese dishes sometimes take more time to cook or eat than their lunch customers have. "Lunchtime, people eat really quickly, and I think, you know, some people, like office people, they will sit down and say, 'Oh, a whole fish! That fish has bones.' Lunchtime is a little bit rushed, you know. Just eat it and go," Sherry says.

Although the quick lunch is a business necessity, it is not Mr. Chen's preferred approach to cooking. He would rather prepare each dish individually. "The difference is, most of the restaurants, they mix all the sauces at one time. So, for example, for Mongolian beef or something, they pool all the sauce. That's it. It's easy. But in here, you have the chef's experience, and you pick up each sauce by itself. This is a really Chinese way to cook because he has forty years of experience," Sherry says.

For Mr. Chen, experience takes cooking beyond food and makes it art. "For example, after you stir fry the food, and the food is ready, you need to put it on the plate, and it needs to be fresh and look really beautiful. In Chinese food we talk about the color, the smell, and the taste. These three basic things all are very important," Sherry says. "When the customers eat it, they use all the senses. When you see it first, the customers like it. And the smell is so good. And then taste it; it is perfect. That's his goal. So, basically, everything's fresh. Everything should be very clean, perfect." 🥠

MÁPÓ DÒUFǓ (Pockmarked Old Woman's Tofu)

Active cooking time: 20 minutes | Total cooking time: 35 minutes | Yield: 4 main dish servings

While no one can say exactly who served *mápó dòufǔ* for the first time, there is one legend of its origin that explains its highly descriptive name. Once upon a time, an old woman with a very pock-marked face (*mápó*) lived by the side of a busy road. To make a small amount of money, she began serving food to travel-ing merchants. She prepared tofu unlike any the merchants had eaten anywhere else, so they began to call the dish *mápó dòufǔ* in her honor.

Whether the story is true or not, the dish is a wonderfully rich and unique combination of flavors. Mr. Chen loves spicy food, and the pepper provides a spicy bite. The bean sauce adds a pungent tanginess, and the tofu provides a creamy base.

This is a great Szechuan dish with a touch of Mr. Chen's Taiwanese style. Best of all, you can easily prepare this at home. Heat is a very important element in cooking many Chinese dishes, and most home ranges can't provide the same level

of heat that commercial wok burners achieve. However, with *mápó dòufǔ*, "you don't need a really big fire, big heat," says Mr. Chen.

Even though you're not working with extremely high heat, this dish still comes together very quickly. You will want to have all of your ingredients prepared and in easy reach before you start cooking.

1 pound firm or extra-firm tofu
2 tablespoons peanut or soy oil
¼ pound ground pork
2 cloves garlic, minced (about
　1 teaspoon)
1 (⅓-inch) piece fresh ginger, peeled
　and minced (about 1 teaspoon)
1 Tien Tsin pepper, sliced thin
2 tablespoons chicken broth
2 tablespoons soy sauce
Salt
1 tablespoon cornstarch
2 tablespoons water
1 tablespoon spicy red bean paste
Freshly ground black pepper

TO SERVE
2 green onions, chopped
Cooked white rice

SPECIAL EQUIPMENT
Wok

Drain the tofu in a sieve over a bowl for at least 15 minutes.

Discard any water that comes out of the tofu and cut the tofu into 1-inch cubes.

Heat the wok over high heat and add the oil.

Add the pork and cook for 1 minute, moving constantly to break up any clumps.

Add the garlic, ginger, and Tien Tsin pepper and continue cooking for 1 minute.

Add the tofu cubes and stir to combine. Add the chicken broth, soy sauce, and a pinch of salt, stirring to coat.

Reduce the heat to medium.

Continue cooking, stirring often, for 5 minutes to allow the chicken broth to reduce.

Whisk together the cornstarch and water. Add to the wok and stir to combine with the sauce.

Stir in the bean paste.

Season with black pepper to taste.

Garnish with green onions and serve with cooked white rice.

Kitchen Passport For a vegetarian version, substitute diced shiitake mushrooms for the pork and omit the chicken broth. Cook the mushrooms until any moisture released has evaporated before adding the tofu cubes to the wok. A softer tofu will result in a smoother, soupier version.

Yumei Ulu first came to the United States as a high school student in 1992. After receiving her diploma in San Francisco, she moved all over the country before finally settling in Atlanta, Georgia. She lives there now, working as a translator for the Chinese community, but on the weekends she has another life.

Yumei has been in the restaurant business since 1998 and opened her first restaurant in 2000. She is pragmatic about the ownership of Chinese restaurants. "Chinese people have restaurants for two reasons. One is most of the people don't speak English, and they find a job that they can make a living at. The other thing is that if you have a family, it's a great place."

One hour north of Atlanta is Hiawassee. It's a typical southern small town, with the older part in the center and the newer sprawl radiating out. Hiawassee is a tourist town; the visitors drawn by Lake Chatuge in the summer are the backbone of the economy that helps Hiawassee's small businesses stay open through the winters. It is here that Yumei owns and manages China Grill, a small restaurant in the newer part of the town.

She found the restaurant through her job as a translator. "The previous owner of this restaurant and the owner before, they are all my clients. So I got to know this place, and I kind of like this place."

Yumei now spends every weekend in Hiawassee. While she does have some authentic Chinese cuisine on the menu, most of the food she serves is American Chinese food. "Chinese food is two types. One you find in Chinatown—it's served to Chinese people—and the other is Americanized."

She sees a lot of difference between life in Hiawassee and life in Atlanta. Changes in the economy affect the community more directly in Hiawassee. "In small towns, it's slow right now for everybody, so we've been hanging on like that. Hiawassee is a very hard place because everybody, most of the men, their jobs depend on construction. That's why right now we're not doing good. We're just hanging in there."

As Yumei seats guests after her lunch buffet has been set up, her cooks come out to sit at a dining room table to take a break and enjoy their lunch. Instead of eating the food they've set out on the buffet, they are eating lighter, simpler fare—a bowl of rice porridge, or congee, with pickled vegetables and dried shrimp to scatter over it. Yumei notices what they've brought out. "Chinese people eat not so much oil. Restaurants use lots of oil—you have deep fryers. We like to eat something light. Rice with some pickles, something like that."

Yumei enjoys serving and eating authentic Chinese cuisine, but she also takes a lot of pride in the inventiveness of Chinese cooks who have immigrated and adapted their culinary talents to provide food that their new communities will enjoy. "Chinese people start to make lots of chicken wings and stuff, especially chicken wings. That's one thing, but they add Chinese flavor on the chicken wings instead of only hot wings. That's the trend everybody's trying to do now."

She also sees how American-style Chinese food can make it easier for immigrants to open a restaurant that will succeed. "Everything's pretty standard, I guess. And so, more or less, everybody makes the same stuff, because all the cooks learn it. It's just a little bit different in the flavor, but the major taste, like General Tso's chicken, is sweet. You know, the major taste is the same, and everybody has the same thing on the menu."

Yumei's weekends are her escape now. "A restaurant is a fun job. It's very hard work, but people come in and they're hungry; they want to eat. And when they leave, they're happy. It's not like my other job. People come in because they got in trouble. They need to go to court. They need to go to the hospital. It's very stressful. A restaurant, if your business is okay, it's a fun job." ⑤

CRAB RANGOON

Active cooking time: 1 hour | Total cooking time: 1 hour | Yield: 4 dozen crab rangoon

Crab rangoon is a uniquely American Chinese creation. While no one is sure about the dish's actual origin, there are two leading theories. One is that it originated at the 1904 Chicago World's Fair. The other is that it was developed in the 1950s by Trader Vic's restaurant. No matter its origin, it has become one of the staples of American Chinese cuisine.

It's easy to think of crab rangoon as just a filler for buffets and an American attempt at Chinese technique. The only thing Chinese about crab rangoon is the use of a wonton or spring roll pastry. Cream cheese and the artificial crab that make the filling for the dish cannot be found anywhere in authentic Chinese cooking.

And yet, crab rangoon is the dish Yumei thinks about first when she thinks of American Chinese cuisine. "I think the most creative thing in Chinese restaurants here is the crab rangoon. It's simple. It tastes good. It's popular. Some places they put in sugar; some places they put in salt. It depends on the area. I think that's very smart. People like it. It mixes with American style very well. And American people just don't make that. It's Chinese that are making American-style food. That's very smart. I like it."

Crab rangoon is an easy appetizer that will tempt you to turn it into a meal. The creamy filling spiced with fresh green onions and dotted with crab is almost sinfully delicious. When complemented by the tangy sweet flavor of the plum sauce and the thin crispy wrappers, it becomes an almost irresistible treat.

Peanut or soy oil

16 ounces cream cheese, softened

8 ounces artificial crab, minced

1 bunch green onions, chopped
(about 1 cup)

½ teaspoon salt

48 5-inch spring roll pastries

Using a deep pot or deep-fat fryer, heat at least 3 inches of oil to 375 degrees.

In a large bowl, whip the cream cheese until it is light and fluffy. Add the crab, green onions, and salt, stirring well to combine evenly.

Place 2 teaspoons of the cream cheese mixture in the center of a spring roll pastry. Gather the edges of the pastry over the filling and twist, squeezing lightly, to secure the filling. Repeat until all pastries and filling are used.

Working in batches, carefully lower the filled pastries into the hot oil. Cook the pastries for 1 to 2 minutes and lift them from the oil with a strainer. Place cooked pastries on a paper-towel-lined plate to drain and cool.

Serve with plum sauce (recipe follows) for dipping.

Kitchen Passport It's tempting to substitute real crab for the artificial crab in this recipe. While that is perfectly acceptable, make sure that you drain as much liquid as possible from the crab before adding it to the cream cheese mixture.

You can also spike the cream cheese with spices like ginger, coriander, or hot red pepper. The salt in the filling can be replaced with sugar if you prefer a sweeter flavor. You can also use wonton wrappers instead of spring roll wrappers if you prefer a thicker pastry.

To prepare a vegetarian version, sauté the smallest red radishes you can find with their greens. Chop the radishes and greens and substitute them for the crab. The small radishes will provide the typical red color of the crab, and sautéing the radishes will make them softer and sweeter. Larger radishes will have a sharper flavor and woodier texture, and their presence will be more pronounced in the finished rangoons.

PLUM SAUCE

Active cooking time: 35 minutes | Total cooking time: 1 hour, 15 minutes + 8 hours | Yield: 3 pints

Plum sauce is very versatile. Any extra sauce can be used to glaze grilled chicken or pork. It can also be made sweeter or spicier, as you prefer.

2 pounds ripe plums, pitted and
    chopped (about 5 cups)
½ pound apricots, pitted and
    chopped (about 1¼ cups)
½ cup honey
1 (1-inch) piece fresh ginger, peeled
    and grated (about 1 tablespoon)
¼ teaspoon ground cinnamon
1 teaspoon oriental mustard powder
1 tablespoon water
3 cloves garlic, minced (about
    1½ teaspoons)
½ teaspoon red chile paste, or more
    to taste
¼ cup light soy sauce

Combine all of the ingredients in a large pot, stirring to blend.

Bring the mixture to a boil over medium heat.

Reduce the heat to low. Simmer the mixture, covered, for 30 minutes.

Working in batches, puree the mixture in a blender until smooth.

Allow the plum sauce to cool to room temperature before refrigerating. Allow the sauce to rest in the refrigerator for at least 8 hours or overnight. The flavor of the sauce will develop as it cools, and is actually best the day after being made.

Extra plum sauce can be frozen in sealed containers for up to 6 months.

Wally Joe,
Memphis,
Tennessee

Chef Wally Joe personifies the dual menu. Born in Hong Kong, he immigrated to the United States with his family at the age of four. By the time Wally was ten years old, his family was operating a traditional American fine dining restaurant in Cleveland, Mississippi. But in their home kitchen, Wally was learning to prepare traditional Chinese cuisine from his mother and grandmother.

Wally's family didn't come to the United States to work with food. "My dad's brother had been here since he was a teenager. He fought in World War II for the United States. I guess my parents were probably looking for a change—just something different, not necessarily a better life. My dad was a dentist in Hong Kong."

Because Wally's father didn't speak English, however, he was forced to change careers when he moved his family to the Mississippi Delta. "At that time, all the Chinese in the Delta had grocery stores. In Cleveland, there was one on every corner, practically. So that's what we did, because everyone else was doing it, basically, and it was just a way to make a living for us."

Six years after coming to the United States, Wally's family saw an opportunity to get into a new business—the restaurant business. "There was an existing restaurant called Michael's Fine Food, and it was pretty well known all over the Delta. It was a good business, but the owner was getting up there in age, and he wanted to sell it and retire. So the opportunity came for us to buy it, and we did."

From that time on, Wally was part of the business, but food had already been an important part of his life. "When we had the grocery store, my dad raised chicken and squabs and pheasants and quail in the backyard, and we always had a garden. I learned to slaughter a chicken when I was probably seven or eight years old, and for a young kid, I probably thought that was the coolest thing."

He also had the influence of his grandmother living in their home. "I learned to make traditional Chinese food alongside my grandmother and my mom. Really, at a young age, I had an interest in it."

Despite his interest and experience, when Wally went to college he decided that he didn't want a career that had anything to do with restaurants or food. "I tried to get as far away from it as possible, so I got a degree in banking and finance from Ole Miss. But it's hard to get this business out of your system; it gets in your blood."

Still, he didn't jump straight back into his family's restaurant. "I started traveling around a little bit, going to nice restaurants, visiting northern California wine country. And you know, it just struck me that I really love wine, I really love food, and I just wanted to do that."

As it turned out, this realization came at an opportune time. His father needed help in the restaurant and asked him to come back. "I was going to do it maybe three, six months, maybe a year. But a year turned into two years, and I decided that if I was going to be there, I was really going to make something out of it."

The changes happened slowly. They remodeled the building. They built a wine cellar, an oddity in the Delta, and dramatically increased their selection of wines. They received their first national recognition, and slowly but surely, for the first time since they bought the restaurant, they began to change the menu to include the more exotic dishes that Wally wanted to experiment with. "Little by little, my dad started trusting me. He saw that people were embracing what we did."

To celebrate the success of their changes, they made one more very important alteration: Michael's Fine Food became KC's. "KC's my dad. That's his name. It stands for Kay Cheung."

Wally Joe outside
Brushmark Restaurant.

Wally began serving modern, continentally inspired cuisine, but there were still hints of his Chinese food background. "It's just natural for me. These are the flavors I grew up with. Just from childhood memories and growing up eating that food, being around it, it's always going to be a part of my cooking and my cuisine."

He was also influenced by the food of the South. "I'm Chinese by birth, but I'm southern just by growing up here. I've always termed my cuisine to be 'Modern American.' It's a reflection of growing up in the South as a Chinese immigrant and the result of my travels throughout not just America but South America, all over." 🐉

WALLY'S BRAISED PORK BELLY ON SWEET CORN PUDDING WITH GREEN TOMATO MARMALADE

Active cooking time: 2 hours | Total cooking time: 5 hours + 12 hours | Yield: 4 main dish servings

Wally likes to integrate the style of continental cuisine with southern ingredients and Chinese flavors. This recipe is built around one of his favorite ingredients—pork belly. Pork shows up often in Wally's repertoire. Even he admits, "Pork is really my thing."

The first step for this dish is to mildly cure the pork belly. Curing not only allows the flavors of the pepper, coriander, and fennel seed to penetrate the meat but also draws some of the water from it. That lack of water won't mean dry meat. On the contrary, it pulls the meat fibers tighter around the internal fat to produce an exceptionally tender piece of pork. After braising in wine and soy sauce, this meat will literally melt in your mouth.

Wally's corn pudding is a lighter version of the southern classic, relying more on the flavors and juices of the corn itself than on heavy cream and butter. The cumin gives it an Asian touch.

The green tomato marmalade makes a delicious condiment that you'll want to keep on hand. The rice vinegar adds a light tartness that complements the green tomatoes, and the basil adds a note of brightness. If you prefer less spicy food, don't use the full amount of red pepper flakes.

While you could prepare this recipe at any time of year, you'll have the best results at the height of summer when fresh corn and green tomatoes are readily available.

FOR THE PORK BELLY

1 tablespoon coriander seeds

1 tablespoon fennel seeds

½ tablespoon black peppercorns

½ cup salt

½ cup sugar

2 pounds skinless pork belly,
   preferably organic

2 tablespoons canola or vegetable oil

1 small yellow onion, diced (about ½ cup)

1 medium carrot, peeled and diced
   (about ½ cup)

2 ribs celery, diced (about 1 cup)

4 cloves garlic, roughly chopped

2 tablespoons tomato paste

2 cups dry red wine

1 cup soy sauce

2 cups beef broth

1 cup chicken broth

FOR THE CORN PUDDING

8 ears fresh corn

2 tablespoons unsalted butter

1 small yellow onion, diced
   (about ½ cup)

1 teaspoon ground cumin

1 cup heavy whipping cream

½ cup yellow cornmeal

1 teaspoon fresh thyme leaves, chopped

1 cup water

Salt

Freshly ground black pepper

1 tablespoon Parmesan cheese

FOR THE GREEN TOMATO MARMALADE

1 tablespoon canola or vegetable oil

1 shallot, minced

3 medium green tomatoes, diced

1 teaspoon crushed red pepper

½ cup sugar

1 cup rice vinegar

6 fresh basil leaves

TO PREPARE THE PORK BELLY

Heat a skillet over medium heat.

Add the coriander seeds, fennel seeds, and black peppercorns. Cook the spices, stirring constantly, for 5 minutes or until the spices are toasted.

Using a mortar and pestle or spice grinder, grind the toasted spices.

Combine the ground spices with the salt and sugar in a small mixing bowl. Rub a thick coating of the spice mixture onto the pork belly. Place the pork belly in a baking dish and cover the dish tightly with plastic wrap. Place the dish in your refrigerator for at least 12 hours to allow the spice mixture to penetrate the meat.

Preheat the oven to 200 degrees.

Using paper towels, wipe the spice mixture off of the pork belly.

Heat the oil in a large skillet over medium heat.

Place the pork belly in the hot skillet and cook for 5 to 7 minutes.

Flip the pork belly over and cook for an additional 5 to 7 minutes or until both sides are golden brown. Transfer the pork belly to a large Dutch oven.

Add the onion, carrot, celery, and garlic to the skillet. Cook, stirring constantly, for 15 minutes or until the vegetables are golden brown.

Stir the tomato paste into the cooked vegetables. Transfer the vegetables to the Dutch oven with the pork belly.

Add the red wine, soy sauce, beef broth, and chicken broth to the Dutch oven. Add water if needed to cover the pork belly.

Cover the Dutch oven and bake in the oven for 4 hours or until the pork belly is tender. Prepare the sweet corn pudding and green tomato marmalade while the pork belly is cooking.

Remove the pork belly from the Dutch oven and reserve, covering loosely with aluminum foil to keep warm.

Degrease the cooking liquid by skimming any fat from the top or by using a gravy separator.

Carefully strain the remaining cooking liquid from the Dutch oven into a medium saucepan, discarding any solids.

Cook the liquid over medium heat for 20 minutes or until the liquid has reduced to 1½ cups of thickened sauce.

TO PREPARE THE SWEET CORN PUDDING

While the pork belly is cooking, grate the corn into a large mixing bowl, including any liquid. Consider using a box grater for the best results.

Melt the butter in a large skillet over medium heat.

Add the onion and cook, stirring constantly, for 5 minutes or until the onion is translucent.

Add the corn and cumin to the skillet and stir in the heavy whipping cream. Cook, stirring often, for 10 minutes or until the mixture has come to a simmer.

Stir in the cornmeal and thyme leaves along with the cup of water.

Reduce the heat to medium low.

Allow the mixture to cook for 30 minutes or until most of the liquid has been absorbed.

Season to taste with salt and black pepper.

Sprinkle the Parmesan cheese over the corn pudding.

Cover the corn pudding to keep it warm.

TO PREPARE THE GREEN TOMATO MARMALADE

While the pork belly is cooking, heat the oil in a medium saucepan over medium-low heat.

Add the shallot and cook, stirring often, for 10 to 15 minutes or until the shallot is soft.

Add the green tomatoes, crushed red pepper, sugar, rice vinegar, and basil leaves to the softened shallot.

Increase the heat to medium.

Cook for 10 minutes or until the mixture has reached a simmer.

Cover the saucepan and reduce the heat to low.

Cook the mixture, stirring occasionally, for 45 minutes or until the mixture has a jam-like consistency.

TO FINISH THE DISH

Slice the pork belly into 4 equal portions.

Mound the sweet corn pudding in the centers of 4 large dinner plates.

Place a serving of pork belly on top of the corn pudding.

Drizzle the reduced sauce over the pork belly and around the corn pudding. Top the pork belly with green tomato marmalade.

Kosher and Halal
Keeping the Faith in the Land of Pork

Each of the three great religions of the Middle East has some form of dietary restriction. Christianity has Lent, the forty days of prayer, meditation, and self-denial leading up to Easter. Judaism and Islam have dietary laws in effect year-round. Jewish kosher and Islamic halal laws are complex sets of rules that cover everything from the raising of food to its harvest to its preparation.

Although kosher and halal are different, they do have similarities. One area where they agree is pork; both religions strictly forbid the consumption of this food. How, then, do immigrants from the Middle East deal with life in the South, where pork reigns as the king of meats?

Moumen Hamwi, Little Rock, Arkansas "Everybody has some kind of adventure," says Moumen Hamwi, talking about how he became a restaurateur in Little Rock. Moumen came to the South from Damascus, Syria, in 1988 to study systems engineering at the University of Arkansas at Little Rock. He made Little Rock his home, marrying a local girl and choosing to stay in the city to raise his children.

His eyes twinkle with laughter as he recounts his most memorable meal, a very unexpected meal for a man who has traveled halfway around the world but one that was most certainly an adventure. "It was a catfish. I went to my wife's grandma's farm, and we caught a catfish. We took it home, and we fried it, and we ate it. We ate and ate, and I still remember it. This was the first fish I ever caught, and this was the first fish my wife ever cooked. It was awesome. It was great. Great catfish."

For Moumen, that catfish might be very different from the meals he grew up with in Damascus, but the spirit of freshness is very much the same. "In Syria, the food is based on the weather. Like in the summertime, we have fava beans. And my mama, she used to cook the green fava beans with olive oil and yogurt and cilantro and garlic. This is the summer meal. No meat, straight vegetarian, and very fresh olive oil. In

Moumen Hamwi at Layla's.

the wintertime, my mother used to cook kibbeh, which is bulgur wheat stuffed with walnuts, meat, and onion."

Now Moumen serves some of these dishes in his restaurant, Layla's, but his first restaurant wasn't Syrian. Instead, it was a pizzeria. "I started working downtown as a programmer. And at the River Market they have a small pizza store. The owner wanted to sell it. So I said, 'Well, I'll do it.' And the pizza itself is easy. I can make the dough, the sauce, the cheese; everything is ready for you. The oven's there, so you don't have so much prep," he says. "So I started with that. And I enjoyed it. I liked it. I worked every day there at lunchtime because it was close to the office where I worked."

The name of a restaurant is what first attracts customers; it's what will be associated with the memories of the food. For Moumen, choosing the name for his restaurant was easy. "My little girl, Layla, she's seven years old now. When I got the pizza store at the beginning, I wanted to give it a name that meant something to me. So I just got my first child after I had been married for fifteen years, and my wife named her Layla. It's a beautiful name, so I said, 'Okay, I'm gonna call it Layla's.'"

As his family and enjoyment of the restaurant business grew, Moumen had an opportunity to start serving the foods of his homeland. A friend approached him with a business offer that would be beneficial to both of them. "My partner had a butcher shop that he had to move, so we decided to open a shop where we would have the meat and a restaurant. And that's how we came up with the restaurant."

The butcher shop at Layla's is one of only a few sources of halal meats for the Muslim population of Little Rock. Moumen compares halal meat to kosher food. "A kosher meal in the Jewish community, in order for them to eat it, a rabbi's got to come and look at the animal and pray over it, and then the rabbi says this is kosher, now everybody can eat it. Islamic is the same thing. This is one way that we follow that tradition."

While halal is primarily associated with the Islamic faith, Moumen has found that people of other faiths appreciate having a source for halal meats. "We are trying to provide a service for the Muslim community and the non-Muslim community. We have some in the non-Muslim community who are very interested in halal meat because it is more healthy."

The health benefits of halal meats are the result of the extra care given to animals raised for meat. That care can be seen in the butchering process. Moumen describes it in detail. "The process goes with the animal, looking at the animal. You have to have a knife, it's got to be cut from the neck, and—the important thing—it has to bleed. That gets rid of all the bad blood. And before you actually slaughter it, there's a saying, 'We are going to do this in the name of Allah,' and it's going to be directed on the calf. This is the Islamic condition to make it healthy," he says.

"It is very important that whenever you slaughter the animal by the knife, you have to do it the best possible way. Your knife's got to be sharp, and it's got to be cut in one slice. You cannot produce any pain, other than what you have to. There's going to be just one chance. And you have to be as fast as possible," he continues. "My partner does the slaughter. Before he even brings out the knife, he'll relax the animal, and he hides the knife. He won't even let the animal see the knife. He looks the animal in the eye and comforts him. Then you do what you have to do. But it's got to be fast and precise. You cannot harm or make him suffer more than he has to."

These are the meats that Moumen serves at Layla's, with specialty dishes like goat available only when the animal has been freshly butchered. Most Americans are not used to this type of constraint, but for Moumen, it's more like the way he grew up in Syria. Moumen describes how availability and access shaped the way his family ate back home. "Around fall, we made a yogurt dish with a big chunk of lamb and rice on the side. My mom would take at least six hours to cook it. And you remember that because you lived the experience of your mother," he says.

"From the moment you wake up, from the moment she wakes up, you have to go. You have to remember that we didn't have a supermarket that has everything like a Wal-Mart. The yogurt you have to go to get from the yogurt guy, the meat you have to go to the butcher to get, the vegetables you have to go to the vegetable guy. The rice, you're going to go to another guy who specializes in rice and bulgur and spaghetti and sauce. So you're going to visit five or six different shops to come home with the ingredients," he recalls.

"So from seven o'clock in the morning, you have to make sure that the yogurt's ready, the meat is chopped, whatever Mama needs. It's not some simple meal! You have to have low heat, and you have to keep it stirred. So I remember those things. They are beautiful memories to carry."

Growing up in a strong Muslim family in Syria made Muslim dietary restrictions, such as not eating pork, a natural part of life for Moumen. Living in a part of the South where there is not a large Islamic population makes it more difficult to stay away from such restricted foods, but Moumen says that it's not so hard on him. Instead, it's hard on his children, who were born and raised in the South. "My kids, they're young. It's hard for me to explain to them why we should not eat pork. It's hard for me to tell them, 'Well, if you go to school, and they say they're going to have cheeseburgers with bacon, you've got to tell them, no, you cannot eat bacon and you have to explain to them why you cannot eat bacon.' This makes it hard as a parent for me to explain that to my kids."

Even Moumen and his wife have to be careful what they eat in restaurants because pork is such a common ingredient in the region. "It's hard for me when I go to a public restaurant. I always have to ask about their grill. If I want to get a burger that's cooked on the grill, I have to ask, 'Could you please clean that grill after you cook the bacon? Because I cannot eat pork.' This is the hard thing of it: you've got to make sure it's not pork, and it can't touch pork or any element of pork. And it's not just me, not just because I am Muslim! There are a lot of different cultures that don't eat pork; it's not just one culture."

Of course, being Muslim, like being Jewish or Christian, is about more than the foods that are off-limits or butchering traditions and methods. Faith of any variety is a part of everyday life. For Moumen, his faith is as much a part of the food he serves as the garlic and onions are. "Whenever I cook, I always do it in the name of Allah. I start with that, so I will be pleased and blessed by Allah to perform my job and everybody'll be happy with my food."

And that happiness is really why Moumen is cooking instead of working with computers. The happiness of his customers brings happiness to him. He describes simply what he loves most about being a restaurateur. "Meeting people. Seeing people come back, seeing people tell you the food was good, the food was excellent. It gives you a great feeling that you're cooking and people come in and buy from you," he says.

"Everybody can cook, but not everybody can sell their food. And here I feel like I'm doing really good when the people like my food and they come back and request more of it. And this gives me self-confidence and self-pleasure that people enjoy what I'm providing." ❦

HUMMUS (Chickpea Dip)

Active cooking time: 10 minutes | Total cooking time: 10 minutes | Yield: 4 side dish servings

Hummus can be found in almost every Middle Eastern restaurant. This garlicky, tangy, creamy dish is used as a dip, a spread, a filling, and a base for kebabs and other meat dishes.

It's a simple dish, but for Moumen, this recipe represents home more than any other. "It is part of the culture. Just like how we are living here, you eat at least one burger a week. Back home you got to eat hummus once a week. Somehow, somewhere, the hummus becomes part of it," he says. "And that's what I remember. Every Friday, which is our holy day, we go buy the chickpeas, we boil them up, we fix it up, and we make our meal for the morning. And that's what I remember the most. The first one I ever ate, I remember."

Even though it is a simple dish, hummus is not taken lightly in the Middle East. Use your best olive oil for hummus. Of course, good chickpeas, also known as garbanzo beans, help a lot, too. Canned chickpeas make it easy to whip up hummus in a pinch, but when you have time, it's worth the effort to soak dry chickpeas and cook them yourself to get the seasonings just right.

So what's so special about chickpeas? For one thing, they're an ancient staple of the Mediterranean and Middle Eastern regions, even garnering a mention in the *Iliad*. Cicero, the famous Roman senator, was named from the Latin word *cicer*, meaning chickpea, because of a chickpea-shaped growth on his nose.

This recipe uses tahini, a sesame seed paste, to thicken the hummus and add a nutty flavor. Tahini can be found in Middle Eastern markets and most supermarkets.

2 cups cooked chickpeas (8 ounces dry)
   or 1 (15-ounce) can
4 cloves garlic, minced (about 2 teaspoons)
2 tablespoons lemon juice
4 tablespoons tahini
2 teaspoons salt

TO SERVE

Olive oil
Paprika

Drain the chickpeas, reserving 2 tablespoons of the liquid from the can or pot.

Place the chickpeas, garlic, lemon juice, and reserved cooking liquid in a blender or food processor and process until smooth.

Add the tahini and salt to the chickpeas. Continue blending until well combined.

To serve, spread the hummus on a flat dish. Drizzle with olive oil and sprinkle with paprika.

Kitchen Passport Hummus is a very versatile dish. While the recipe originated in the Middle East with chickpeas, it can be easily adapted to other legumes. Try a variation like fresh lima beans with coriander and a little bit of white onion; black-eyed peas with vinegar instead of lemon juice; or black beans with lime juice and a touch of cayenne pepper.

You can also add in ¼ to ½ cup sundried tomatoes, pitted olives, or spinach for additional flavor. Another great option is to roast your garlic before adding it to the hummus. Roasted garlic will add a complex sweetness that is beautifully complemented by the creaminess of the chickpeas.

Olive Oil

Olive oil is the darling of the culinary world. With its extremely high level of monounsaturated fats, olive oil has been shown to reduce the risk of heart disease. The flavors of a good olive oil can be as complex as wine; tastings are often held to compare different pressings of oil.

Production ranges from the massive output of olive oil as a commodity down to very small artisanal pressings that celebrate the particular flavors and textures of different olive varieties and specific regions.

The process used to make olive oil is surprisingly simple. Olive oil is extracted by grinding ripe olives into paste. This paste is then pressed to expel the liquid. Finally, this liquid is spun to separate the oil from the water the olives contained.

Olive oil produced in this manner is classified as either virgin or extra virgin. Extra virgin olive oil has an intense fruity flavor and is best for applications like salad dressing or a dip for bread where the oil itself is a primary flavor. Virgin olive oil has a milder flavor and is ideal for sautés. Any olive oil that is not labeled virgin or extra virgin contains oil that has been chemically refined and should be avoided.

Over 90 percent of the world's olive oil is produced in the Mediterranean. The first olive oil was made over 6,000 years ago in either Greece or Israel. Beyond its culinary uses, olive oil plays an important part in the three major religions of the Middle East.

The Jewish holiday Hanukkah celebrates the "miracle of the container of oil." After the Jews drove the Seleucids from Jerusalem, they moved immediately to reconsecrate the temple there. However, there was only enough oil to burn the temple's eternal flame for one day. Miraculously, that oil lasted for eight days, long enough for more oil to be pressed and consecrated. That oil was olive oil.

In Christianity, the Catholic and Orthodox churches use olive oil for anointment and consecrations. In Islam, the Qur'an says, "Allah is the light of the Heavens and the Earth. An example of His light is like a lantern inside which there is a torch, the torch is in a glass bulb, the glass bulb is like a bright planet lit by a blessed olive tree, neither Eastern nor Western, its oil almost glows, even without fire touching it, light upon light."

When Memet Arslan was chosen in the green card lottery of 1991, it was a bittersweet success. He left Turkey, his home country, to prepare a place for his family, but he had to leave his wife behind while she was pregnant with their first child. That child, Yusuf, was born in Turkey, and Memet didn't get to meet his oldest son until he was two months old.

Memet chose to make his home in Nashville, Tennessee, because he already had connections to the city through a friend. At that time, the Muslim community in Nashville was small but growing rapidly. His next choice was how to support himself and his family. Unlike immigrants who come to the United States with specific work visas, Memet's green card left him free to choose any job once he reached his new home.

Before he left Turkey, Memet had opened a coffee shop of his own in Izmir at the age of seventeen. In the United States, he decided to continue working with food because he already had experience. He worked at Luby's Cafeteria for seven years while he saved the funds to open a restaurant of his own, which would have a ready audience in Nashville with its growing community of Muslims.

Today, Memet's Istanbul Turkish Restaurant is a place where his food brings smiles to the faces of his patrons. "It's a very hard job. But I like all kinds of people. I love my customers to be happy all the time," he says. In addition to an almost endless variety of grilled meats, he serves traditional dishes like *tarhana çorbasi*, a tangy yogurt soup. He would like to regularly serve other dishes like *lahmajun*, a dish he describes as Turkish pizza, but the time and cost needed to prepare them allow him to offer them only as specials. However, he is able to offer delicious traditional desserts every day prepared fresh in the restaurant.

As a Muslim, Memet doesn't offer pork on his menu. But his reasons for avoiding pork go beyond religion. "Pork for eating is not healthy. That's why they do not eat, you know. Cholesterol, maybe blood pressure, too fatty—that's why. Some people say religion. But it's not. In my opinion, no."

The restaurant is now a family business. When Yusuf has breaks from college, he works with his father, learning Memet's skills as a great cook. But beyond acquiring knowledge and experience at the restaurant, growing up Muslim in the South has meant that Yusuf has always been more aware of his food than most Americans. "I didn't have that much trouble, but, like, when I went to play soccer and to soccer parties, they would always have pepperoni pizza and cheese pizza. I mean, as long as they also had cheese, I would have cheese.

Memet Arslan at Istanbul Turkish Restaurant.

And at school it wasn't that big of a problem because there were always choices. I just chose my way around it," he says.

Like his father, Yusuf is pragmatic about pork. "It's more visual for me. If I can see it in what I'm eating, I try not to eat it. Accidents have happened. I mean, sometimes I buy something or someone gives me something, and I eat it to make them happy."

When Yusuf was younger, his parents helped people understand his dietary restrictions. "When I was in elementary school, they actually did go to the school and explain to them. Some days I would have different meals."

Memet is happy and proud that meals were the only things his children had to deal with in school. They never experienced religious intolerance, and their friends and those friends' families welcomed them into the community and into their homes. "They make friends. They go out. Their friends have family—they don't care, no, no, not for religion, no."

Perhaps as a result of raising his children in such a friendly and accepting environment, Memet truly feels at home in Nashville. "I love this country; I stay in this country. I have lived in this country for nineteen years, and for religion, anything, no problems. Absolutely."

TARHANA ÇORBASI (Turkish-Style Yogurt Soup)

Active cooking time: 25 minutes | Total cooking time: 1 hour, 30 minutes | Yield: 4 to 6 main dish servings

People have been making and eating yogurt for almost 6,000 years. As a cultured dairy product, yogurt has nutritional benefits that milk alone does not. Because most of the lactose in the milk used for yogurt is converted to lactic acid, yogurt is a dairy product that even the lactose-intolerant can enjoy.

While it is commonly believed that yogurt originated in Eastern Europe, it is the base for many soups, dips, spreads, and beverages throughout the Middle East. In fact, the English word "yogurt" comes from the Turkish name for the dish, *yoğurt*.

Normally, Turkish meals begin with a soup, and *tarhana* is one of the more common soups served in Turkey. Made with flour, yogurt, and spices, it is traditionally fermented and dried to be reconstituted into a thick soup with just the addition of hot water.

Don't be tempted to use low-fat or fat-free yogurt. The dish needs the fat from the yogurt to make a rich and creamy soup. Strained yogurt will produce a thicker soup with a tangier flavor.

4 cups plain yogurt

½ cup vegetable oil

1½ teaspoons mint, minced

½ teaspoon Aleppo pepper

3 cloves garlic, minced
(about 1½ teaspoons)

1 cup all-purpose flour

¼ cup paprika (half-sharp
if available)

½ gallon water

Salt

Kitchen Passport Paprika is the dominant spice flavor in this soup. A sweeter paprika will yield a sweeter soup, and a sharp paprika will add heat. Consider using smoked Spanish paprika, sometimes labeled pimentón, for its smoky heat.

Aleppo pepper is an unusual ingredient, but it can be found at specialty spice stores or in some Middle Eastern markets. If you can't find it, substitute ¼ teaspoon cayenne pepper or ancho chile powder.

Strain the yogurt by pouring it into a fine-mesh sieve placed over a bowl; let it drain for 30 minutes.

Discard any liquid that collects in the bowl. You should have approximately 3 cups of strained yogurt when you continue with the recipe.

Heat the oil in a stockpot over medium heat.

Add the mint, Aleppo pepper, and garlic and cook, stirring constantly, for 2 minutes or until the garlic is tender and fragrant.

Add the flour and continue to cook, stirring constantly, for 3 minutes or until the flour mixture begins to brown.

Add the paprika to the flour and stir to form a thick paste.

Gradually add the water, stirring in a small amount before adding more in order to prevent lumps. Bring the mixture to a boil and then reduce the heat to low.

Transfer the yogurt to a large bowl. Add ½ cup of the soup mixture to the strained yogurt, stirring to combine thoroughly. Repeat until the yogurt mixture has the same consistency as the soup.

Add the yogurt mixture to the stockpot and stir in thoroughly. Continue cooking for 20 minutes or until the yogurt has warmed through without coming to a boil.

Add salt to taste.

Most great New Orleans restaurants have a great bar. Domenica in the Roosevelt Hotel is no exception. A long oak bar overlooks the modern and comfortable dining space. At one end, however, the bar transforms. The oak top gives way to granite, and shelves of bottles give way to glass-fronted cases filled with a remarkable assortment of *salumi*, Italian cured meats, many of them made from pork.

*Alon Shaya,
New Orleans,
Louisiana*

Sitting in front of these cases filled with his work, Chef Alon Shaya speaks passionately about food and life. All the while, the listener can't help but observe the paradox of Alon, a Jewish immigrant who has become a master of pork.

Alon was born in Bat Yam, Israel, a beach town just south of Tel Aviv. He was only four years old when he came to the United States. His father was the one who lived the true immigrant experience. "My dad was kind of in search of the American dream, a better life. He had a business in Israel that he wasn't very happy with, and he came to America to start a new life for him and his family. At the time, he couldn't afford to bring the entire family along, so he came to America by himself. He didn't speak a lick of English. He went to Philadelphia and had, I think, $200 in his pocket and just started from scratch."

By chance, Alon's father met people who spoke Hungarian, his native language. They were seeking someone with his mechanical skills, so he found a job. "That was in 1979. I was only one year old," Alon says. "And it took him about three years of working and raising money to move the rest of the family."

It might seem that since Alon was very young when he came to the United States, he would have been able to ease into life in America. But from an early age, he too worked hard to achieve the American dream. "About a year after we were back together, my parents got divorced, so then my mom took my sister and me and moved to another part of town. My mom was working two jobs. My older sister and I fended for ourselves growing up."

Fending for themselves included cooking, and he will always carry that with him. "From the time I was nine, I was cooking for the family while my mom was working. I was preheating the oven and baking cookies and making potatoes and chicken and all these different things."

As taking care of himself increasingly became taking care of his family, Alon began to delve further into food. "I was fourteen when I got my first job in an Italian butcher shop. It was really to take some stress off of my mother financially. I was also, at that point in my life, getting into a lot of trouble, kind of going down the wrong path, and it was a way for me to get back on track," he says.

"At the time, I was just doing it to make money—but now that I look back at it, I realize that cooking really saved me from ending up either in jail or dead. So once I found food, I was able to kind of regain focus and get excited about something other than getting in trouble."

For Alon, food, which had gotten him back on track, was soon to become his career path. All it took was one teacher who saw his potential. "I was in high school, and I took a home economics class so that I didn't have to sit in real class, you know, and my home ec teacher really saw something in me. She's the one that got me my first job at a restaurant when I was sixteen," he says. "She was really one of the first teachers I had that complimented me and believed in me. I think that everybody else just kind of wrote me off as the bad kid. All they wanted to do was keep me quiet. She really wanted to let my talents shine."

After high school, Alon worked his way through the Culinary Institute of America in Hyde Park, New York. Not knowing from semester to semester whether he would have enough money to continue, he made it through with occasional loans from his family. After graduating, he moved to Las Vegas with a friend to work in casino kitchens.

Once there, Alon's career began to skyrocket. He worked for the great chef Jean Louis Palladin, then landed a job at the Rio in its Italian restaurant, Antonio's, where his efforts earned him a sous chef position. This hard work led him to the next steps along his path. "Harrah's Corporation bought the Rio where I was working. Harrah's had a property in St. Louis, where they wanted to open an Antonio's because it was such a huge hit in Las Vegas. They transferred me out there to be the chef of that restaurant at the age of twenty-one," he says.

"Up there I met a friend named Octavio Mantilla, who is now John Besh's business partner in his restaurant group. When Octavio came back to New Orleans to work with John, he enticed me to come and work down here.

"So that's what happened. I came down here, met John, started working with them, and I've been in New Orleans ever since. And I really fell in love with the South, fell in love with New Orleans and the lifestyle and the culture down here. It was really something that appealed to me."

Like his father, Alon succeeded with hard work and a bit of luck. Thanks to a push in the right direction from a good teacher, he is now a celebrated young chef in one of the world's premiere food towns. But still, how did an immigrant from Israel who grew up in Philadelphia end up serving authentically prepared regional Italian cuisine?

The way Alon explains it, it started with flavor. "I grew up eating traditional Israeli food, and those flavors and the Italian flavors are very similar. It's Mediterranean. It's eggplant. It's roasted peppers. It's olive oil. It's chickpeas. It's garlic. All these different spices and vegetables that I grew up with are very similar in Italian cuisine."

His interest in Italian food was born in Philadelphia. "There were a lot of Italians in Philadelphia. I wouldn't necessarily call the neighborhood I grew up in an Italian neighborhood, but there was a lot of great Italian food there, which I started cooking."

When Alon was offered the opportunity to become the executive chef at Domenica, he decided that he needed to learn more about true Italian cuisine than he could gather from books or from restaurants in America. He spent a year in Italy, working at small regional restaurants, learning how Italians used the ingredients available locally.

When he came back to Domenica, he brought that knowledge with him. "The *polenta e osei* on the menu is only found in a town called Bergamo in northern Italy. It doesn't exist anywhere else in the country. You don't see it in Sicily; you don't see it anywhere else. The octopus carpaccio I serve comes from the shores along Tuscany. So that's really the approach that I've tried to take with the restaurant," he explains.

"The menu is very reflective of my personal history and travels. There are a couple of odes to my grandmother on the menu—the caponata is something she used to make a version of. I'm really having fun with playing off of my history and the history of these small towns in Italy and then bringing it to New Orleans and introducing people to it."

But he's also teaching his diners that Italian food is more than garlic, oregano, and olive oil. It's even more than regional differences. "There's no secret ingredient that makes something Italian. It's a combination of culture and history that defines what Italian food is."

In his restaurant, Alon presents the Italian food born of that combination. He also uses his platform to present another combination: that of Jewish culture and Roman cuisine. "We did a Passover menu here at Domenica that was Roman-style Passover. We were baking matzo in our wood-burning oven. We made *haroset* from my grandmother's *haroset* recipe and did gefilte fish with Mediterranean *branzino*. And it was kosher-style, meaning that there wasn't any meat and dairy mixed and there wasn't any shellfish or pork products. We didn't serve any type of leavened products with the menu. So it was kosher style in an Italian way in New Orleans."

He wasn't sure how the menu would be received, but it was such a success that he plans to offer it again. "We had people in here eating the Passover menu who were in tears because they thought it was just great that a restaurant would bake matzo in a wood-burning oven or because the *haroset* reminded them of their grandmother's," he says.

"As a chef, I want to taste something that reminds me of something. If your grandmother used to make *haroset* a certain way and you haven't had it since she made it, then to taste it again somewhere that you never thought you would even experience it, that can really bring back some strong feelings. And that's why I think food is beautiful—because it can touch emotions."

Alon is more than a success; he may very well be the epitome of the American dream. "I think one of the beauties of all this is that I'm an Israeli person cooking regional Italian food in the south of America. I would say that America is such a wonderful place because it allows this type of stuff to happen," he explains. "You know, if I went to Italy as an Israeli and opened up a southern fried chicken shop, it probably wouldn't take off very well because people are very close to their traditions and their customs, and that's the beauty of that area. That's why we go out there to learn what they've been doing for a couple hundred years," he says.

"But that's why I think it's so interesting here; it really allows us to do these kinds of things and have fun with it. And that's why I love food. I'm a poor kid that was on the wrong side of the tracks in Philadelphia that has made friends and had very interesting conversations with some very, very influential people in the world. And that's not because I won the Nobel Peace Prize. It's because I've learned how to cook, and you never know who you're going to touch in what way, but I've found connections with people through food, and that is priceless to me." ✎

CARCIOFI ALLA GUIDEA (Roman-Style Fried Artichokes)

Active cooking time: 35 minutes | Total cooking time: 1 hour, 25 minutes
Yield: 4 appetizer or side dish servings

Alon first encountered these delicious treats as street food in the Jewish quarter of Rome. They're a specialty of that particular area and are rarely found outside of it. This was the dish that made him feel most connected to his Jewish roots while he was studying the cuisine of Italy. "To me, it is a dish of a group of people moving to an unfamiliar land and mixing what they know with the ingredients that are locally available and creating a cuisine out of that. And that dish you don't find in Israel. You only find it in Rome, or in Italy. But it wouldn't be there if the Jews never immigrated there," he says. "So that's what I love about food. And that's why I hope I'm creating a little bit of an influence in New Orleans with food that way."

You may not be familiar with preparing artichokes in your kitchen. They aren't very common in American cuisine. Alon puts it simply, "I think a lot of people get very nervous when they cook things that they haven't cooked before. But if you have a fundamental base of cooking knowledge, you can really use that for anything."

When you're buying artichokes, look for ones with tight leaves. If the outer leaves are loose, the artichoke is not as fresh and will fall apart when you prepare it. This is a dish that takes some effort, especially with a potentially unfamiliar ingredient, but the treat you end up with is crispy on the outside and almost creamy on the inside. The contrast of the fresh flavor of the artichoke with the sweetness of balsamic vinegar makes a perfect combination.

Alon's final advice for the home cook is advice that is close to his own heart. "I would say the most important thing is keep it simple, buy local, and really just have fun with it. But do something that means something to you."

4 Roman or globe artichokes

1 cup lemon juice

1 bottle dry white Italian wine

2 whole lemons

7 tablespoons salt, divided

Peanut or soy oil

1 teaspoon freshly ground black
  pepper

TO SERVE

Aged balsamic vinegar

SPECIAL EQUIPMENT

4 10-inch wooden or bamboo
  skewers

To clean the artichokes, start by peeling off and discarding the hard outer leaves. Cut at least 2 inches from the top of each artichoke so that you have removed the pointed tips from the majority of the remaining leaves and have exposed the purple-tipped inner leaves.

Using a paring knife, peel the hard skin from the artichoke stem until the white inner meat of the stem is exposed. Trim off any remaining pieces of the hard leaves around the base of the artichoke heart.

Place the prepared artichokes in a bowl of water with the lemon juice to prevent discoloration.

In a large stockpot, bring 1 gallon of water and the white wine to a simmer with the lemons and 6 tablespoons of salt.

Add the artichokes and poach in the simmering liquid for 15 minutes or until tender enough to poke a knife tip into the heart.

Place the artichokes cut side down on your work surface to allow any excess liquid to drain.

In a deep pot or deep fat fryer, heat at least 3 inches of oil to 360 degrees.

When the artichokes have cooled enough to handle, spread the leaves apart gently to expose the purple-tipped inner leaves. Using your fingers, carefully pull out these leaves to expose the choke, the hairy, inedible part at the center of the artichoke. Use a teaspoon to scrape out all of the choke, leaving a smooth base of artichoke heart.

Hold the artichoke gently in your hand. Insert a 10-inch wooden skewer into the stem of each artichoke. Gently spread the leaves so that the artichoke will "bloom" in the hot oil.

Holding the skewer, carefully lower the artichokes one at a time into the hot oil. The artichokes will have retained a lot of liquid, so there will be popping oil. Allow the artichoke to cook for 3 to 4 minutes or until golden brown and crispy. Transfer the artichokes to a paper-towel-lined plate and sprinkle with the remaining salt and black pepper.

Allow the artichokes to rest for 10 minutes.

Serve the artichokes with a drizzle of aged balsamic vinegar.

"In Lebanon, we don't even have pies!" Marie Husni exclaims, laughing. She's describing how she's tried to teach her family in Lebanon to make some of the American dishes she has come to love since she made her home in Oxford, Mississippi.

Pies weren't the only American food that her family was unfamiliar with. "I had to take them the chocolate chip bag to show them what it is; then we had to go find it. That was the first time they tasted chocolate chip cookies."

It may seem odd that Marie would take American dishes to Lebanon, but it's just in her nature to want to experience new flavors and share them with the people she loves. "I was always very curious. I always ask questions, especially about cooking. 'Oh, I love this! How did you make it?' You know, that's how I do. I always did."

That openness and natural curiosity served Marie well when she and her husband moved to the South in 1978. They didn't get a lot of time to make a decision about coming to the United States. "He got a scholarship they hadn't told him about. So, they said, 'You have three weeks to decide if you're gonna take it or leave it.'"

They came directly to the South, making their first home in the United States in Denton, Texas. "We stayed there one year and a half while he finished his master's degree and I had a child."

One of Marie's most vivid memories of Denton is learning to speak English. "I started learning English at that time because I knew no English. I took a mini course, a $10 course. And then I would hold onto my husband's arm, going around to just talk to people. I would talk to him in Arabic, and he would state my words in English. I would try to listen as much as I could," she recalls. "I knew a lot of French, and my parents were in Africa, so they spoke Creole. So I'd heard them speak a little English, but it's not something that I spoke at all."

Learning English was an important step for Marie. When her husband applied for his Ph.D. at a school in Columbia, Missouri, she decided to go to school as well. "I had another child there, and I got my bachelor's degree over there, a Bachelor of Science in Mathematics."

Her husband finished his Ph.D. and took a job in Oxford, Mississippi, in 1984. Marie continued her education: "I decided to go to school and finish my master's degree; I was pregnant at the time when I was defending my thesis. After that, I was teaching as an instructor off and on. Then I decided to go on for my Ph.D., and I worked three years. I had one course left; I did not finish it." In 2001, Marie decided to start over on her doctorate, earning her degree in higher education in 2006.

Food remained an important part of Marie's life, no matter where she lived or how busy she was. After all, feeding a large, busy family was nothing new to her. "I have loved to cook since I was twelve years old. There were ten kids in my family, so my mom used to put me down for three hours with the grape leaves and the stuffing and everything, and I would be rolling them. I didn't cook, but I did all the material preparation for her."

Marie used food to get to know her neighbors in Oxford and to practice Lebanese hospitality. "Twice a week I invited people to my house. They loved it. I always invited people. That's how we are, the Lebanese. You know, we invite people all the time."

Food was the reason Marie stayed in Oxford after she stopped working on her first Ph.D. in 1991. She had considered moving away with the children to finish her degree somewhere else, but her husband had a different idea. "That's when he said, 'Okay, I know you're a good cook; everybody keeps praising your cooking. Let's open up a restaurant.' So, at that point, there was a place off the Oxford town square, and the rent was $500. So I sat down for two months, decorating and designing, deciding the menu, and that was it."

Her restaurant, Marie's Lebanese Cuisine, has since moved from its original location, but the menu has remained the same. That menu includes no dishes containing pork, prohibited by the laws of both kosher and halal, but Marie is Christian. For her, leaving out pork is not a religious or taste decision; instead, it's a matter of tradition. "It's just that Lebanese don't have dishes with pork at all, because it's not available. My sister knew somebody who raised pigs and she brought something once to eat, but I never tasted it."

Marie's first taste of pork didn't come until later in her life. "When we were married, we went for our honeymoon in Greece, and they had meat on skewers on the street where you would buy it and eat it. We asked them, 'What is that?' and they made an 'oink oink' noise because they didn't speak any English. It was the first time we tasted it."

As a first-generation immigrant, Lebanese tradition is very strong for Marie. But she has learned that for Lebanese families who have lived in the South for generations, the lines between Lebanese tradition and southern tradition have blurred. "People come into the restaurant and say, 'Ohhh, but my grandma, the second or third generation of Lebanese in Mississippi, used pecans in her baklava. That was real baklava.' But in Lebanon, we don't even have pecans!"

Serving authentic Lebanese cuisine is very important to Marie, but she admits that it does mean putting her heart on her sleeve. "Sometimes when people come, they look at the menu and say, 'Oh, you don't have pizza?' and get up and leave. That's really awful to do, to come in and say that! And I say, 'Why did you come in to tell me that?' That hurts my feelings! It does! Because you knew it's Lebanese, not Italian. We do pizza for the kids. But you know you have to accept to sit down first before we can treat you right. So that's what happens. Oh yeah, we get hurt all the time!"

But there are also great rewards for Marie. "You have to have your own niche. You have to have your own taste, your own flavor, your own love for those people. You have to enjoy them. I enjoy every single one of them when they come in, I really do. And Lebanese cuisine is just delicious and exquisite. I really think so. I love Lebanese food. So, I just won't replace it for anything else. I won't." 🖬

KIBBEH (Lebanese-Style Meat Pie)

Active cooking time: 1 hour | Total cooking time: 2 hours | Yield: 8 to 10 main dish servings

Kibbeh is a deceptively simple dish found in different forms all over the Middle East. The blend of meat, spices, and bulgur provides contrasts of flavors and textures that are the result of millennia of practice in the home kitchens of the region. While no single nation can claim to be the originator of kibbeh, it is most closely associated with Lebanon, where it has been named the country's national dish.

The word "kibbeh" is derived from the Arabic word *kubbah*, meaning "ball." Kibbeh itself can be served as balls, patties, or football-shaped croquettes or pressed into pies. It can be fried, baked, boiled in broth, or served raw. The fried croquettes are perhaps the most popular presentation of the dish in the United States, but Marie has a different view on that technique. "Everyone that comes from Lebanon says that my food is 100 percent authentic. It did not change when I came here. In fact, many times they have asked me, 'Can you serve only fried kibbeh?' I tell them, 'Nope, we only do fried kibbeh for parties!' I have raw kibbeh in the freezer, so I'm ready whenever somebody comes and wants fried kibbeh. I could fry it for them. But we don't serve it that way all the time. I don't change."

FOR THE CRUST

2 medium yellow onions, roughly chopped

2 cups cracked wheat (bulgur)

2 pounds ground lamb

2 teaspoons oregano

2 teaspoons ground cumin

¼ teaspoon ground cayenne pepper

1 tablespoon salt

1 teaspoon freshly ground black pepper

1 cup ice water

TO PREPARE THE CRUST

Preheat the oven to 350 degrees.

Add the roughly chopped onions to a food processor and process until the onions are diced. Transfer the diced onions to a large bowl.

Rinse the bulgur in a fine mesh sieve. Transfer the bulgur to the bowl with the onions one handful at a time, squeezing tightly to remove any excess water.

FOR THE FILLING

¼ cup olive or vegetable oil

1 large yellow onion, chopped
   (about 1 cup)

½ cup pine nuts

1 pound ground lamb

½ teaspoon cinnamon

½ teaspoon nutmeg

½ teaspoon allspice

1½ teaspoons salt

1 teaspoon freshly ground black
   pepper

TO FINISH

8 tablespoons butter, softened
   (1 stick)

Add the 2 pounds of ground lamb, oregano, cumin, cayenne pepper, salt, and black pepper to the bowl with the onions and bulgur. Stir to combine.

Working in batches, process the ingredients in the food processor, adding the ice water as needed, until a smooth paste is formed. Combine all batches into one, stirring to combine.

TO PREPARE THE FILLING

Heat the oil in a large skillet over medium heat.

Cook the chopped onion, stirring constantly, for 5 minutes or until soft and translucent.

Add the pine nuts and cook for another 5 minutes or until the pine nuts have browned.

Add the pound of ground lamb and continue cooking for another 5 minutes or until the meat has browned.

Drain off and discard all excess juices and oil. Add the cinnamon, nutmeg, allspice, salt, and black pepper, stirring to combine.

TO FINISH THE DISH

In a 9-by-13-inch baking dish, spread half of the crust mixture evenly over the bottom using wet hands, pressing up at the sides as you would a pie crust.

Spread the filling evenly over the crust mixture.

Top the filling with an even layer of the remaining crust mixture, using wet hands to form a smooth surface.

With a wet, sharp knife, gently cut the kibbeh with evenly spaced diagonal lines, making large diamond-shaped pieces.

With a wet knife, gently loosen the kibbeh from the edges of the pan. Score the center of each diamond-shaped piece by shallowly inserting the knife and removing it.

Spread the butter evenly across the top of the scored kibbeh.

Place the kibbeh on the bottom shelf of the oven and cook for 45 to 60 minutes or until the kibbeh moves when you move the pan.

Transfer the kibbeh to a hot broiler and cook for 3 minutes to brown and crisp the top.

Remove the kibbeh from the oven, drain off any excess fat, and cover until ready to serve.

Europe
Haute Cuisine and Double Standards?

Spectacular food is prepared in every corner of the world. Dishes from the simplest stews to the most complexly seasoned curries make superb meals. But in spite of the ever-increasing availability of delicious international foods in the United States, is there a bias in favor of European cuisine?

When you think of French and Italian food in American pop culture, three icons stand out. One is an improbably tall woman with a distinctive voice; the other two are cartoon dogs. Through her books and television shows, Julia Child demonstrated how remarkable French cuisine could be. Her folksy and endearing manner convinced many Americans that the food of France was not beyond them. And the "Bella Notte" scene in Disney's *Lady and the Tramp* marked Italian food as the food of romance and passion with its starlit serenade, slurped spaghetti, and stolen kisses.

Of course, popular culture shows a negative side, too, from the snooty French maître d' sneering at customers to countless mobster films with signature red-checked tablecloths, candlelight, and breadsticks as the backdrop for deals and death.

But what are the actual experiences of French and Italian restaurant owners in the United States? And what about restaurant owners from other parts of Europe? After all, there's more to Europe and European food than just France and Italy.

Benedicte Cooper owns Café Alsace, a small, well-received French café in Decatur, Georgia. She defies the image of the snooty maître d' in every way. Nonetheless, she is proud of her French heritage and of her particular corner of France. "I come from Colmar, which is in Alsace, which is the northeastern part of France. Alsace-Lorraine is on the border with Germany and Switzerland. So in that specific area, you have a strong German influence since it's been invaded by the Germans back and forth," she explains.

Benedicte Cooper, Decatur, Georgia

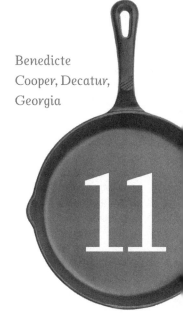

11

Lea and Benedicte Cooper at Café Alsace.

"The food is a little bit different than in the rest of France. You have a little bit more pork. You have the sauerkraut. You have spaetzle. We mix French food with German food. The culture and the mentality are a little bit different, and that's where I come from."

Where she has arrived is a little bit different as well. In the 1830s, the Western and Atlantic Railroad suggested that Decatur be the southern terminus of a line from Chattanooga, Tennessee. The residents of Decatur declined, not wanting their town to be so significantly affected. The railroad then chose to build a new city to the west, a city that was to be called Atlanta.

The residents of Decatur appear to have had the right idea, however. In spite of being a suburb of a sprawling metropolis like Atlanta, Decatur has a culture and mentality all its own. Today, it features elegant old homes and beautiful green spaces. The town square blends quaint bookstores and pubs with a link to the big city, a subway station tucked out of sight under the square.

During the post-9/11 French boycott, Benedicte was part of a survey of French-owned businesses. The survey was to investigate the impact of the boycott on business, and Benedicte's answer was so surprising that the survey's organizer contacted her. "Our sales were higher during that period," Benedicte explains. "People were wonderful. It's such a great community. I think that's why I did stay in the United States. Decatur's like a little European town. People know each other. You help each other." It was that spirit that helped Café Alsace survive when other French-owned businesses—restaurants especially—did not.

Initially, it wasn't the charm of Decatur that led Benedicte here. Rather, it was that her other option was not her style. As a student in France, she took part in a program that provided a green card and a list of potential summer employers in the United States. She sent in applications and got two responses. Ironically, she passed up a chance to work close to the largest reminder of France in the United States: "I could have worked at the gift shop of the Statue of Liberty. I was really scared to move from France, from Alsace, to New York. It was a little bit too radical, so I chose Atlanta."

In Atlanta, she made her first professional foray into the world of food service. "There was an ice cream company that provided trucks and all that. So I chose Atlanta and sold those ice creams in the summer, which was neat because I was not in an office. You meet tons of people all day long. I came back three times, three summers."

After her last summer, she returned to France to begin a career. She found herself stuck in the slow-moving French work environment, wanting to succeed but unable to advance as quickly as she hoped. To her parents' dismay, she quit her job.

When she decided to try something new, she returned to Decatur. "I said, 'I just need to try it. If it doesn't work, I'll do anything, fine. But I need to try it.' And I'm glad I did," she laughs.

During her third summer in the student work program, she had stayed at a youth hostel in Decatur and befriended the owner. "I came here on vacation and stayed at the youth hostel. I went to a party and actually met my husband. And that's how it happened. I moved here and worked at the youth hostel."

At the time, she had no idea that her ice cream truck days were only the beginning of her life in food, but then her friend the hostel owner came to her with an idea—opening a tea room. Although working with food wasn't part of her plan, Benedicte already had a very definite opinion about the French food she encountered in the United States. "I was so disappointed when I moved here because all the French restaurants were upscale and very old France and very dramatic and expensive and not fun. You would always find the same food. You would find French onion soup and crème brûlée."

But while that stiff formality wasn't what she wanted, she wasn't willing to give in to the American idea of convenience either. "He wanted to do a drive-through kind of tea room, and I didn't agree with that. I said if you want to do a tea room, you should do it the European way where you sit down and have tea and relax and have a pastry."

The business grew until her hard work led to the sort of opportunity that had eluded her in France. "One day the owner of the building here, who was one of our regular customers at the tea room, approached me and said, 'I love what you have done with the tea room. I have an open space, and I would like to do something friendly like that. Would you come and visit that place and tell me what to do?'" she says.

"I had never thought of opening a place. But I worked long hours at the tea room, and it was not mine, and so I was a bit frustrated there. Then I visited here, and I said, 'Well, you know, I think I can do something with it.' So that's how it started."

From the beginning, Benedicte had a sensible business plan, choosing not to overextend her finances. "I just wanted it small because I could control it and manage it. The costs were low."

She wanted to keep her menu in line as well. "I said, 'I want to do something very homey and very simple, and then we'll see.' So we started with just quiches and soups and salads, just very casual, lower prices." Initially, she also refused to include some things on her menu. "When we first opened here, I said no crème brûlée, no French onion soup, because you don't necessarily have it in France. I think I had my first crème brûlée here in the U.S.," she laughs.

The menu was a success, but her customers also came to her with unexpected requests. "At the beginning, I had a business partner, and we both came from Alsace, and we were looking for a name, and we said, 'Let's do Café Alsace.' We wanted to do a French restaurant, but then we realized that when the people saw Café Alsace, they wanted something from Alsace. We had that feedback constantly, so we said, 'I guess we need to do something from Alsace.'"

Now her menu offers traditional French and Alsatian dishes. Her customers leave full and happy and come back gladly. And she has found success defying even her own expectations of a French restaurant. "I think the restaurant was successful because it was a French restaurant showing something a little bit different than what people were used to," she says. "I think the food contributes a lot because it's different, but I think it's the atmosphere, too, and me and the waitresses. And people can just peek in and talk with the chef, and he's fine with that. It's like a big family." 🍃

TARTE FLAMBÉE (Alsatian-Style Flatbread with Bacon and Onions)

Active cooking time: 1 hour, 10 minutes | Total cooking time: 1 hour, 25 minutes + 2 hours
Yield: 4 main dish servings

Throughout Alsace, small cafés often transform their bread ovens in the evenings. The brick hearths stay hot and ready to quickly toast the thin crusts of *tartes flambées*. This pizza-like dish is a favorite of casual weekend diners and tourists alike.

Benedicte remembers going out on Friday evenings to share a *tarte flambée* with friends. Each café has a slightly different version. It's a simple dish, and yet the combination of flavors is uniquely Alsatian.

In this version, beer adds a slightly bitter flavor to the crust. The thickness and crispiness is reminiscent of New York–style pizza. You should be able to fold the slices.

For the topping, sweet caramelized onions blend with rich cream before being topped with smoky bacon. It may seem unorthodox, but it's a perfect comfort food.

FOR THE CRUST

1 teaspoon active dry yeast (½ packet)
1½ cups (about 7 ounces)
    all-purpose flour
1 teaspoon salt
½ cup beer, room temperature
1 tablespoon unsalted butter, melted

TO PREPARE THE CRUST

Combine the yeast, flour, and salt in a large bowl, stirring with a fork to distribute the yeast and salt evenly through the flour.

Create a well in the center of the flour mixture. Add the beer gradually, stirring to create a paste in the well. Add the butter

FOR THE TOPPING

8 ounces bacon, cut into
    ¼-inch strips
1 medium yellow onion,
    minced (about ⅔ cup)
1 cup crème fraîche
¼ teaspoon freshly ground
    nutmeg
Salt
Freshly ground black pepper

Kitchen Passport If you have a favorite pizza crust recipe, feel free to use it instead of the one given here. The only requirement is that the crust should be thin.

The toppings can be varied as well. Try replacing ¼ cup crème fraîche with quark cheese or whipped Neufchâtel. Add aromatic herbs like thyme or rosemary to the onion as it browns. Try using thin slices of pork jowl or ham instead of the bacon, or leave the meat out entirely for a vegetarian version.

and work the paste into the remaining flour mixture.

Turn the dough out onto a floured work surface and knead for 5 to 8 minutes.

Form the dough into a ball and place it in a bowl. Cover the bowl with a damp cloth and allow the dough to rise for 2 hours.

Flour your hands and knead the dough for 1 to 2 minutes, just enough to deflate it.

The dough can be used immediately or wrapped tightly in plastic wrap and refrigerated for up to 3 days. Bring the dough to room temperature before rolling if refrigerated.

TO PREPARE THE TOPPING

Heat a heavy-bottomed skillet over medium heat.

Add the bacon strips and cook for 10 minutes or until the bacon is beginning to crisp. Transfer the bacon to a paper-towel-lined plate to drain. Retain the bacon drippings in the skillet.

Add the onion to the skillet and cook, stirring often, for 30 minutes or until the onion is light brown.

In a large bowl, stir the crème fraîche until smooth. Add the ground nutmeg and the cooked onion. Stir to combine and add salt and black pepper to taste.

TO FINISH THE DISH

Preheat the oven to 450 degrees.

Roll the prepared dough into a thin round.

Spread the crème fraîche mixture over the round, leaving a ½-inch border. Sprinkle the bacon over the top.

Bake the *tarte* on a pizza stone, pizza pan, or baking sheet for 12 to 15 minutes or until the crust is golden brown but still tender.

Laurent Desmet and his parents, Clementine and Daniel, came to the United States from Belgium in order to open a restaurant. After visiting several cities, they settled on Gretna, Louisiana, just across the Mississippi River from New Orleans. "We knew somebody who was living here. I guess the atmosphere, the friendliness of people, was the main factor that made us choose the city. Plus, economically, it's much more affordable than a large city," Laurent says.

A restaurant was a natural choice, an obvious choice, for the Desmet family. Speaking about his mother, Laurent says, "It's a long family tradition. She was in the restaurant business since she was a kid because her parents had a restaurant, too."

Clementine says, "My father and mama had a restaurant—my sister, too, my brother." She is happy that the tradition is being carried on by at least part of her family. "My three daughters did not get the restaurant from me. Two are teachers; one is a decorator. I give my savoir faire to my son."

Laurent sees it slightly differently. "I'm the one that got cursed," he laughs.

Whether they are in the restaurant business or not, each member of the family has a passion for creativity and for working with people. Translating for his mother, Laurent says, "Cooking was the only thing she ever did, cooking and operating a business, a restaurant. If she had to do something different, it would be something in connection with people. She needs an audience."

Laurent demonstrates his creativity both in and out of the kitchen. His handiwork is evident in the restaurant, Clementine Belgian Bistrot, particularly on one wall where he has painted a mural of the city of Brussels. "You see the painting there? I did it. I did the floor, the concrete. I do a lot of different things."

Still, Laurent's heart is in the kitchen because of a love for food he learned early on. "You're not going to believe me, but every day I had fresh vegetables. Even though they were working—and maybe it's an advantage to parents working in the restaurant business—every day I had leeks or broccoli or fresh vegetables," he says. "That means going to get them, washing them, and cooking them. It's work, you know. The modern life doesn't really allow everybody to do that. Now when I think about it, it's really something amazing."

Bringing Belgian cuisine to the United States has not been easy, because some ingredients are difficult to find. "There's a traditional dish in Belgium made with eel, and it's very popular. I mean, it's delicious. We couldn't find it. I found frozen eel in an Asian market, but it was

Laurent Desmet
at Clementine
Belgian Bistrot.

not the same, not at all. And when I asked my seafood supplier for eel,
he almost laughed. 'Eel?' He was very surprised," Laurent says.

"It's more difficult to find rabbit. You can find rabbit in grocery
stores in Belgium. Here, it is more like a specialty item that you need
to hunt for." But not a literal hunt. "You can find people hunting rabbit,
and they can sell it to you, but I'm not speaking about the wild rabbit.
I'm speaking about the domestic rabbit," Laurent explains.

One ingredient that has been available is a crucial one—mussels. Mussels are the main ingredient in Clementine's signature dish,
moules frites, mussels and fried potatoes. Still, in an area so famous
for seafood, the mussels aren't local. "That type of mussels, the blue
mussels, needs the colder water. The ones from Canada are really good.
They're as good as the ones we find in Europe. That was a good surprise," Laurent says.

Ingredients aside, surely life was made easier for a French-speaking
family starting a business just a few miles from the French Quarter.
As it turns out, no. "I never met anybody who spoke French with me,
and sometimes my feeling is it's almost more a folkloric tourist picture,

that French background about New Orleans," Laurent says. "It existed; although historically, the Spanish influence is stronger than the French one. But you never meet it in your daily life. I met a few people speaking Cajun, my neighbor across the street. My sister in Lafayette, she felt that influence much more. French is alive there."

Now that the business is started, does the glamour of being a European restaurant give Clementine's an advantage? "I don't know that we have any advantage. We're Belgian. A lot of people wouldn't know what that means."

Even for a Belgian chef, it's not necessarily easy to explain the cuisine of his native land. "Belgium is famous for the beers, chocolate, and fries. We have shops where they sell fries in the street in Brussels," Laurent says. Yes, French fries are a Belgian invention, and they are every bit as popular there as they are here.

Beyond that, Laurent doesn't provide specifics. He isn't stumped. He just acknowledges the difficulty of categorizing anything as local when the world has always been in motion. "There's not one ingredient that would summarize the Belgian gastronomy. The potato is very present, but that would be the answer from somebody from Germany, too. It's probably more complex than what people think with so many influences."

The complexities of Belgian cuisine are forgotten when Laurent describes his favorite family meal. "It would be at my parents'. We have a lot of dishes, like the rabbit, that take simmering, that take a lot of time. The easy way to say it, I guess, is patience," Laurent says.

"You can make a huge pot and feed a lot of people. And it's something that would be very warm. It's that idea of getting together. I grew up with an open house," he continues. "I always had all these friends stopping by, and if there's dinner for five, there's dinner for ten or fifteen. It was like that. That's the kind of food and atmosphere I like." ▧

BELGIAN-STYLE CRÊPES

Active cooking time: 1 hour | Total cooking time: 2 hours | Yield: 18 crêpes

Another favorite for Laurent that can stretch to serve a larger than expected crowd is crêpes. Crêpes originated in Brittany, a region in the northwest part of France. While they are especially popular throughout France, they are also prevalent in Belgian kitchens. They're often served at fast food stands in both France and Belgium.

Their popularity can be attributed to their versatility. As Laurent says, "It's like a pizza. Basically you can add anything you like—ice cream, chocolate, there's no limit. You can make it salty." At Clementine's, savory crêpes stuffed with spinach or chicken and cheese are served as appetizers. Crêpes appear again on the dessert menu with sweeter options.

While Belgian crêpes appear to be identical to their French siblings, they have an important difference. "To help it rise, some people add baking powder, but in Belgium, we add beer to make the batter rise. That gives a little bitter flavor to it, which is what makes it a little different."

4 tablespoons unsalted butter, divided
1 cup whole milk
1¼ cups (12 ounces) Belgian beer
4 eggs
½ teaspoon salt
1¾ cups all-purpose flour

Kitchen Passport Crêpes are such a versatile backdrop for any combination of flavors. One classic option requires nothing more than fresh lemon juice and sugar. Squeeze lemon juice over the crêpe and dust with sugar before folding into fourths.

At Clementine's, the signature crêpe is topped with thin slices of apple and sugar. Flaming rum is poured over to caramelize the sugar, and the resulting combination is topped with a scoop of vanilla ice cream.

Crêpes can also be great building blocks. In France, a cake known as *gâteau de crêpes* is made by layering crêpes with jelly, pastry cream, sweetened mascarpone, or chocolate sauce until they reach the height of a typical layer cake. Allow your finished cake to rest for at least 2 hours to allow the flavors to soak into the crêpes for a truly decadent treat.

In a small saucepan, melt 2 tablespoons butter over medium heat.

Transfer the butter to a large bowl and add the milk and beer, whisking to combine. Whisk in the eggs one at a time, making sure each is combined with the milk mixture before adding the next egg. Add the salt and flour. Continue whisking until the batter is smooth.

Cover the bowl with a towel and allow the batter to rest at room temperature for at least 1 hour. The batter can be prepared and refrigerated for up to 12 hours in advance.

Heat a 10-inch non-stick skillet or crêpe pan over medium heat.

When the skillet is hot, brush with butter and pour in a scant ⅓ cup batter. Lift the skillet and swirl to distribute the batter evenly in as thin a layer as possible. Pour any excess batter back into the bowl.

Return the skillet to the heat and cook the crêpe for 2 minutes.

Flip the crêpe using a large turner and cook for an additional 30 seconds.

Transfer the crêpe to a plate and cover the plate with a tent of aluminum foil. Repeat the process until all the batter is used.

Serve the crêpes with your choice of fillings.

Francesco and Jeniffer Fiorello just may be the most romantic couple in food. They met when they worked together in a small Italian restaurant on Williamsburg Road in Richmond, Virginia. In a twist worthy of a fairy tale, they now have their own Italian restaurant, Francesco's Ristorante Italiano, on Richmond Road in Williamsburg, Virginia.

Francesco and Jeniffer Fiorello, Williamsburg, Virginia

Their story also has a touch of romance novel, with dashing Sicilian immigrant Francesco meeting lovely southern belle Jeniffer. Even after years of marriage, two children, and the stress of opening their own restaurant, they still have that starry-eyed joy of a twosome who have just fallen in love. Beyond completing one another's sentences, they weave sentences, especially when talking about food. A list of the different sauces Francesco makes in the kitchen practically becomes a duet with each of them complementing the other's statements.

While Francesco is in the kitchen, Jeniffer talks about what they eat at home. "I went to Sicily, and his grandmother showed me a few things. We have this traditional dish called *pasta al forno*. It's made with these little—to you I think they would look like Spaghetti-Os—little round circles. They're called *annelletti*. That means 'rings.' We start from scratch with the meat sauce. We prepare the meat sauce fresh, and then we layer it."

Later, when Francesco has returned to the table, he talks about his favorite meal, which is "anything you put on that table. I enjoy everything. That's a kind of hard question. If it just has to be one, I guess it would be *pasta al forno*." The thought leaves Francesco with a contented look while Jeniffer smiles.

They have their love of one another, but clearly they also have their shared love of food. For Francesco, that love began when he was only eight years old. It was at that age that he began learning to bake bread in a local bakery in Sicily. "When I was a little boy, I was walking, and I saw a man in a truck delivering bread. And I asked him if he needed somebody for working. He said, 'Yeah, come on.' So I just jumped in. Since then, I've been loving making bread, cooking. It became my love." That early introduction to baking left an indelible mark; Francesco bakes his own bread and makes his own pasta in his restaurant today.

Francesco's love of food was also inspired by his grandmother. Jeniffer produces a portrait of a slim and strikingly lovely Sicilian woman. "This is Francesco's grandma. She had fourteen children—six of those were sets of boy-girl twins—and this is her after her children."

Francesco's eyes go cloudy with memory as he looks at the photo. "Oh, my grandma! Oh my God, I loved her cooking. I like my grandma's cooking better than my mother's cooking."

Francesco and Jeniffer Fiorello at Francesco's Ristorante Italiano.

Francesco and Jeniffer eat traditional meals at home, food that customers in the restaurant might not initially recognize as either Italian or Sicilian cuisine. As Jeniffer describes it, "We do a lot of lentils, beans. We do a lot of stuff like that. It's so cheap, but so good once you transform it. Italian people, a lot of them are poverty-stricken, but they've always been able to eat well, so they really didn't notice."

Part of that comes from a different way of looking at food. She continues, "If you think of a steak, and you think, 'Oh, I've only got one steak. I don't think I want to have to eat that alone.' Well, nobody there is looking at it as *my* steak. They take the steak and they dice it up so small, and they put it with some beans so that the whole family can have it. They know exactly how to proportion food, to stretch it."

Francesco always had the dream of having a restaurant of his own. When he came to the United States, he brought that dream with him, although he didn't know how he would ever be able to afford it. His family and friends already in the United States lent him the money for his trip and helped him find a job when he got here. "When I came to this country, the guy from my town, he paid my ticket to get here. He's got restaurants, so I started working for him."

Once his loan was paid off, he continued working in the restaurant, gaining experience and learning new flavors and techniques. His experience formed his philosophy of the kitchen. "I learned as I went. I got more experience, I think, that way. I don't have anybody show me things. I just do and do and do. Making mistakes, I become better out of it. The more mistakes you make, the better you become."

It took an unlikely situation for him and Jeniffer to decide that the time was finally right to open a restaurant. As Jeniffer tells it, "We had a daughter in 2007, born on my mom's birthday, November 27. And then we both lost our jobs at the same time, when our daughter was five weeks old. And so we just looked at each other and said, 'You know, I think we should try now. Now's as good a time as any.' It kind of just clicked, and it was time. And here we are."

Francesco feels that having an Italian restaurant is both an advantage and a disadvantage. On one hand, people are familiar with Italian cuisine. However, some customers also have expectations or built-in misconceptions and dislikes. But since he's been in the United States, he has seen change that allows him to introduce more authentic dishes. "It changed a lot, because back then in the United States, they used to make spaghetti and meatballs and spaghetti and sausage. Now people know what they are talking about with food. So now we have a more fine-type Italian restaurant."

Today Francesco is living his dream. "When I'm standing in there cooking, I do each sauté. It makes me feel good, because I know I can get something good out of the dish. And when I bring it to the table and see people enjoy it so much, I feel even better. I like this inspiration." 🐚

INVOLTINI DI MELANZANE (Eggplant Stuffed with Pasta)

Active cooking time: 45 minutes | Total cooking time: 2 hours, 20 minutes | Yield: 6 to 8 main dish servings

Eggplant is the only member of the nightshade family that is native to the eastern hemisphere. It was first domesticated in the Southeast Asian region of India over 4,000 years ago and was introduced to Europe when the Moors brought the eggplant into Spain sometime between the fourth and seventh centuries. By the sixteenth century, eggplant was a common ingredient in southern European cuisine.

While there are many varieties of eggplant available in markets today, you will want to use the largest specimens you can find for this recipe. The larger slices will make it easier to roll the eggplant over the fillings.

Traditionally, the eggplant is breaded before being used to encase the fillings, but Francesco's baked slices make for a lighter version. The inclusion of the pasta inside the rolls means that less cheese is used as well.

2 large eggplants

2 teaspoons salt

2 tablespoons olive oil

8 ounces angel hair pasta (capellini)

8 ounces ricotta cheese

12 leaves fresh basil, cut into thin ribbons

2 ounces Parmesan cheese, grated

½ teaspoon freshly ground black pepper

4 cups marinara sauce (recipe follows), divided

8 ounces fresh mozzarella, sliced thin

Preheat the oven to 400 degrees.

Peel the eggplants and slice lengthwise into ¼-inch-thick slices. Sprinkle the slices with salt and lay them on a cooling rack over paper towels to drain for 30 minutes. This will leach out any bitterness.

Blot the eggplant slices with paper towels to remove excess moisture and salt.

Coat a baking sheet with oil. Place the eggplant slices on the baking sheet in a single layer and bake in the oven for 10 to 12 minutes or until the eggplant is pliable enough to roll.

Remove from the oven and allow the eggplant to cool to room temperature.

Cook the angel hair pasta to al dente according to package directions. Strain and reserve.

In a large mixing bowl, combine the ricotta cheese with the fresh basil, Parmesan, and black pepper.

Spread 1 cup marinara sauce in the bottom of a baking dish.

Lay out a slice of eggplant on your work surface. Mound roughly 2 tablespoons angel hair pasta in the center of the eggplant slice. Top the pasta with 2 tablespoons of the cheese mixture. Top the cheese mixture with a slice of mozzarella.

Starting at the bottom of the eggplant slice, fold the eggplant over the filling and roll the eggplant. Place the eggplant roll seam-side down in the baking dish. Repeat until all eggplant slices and fillings are used.

Cover the eggplant rolls with the remaining marinara sauce.

Bake in the oven for 1 hour or until the sauce is bubbling and the cheeses have melted.

MARINARA SAUCE (Fresh Tomato Pasta Sauce)

Active cooking time: 25 minutes | Total cooking time: 1 hour, 40 minutes | Yield: 2 quarts

2 tablespoons olive oil
1 large yellow onion, diced (about 1 cup)
3 teaspoons salt, divided
4 cloves garlic, minced (about 2 teaspoons)
¼ cup fresh oregano, minced
12 leaves fresh basil, cut into thin ribbons
¼ teaspoon ground cayenne pepper
¼ teaspoon sage
1 teaspoon freshly ground black pepper
2 (28-ounce) cans whole Italian tomatoes, preferably San Marzano

Heat the oil in a large stockpot over medium heat.

Add the onion and 1 teaspoon salt to the stockpot and cook, stirring constantly, for 5 minutes or until the onion is translucent.

Add the garlic, oregano, basil, cayenne pepper, sage, 2 teaspoons salt, and black pepper to the onion. Continue cooking, stirring constantly, for 2 more minutes.

Add the tomatoes and stir to combine with the onion mixture. Continue cooking over medium heat until the mixture begins to bubble.

Reduce the heat to low and continue simmering for 1 hour.

Blend the sauce for a smoother consistency if desired.

Influences from the New World

Imagine Italian cuisine without tomatoes or corn for polenta, or German cuisine without potatoes, or French desserts without chocolate or vanilla. What we think of today as some of the national dishes of Europe didn't exist there until explorers brought the ingredients back from the New World.

Like the potato and the eggplant, the tomato is a member of the nightshade family. The plant was first cultivated in South America, and it was there that Spanish explorers first encountered the fruit. While no exact date for the tomato's introduction in Spain is known, the plant was first written about by an Italian botanist in 1544. Not only did the Spanish introduce the tomato to Europe, they also carried it with them all over the Caribbean and to the Philippines. From there, it spread across Asia.

Corn was first domesticated in central Mexico at least 7,000 years ago. Columbus's men encountered the grain first in Cuba and carried corn back to Europe with them. It spread quickly throughout Europe, had found its way to China by 1575, and was an important part of the daily diet in the Philippines and the East Indies.

The potato is native to South America and was carried back to Spain in 1536. The Spanish used the potato to help feed their armies across their domain. While it took many years for the tuber to be accepted across Europe as a food source, it had become such a staple item in the Irish diet that a potato crop blight in 1845 contributed to the Great Irish Famine.

Columbus brought the first cocoa beans to the royal court of Spain, and they were spread across Europe by Spanish friars. After the Spanish conquest of the Aztecs, chocolate became a very popular import in Europe, where it was prized as a beverage. Vanilla is derived from a family of orchids native to Mexico. It was introduced to Europe in the 1520s by Spanish explorer Hernán Cortés, and it quickly became a rare treat.

Imports from the New World also included peppers, squash, peanuts, blueberries, and many others. As products from the Americas were integrated into European and other world cuisines, their exoticism was lost to delicious familiarity.

The Outer Banks of North Carolina are a beautiful place with a rich heritage of fishing and sailing. Today, although fishermen still ply the waves there, the area has become better known as a summer tourism destination than as a seaport. However, there is more to the region than seafood, sailing, and tourism. Just slightly inland is some of the richest soil for farming in the United States. It is here, where the breezes are still scented with the salt smell of the ocean, that Weeping Radish Farm, Brewery, and Butchery has become a local institution.

Uli Bennevitz came to the United States not to cook food but to raise it. Although many immigrants have small farms or backyard gardens so that they can enjoy the produce of their homelands, Uli's farming was on a professional level. "In Bavaria, I worked on a small farm, a neighbor's farm. And they basically raised me as their seventh child. My mother was not in farming, but I loved it," he says. "From there, I went to agricultural school, and I didn't like the all-theoretical agricultural university in Munich, so I went to England and went to an agricultural college there. First, you have to have a year practicum before they can let you in, and then you spend fourteen months in college. Then you have to go out for seven months, then you come back to college, so it's an integrated approach to agriculture. I loved it."

After college, Uli chose to come to the United States to manage large-scale farms. But why leave Europe for the United States? And if the United States, why come to the Outer Banks of North Carolina, which are far better known for seafood than for agriculture? Uli moved to the Outer Banks for that rare opportunity—the chance to make a difference.

"I could have stayed in England farming, but the problem is if you stay on a farm, you can't change anything, because the farm's always been in the same management for 200 years, and so you become one link of the chain. What attracted me to this area was that I could truly effect change in agriculture by taking younger land and turning it into farmland," he explains.

"Inland, we have beautiful blackland soils—highly productive blackland soils—and that's why I came down here. They were completely undervalued, underused, not known, and now this is some of the best-known corn and soybean land anywhere in the Southeast."

In those early years of farming in the United States, Uli had a different approach to environmental concerns than he does today. "I was actually one of those environmental bad boys—I was clearing land. I've cleared about 8,000 acres of farmland, and I make no apologies whatsoever, because my concept about land clearing is if it is good farmland,

I'm all in favor of farming it." Uli feels very strongly that the best use of land is what should be considered.

While his farm today is not as large as those he has managed, he still works with the philosophy of getting the best use out of each part of the farm. His farm manager works not only with the seasons and soil of the Outer Banks but also with the phases of the moon, planting and harvesting at the optimal cycles in the lives of the plants. Where land was not optimal for farming, Uli has retention ponds, chickens, and goats.

In addition to his career in agriculture, Uli, like so many immigrants, decided to bring a taste of his homeland to the United States. For twenty-one years, he owned a Bavarian restaurant in the Outer Banks. "It took me that long to figure out that that was a stupid thing to do, have a Bavarian restaurant in the South. There aren't any to speak of, and there's a good reason that there aren't any. In this market, we had a booming business for ninety days every summer when the tourists from Pennsylvania and Ohio came to town."

With the local population, the restaurant seemed to be something more exotic. "It's a bit like going to Disney—you can only go there once or twice. And that's what you do. You don't go there every day. You go to whatever, Applebee's, to eat. But you only go to Disney once or twice a year. Our average customer came from 200 miles, and you can't run a restaurant like that."

His passion had overridden his typical pragmatism. "I should have looked in the Washington, D.C., phone book twenty years ago. Because, you know, in the Washington, D.C., phone book, you will find, under 'Restaurants,' fifty French restaurants, a hundred Italian restaurants and Chinese, Vietnamese, everything under the sun—*one* German restaurant in the whole of Washington, D.C. Now, if they can afford just one German restaurant . . ."

Even if Uli had done more research, he still would likely have opened the restaurant because he frequently sees things differently than most. Uli simply is different from most people. Yes, Uli immigrated to the United States from Germany, but his story doesn't begin there. "I was born in Lima, Peru, South America—German parents, but born in Peru. We lived in Peru for eight years. I have a very different point of view than most other people. I mean, I've lived on three continents in my life, and I always felt—I've never been local in my life. In Peru, I certainly wasn't a local. In Bavaria, I was never really local. And in America, I'm a little bit different again."

It's that difference that has kept him sharing the food traditions of Bavaria with the South, even though he gave up on the restaurant busi-

Seasonal Availability Chart

	jan	feb	mar	apr	may	june	july	aug	sept	oct	nov	dec
Apples							July–December					
Arugula				January–November								
Asparagus				April–June								
Basil						March–November						
Beans						June–September						
Beets			March–June							October–December		
Blackberries						June–July						
Bok Choy		January–May								October–December		
Broccoli					January–December							
Brussel Sprouts	Jan–Feb										Nov–Dec	
Cabbages		January–April								October–December		
Cantaloupes							July–August					
Cilantro					May–June							
Collards		January–May							September–December			
Cucumbers						June–September						
Eggplant					May–November							
Figs								Aug–Sept				
Garlic, Elephant										October–December		
Honeydew							July–August					
Kales		January–May							September–December			
Lettuces		January–June							September–December			
Mushrooms			January–December									
Okra							July–Sep					
Peas					May–July							
Peppers, Bell							June–					
Peppers, Hot							July–O					
Potatoes, Irish		January–April										
Potatoes, Sweet		January–April										
Pumpkins	Jan–Feb											
Radishes			March–June									
Rutabaga		January–April										
Scallions			March–June									
Spinach			March–May									
Sprite Melons							July–					
Sprouts					January–Dece							
Squash, Summer												
Winter		January–April										
rries				April–June								
orn						June–J						
ard			March–June									
				March–August								
		March										
						June–						

Uli Bennevitz at Weeping Radish Farm, Brewery, and Butchery.

ness. Now his focus is on producing authentically brewed German-style beers and providing world-class German-style charcuterie. He also uses both of these endeavors not only to introduce German flavors to the South but also to support the traditions of artisan brewers and butchers.

The butchery also gives him a chance to work with local farmers, encouraging them to produce quality ingredients for his products. And in return, he has introduced the flavors of the South to German charcuterie, using North Carolina apples in his apple bratwurst and creating a sweet potato liverwurst.

It would be easy to think that one of Uli's passions would take precedence over the others. But instead, he sees all of them as portions of his greater passion—a passion to see commonsense environmental practices become an accepted part of the legal regulations governing agriculture.

Uli is still an environmental bad boy, albeit in a completely different sense from when he first came to the United States. He is not one for rules when they're contrary to common sense and their stated purpose. He complains about regulations that don't permit him to use his brewery and butchery wastes to fertilize his farm and about not being allowed to leave an island in his retention pond to act as a bird sanctuary.

One story involving the butchery illustrates the problems he has run into by trying to be truly environmentally responsible. "There were two hogs we picked up from the slaughterhouse, and the inspector forgot to stamp them. Officials quarantined the meat, these beautiful hogs—disinfected my whole place. I mean, it was mayhem. I raised so much hell. I said, 'Okay, what can I do with them?' 'You have to dispose of them.' I said, 'Can I eat them myself?' 'Yes, you can.' I said, 'Well, this is interesting. What about my staff?' 'No you can't give it to your staff, but they can come to your house and eat it.'"

Uli couldn't stand the thought of wasting perfectly good meat. "So what I was going to do was cook them all, turn them all into barbecue, and have a big, big 'Open' sign out front, saying 'Free barbecue for the unemployed, the hungry, and the poor.' And I was going to give them away that way. The officials went nuts. Did you know that it is considered commerce to give away food? I thought commerce meant you have to exchange money."

It was at this point that Uli made his stand. "They came down with a whole delegation. The assistant whatever from the whole inspection bureau came down here. It was a Monday, and we sat down in this office, and they read me the riot act. And when they finished, they said, 'Any comments?' I said, 'Yes, please.'

"I said, 'Today is Monday. Yesterday was Sunday. I am sure you all went to church on Sunday. If you went to church on Sunday, and you're coming in here on Monday, and you're telling me that I cannot give away perfectly good meat—manifested by the fact that I can eat it—to people who need it, obviously you didn't listen to what they said on Sunday, did you?' They went deathly silent. And that's the only time I got through to bureaucrats."

Perhaps an even worse example of the clash between the practical and the regulatory worlds came about when Uli was building the brewery. Because drinking water is a precious resource so close to the ocean, he decided he could route rainwater that falls on the roof into cisterns next to the building. That water could be used to flush the toilets, saving gallons of drinking water. Uli submitted his plan to the state. The response came in the form of a letter. The letter said that he could not use cistern water in his toilets. The water used in toilets must be potable—drinking water going down the toilet. And also in that envelope? A bumper sticker reading "Save North Carolina's Drinking Water."

Somehow, in spite of his frustrations, Uli isn't giving up. He's convinced that eventually practicality will win out and that Weeping Radish can become a truly sustainable system. But for now, he's focusing on making more people in his community aware. "About three years ago, I saw a change. When you talk about beer, people are open. You know, they've had beer before. And then you talk about natural food, and suddenly you get their attention. I thought, 'Wow.' I don't mean to be condescending in any way to anyone, but when you get lower- and middle-income people interested, then you have a chance," he says.

"And I'm trying to do school classes, because that's where it has to start. And farm tours now are getting really, really popular. It's a groundswell movement, no question about it. It's grass roots, and grass roots is winning." ❦

BIERSUPPE MIT MILCH (German-Style Creamy Beer Soup)

Active cooking time: 35 minutes | Total cooking time: 1 hour 35 minutes

Yield: 4 to 6 appetizer or first course servings

At Weeping Radish, Uli is justifiably proud of his award-winning beer. His traditional German recipes and methods produce beer that is unique in the South.

While Uli's beer may not be available to you in your area, this soup can be prepared with any good quality German beer. Oktoberfest beers are recommended because of their milder flavor, but experiment with different types of beer to find the one you like best. This is a very authentic recipe, and as such it may be too bitter for some American tastes. Feel free to add additional sugar.

The spices simmered in the beer and added to the soup give it a subtle holiday flavor. The combination of egg yolks and cream makes this an almost decadent soup. Rye bread croutons add a perfect touch of crispness and dark flavor.

FOR THE SOUP

3 (12-ounce) bottles German beer

Zest of 1 lemon

6 whole cloves

1 4-inch stick cinnamon

4 tablespoons unsalted butter

2 tablespoons all-purpose flour

Pinch of freshly grated nutmeg

Pinch of ground ginger

1 teaspoon salt

4 egg yolks

1 tablespoon sugar

2 cups heavy whipping cream

FOR THE CROUTONS

3 tablespoons unsalted butter

3 to 4 slices dark rye bread

TO PREPARE THE SOUP

Bring the beer to a simmer in a large saucepan over medium heat.

Add the lemon zest, cloves, and cinnamon stick to the beer and continue simmering for 30 minutes.

Strain the beer and reserve. Discard the solids.

Melt the butter in a large saucepan over medium heat.

Add the flour and cook, stirring constantly, for about 15 minutes or until the roux is a light golden brown.

Stir in the nutmeg, ginger, and salt.

Slowly add the hot beer to the roux, stirring constantly to prevent lumps from forming.

Bring the mixture to a boil, then reduce the heat to low.

In a heat-proof mixing bowl, whisk the egg yolks, sugar, and whipping cream until frothy. Gradually add 2 cups of the beer mixture, whisking constantly to prevent the eggs from scrambling.

Add the egg mixture to the saucepan, stirring constantly to combine.

Kitchen Passport This is a very versatile soup. Change the spices to make the soup spicier or more savory. Simmer the beer with herbs and garlic and use spices like dry mustard, sage, or mushroom powder for a completely different version. Simmer Mexican beer with dried peppers and lime zest and use spices like ancho chile powder, black pepper, and onion powder to create a more Mexican-flavored version.

You can also add cheese to this soup if you like. A nutty Swiss cheese would pair well with the recipe as given, but a Dutch cheese like Gouda or a Danish one like Havarti would be delicious too. Cheddar would add a more British flavor, or a Mexican melting cheese like queso quesadilla or queso Chihuahua would be complementary to the Mexican spiced version.

Return the heat to medium and continue cooking, stirring constantly, for 10 minutes or until the soup has heated through. Do not allow the soup to reach the boiling point after adding the egg mixture.

Add salt to taste.

TO PREPARE THE CROUTONS

Melt the butter in a large skillet over medium heat.

Cut the bread into 1-inch cubes.

Add the cubes to the skillet. Cook, moving constantly with a turner, until the bread is crisp.

Serve the soup with a sprinkling of the rye croutons.

Africa
Returning from Gumbo to N'gombo

The American dream represents a second chance for immigrants, a chance for freedom and opportunity that they may not have known otherwise. For African immigrants, however, the American dream can also represent a second chance for the South to be a better host than it was for the first Africans brought here.

Although African food is still one of the most exotic, least understood cuisines in the world, it's more familiar to southerners than they may realize because enslaved African cooks influenced so much of distinctively southern food. Now many contemporary immigrants are bringing with them the original dishes that inspired hoppin' John, gumbo, jambalaya, and more. And that gives southerners the chance to taste actual African cuisine and discover the roots of what they have traditionally eaten.

Yilma Aklilu and Seble Haile-Michael, Memphis, Tennessee

Ethiopia is a land of contrasts. Situated on a plateau with a formidable border of high mountains, the land appears to be secure from hostile invasion. Yet, border skirmishes have marred the history of recent decades. It is a land of fertile soil, but it is better known for mass famine than for its unique cuisine. The country has enjoyed rich trade with India and the Arab world, and yet the majority of its people live in stark poverty.

Yilma Aklilu and his wife, Seble Haile-Michael, fled Ethiopia in 1988. At the time, Mengistu Haile Mariam was the president of Ethiopia, having ruled the nation as a Marxist dictator since 1974. Mengistu's tenure was marked by atrocities. He led a bloody campaign against those who opposed him, killing thousands before his government was overthrown and he fled to exile in Zimbabwe in 1991. In 2006, he was convicted, in absentia, of genocide and sentenced to life in prison, a sentence he has yet to begin serving.

Yilma is a soft-spoken man, not the sort of man who might be expected to land in trouble with his government. But he did. He was arrested and tortured because of his political views. When he was

12

released, he was threatened with death if he spoke about what had happened to him. He and Seble felt that they had no choice. They left for the United States and were granted political asylum.

Their first home in America was in Virginia, where Seble worked in a large hotel restaurant, as she had in Ethiopia. "I went to school for hotel management, and when I got out, I worked at the government hotel in Ethiopia. All my life I have been cooking," she says.

They found their way to Memphis when they visited a friend in Pine Bluff, Arkansas. When they passed through Memphis, they noticed that there were no Ethiopian restaurants or groceries. They did some research on the area and decided to move there, having a plan to invest in service stations.

When that didn't work out as expected, Seble suggested they open Abyssinia Ethiopian Restaurant, a restaurant where she could use her skills to prepare food that would be unique in Memphis. Yilma says, "She came up with the idea of opening this restaurant because she wanted to do something in her field. We opened up here in 2000, and then, here we are."

Seble's skills are a result of a lifetime of learning. As Yilma says, "She knows everything. She knows how much to put in, how many hours it needs to be cooked, temperature, everything. She knows enough to manage any restaurant."

Seble is more modest about her skills. "My grandfather was a very, very good cook. We had a big family, and every time we got together there was very, very good food. I like cooking everything, but mostly I like cooking vegetarian. I just like cooking. It's my hobby."

Memphians have come to appreciate Seble's delicious food. While there are approximately 2,000 Ethiopian families living in the Memphis area, the majority of customers at Abyssinia are Memphis natives. "I would say 95 percent are not Ethiopian," Yilma says.

As Yilma tells it, it's not that the local Ethiopian population doesn't eat at their restaurant; they just mainly pick up food to take with them. "People don't have time. They can't sit down and eat. Cab drivers, grocery store owners—they do not have time. They don't have people to stay there and work for them, so they have to just get and go."

Yilma has seen many people coming into the restaurant and trying Ethiopian food for the first time. "Everybody likes the taste. They like to try something different."

This food is unlike any other in Africa. Injera, a spongy, sourdough flatbread made with the grain teff, is served with every meal to be used not only as food but also as a utensil. Traditionally, diners pick up food with pieces of injera instead of with a fork or spoon, then eat the food

Seble Haile-Michael and Yilma Aklilu at Abyssinia Ethiopian Restaurant.

and bread in the same bite. Many dishes are based on *nit'r qibe*, a spiced, clarified butter. Complex blends of spices flavor the dishes. Trade with India brought Indian spices to the region, and ingenious Ethiopian cooks used those spices to create a cuisine that may be reminiscent of some Indian dishes but is unique.

No matter how exotic their food, though, Yilma and Seble are true southerners now. When talking about Ethiopian food, Yilma espouses one tenet dear to the hearts of southerners everywhere. "I tell people when they are eating the chicken stew—the meat is good, but the gravy is what is important. You can ignore the meat, but you have to sop up the gravy." 🍲

MISR WOT (Ethiopian-Style Lentil Stew)

Active cooking time: 20 minutes | Total cooking time: 1 hour, 50 minutes | Yield: 6 main dish servings

When Yilma describes Ethiopian cuisine, he uses simple words that belie the complexity of the flavors behind them. He says that Ethiopian food is "spicy, tasty, just different. It's very authentic." This lentil stew, while appearing to be a simple dish, actually layers flavors to create a lentil stew like no other.

Berbere, the spice blend used in this dish, will likely be hard to locate on supermarket shelves. Most African markets will carry it, and some sources will deliver it to your door. Even restaurateurs like Yilma and Seble have a hard time finding some of their ingredients. "There are a lot of things which I can't find usually that I have to import from Ethiopia, like hot pepper. It's not just the pepper but the mixture to make it taste the way we want. You can get it, but you have to dry it and crush it to get the right flavor. To get it together is hard," Yilma says.

The flavors you will find layered in this dish are those you will find in most Ethiopian cuisine. Seble says that you can't have Ethiopian dishes without "garlic, ginger, and hot pepper." As she describes these ingredients and how they work together, Yilma sighs a contented "yes" with a huge smile. Once you taste this, you'll be able to smile in contentment as well.

1 medium white onion, roughly chopped

2 cloves garlic, peeled

1 (¼-inch) piece fresh ginger, peeled

¼ cup *nit'r qibe* (recipe follows)

2 tablespoons *berbere*

2 cups red lentils

Salt

> **Kitchen Passport** This recipe can also be made with yellow lentils, split green peas, or mung beans. For a different flavor and texture, try using dried white beans or pinto beans. When using these beans, you will need to soak them for at least 8 hours or overnight.

In a food processor, combine the onion, garlic, and ginger. Process until the vegetables form a puree, scraping the sides of the food processor bowl as needed. There should be no large pieces of onion, garlic, or ginger when you are done.

In a large heavy pot, heat the *nit'r qibe* over medium heat.

Add the *berbere* and stir to combine. Cook for 1 minute.

Add the vegetable puree to the spiced *nit'r qibe*. Stir to combine and continue cooking over medium heat for 5 minutes.

Add the lentils to the vegetable puree, stirring to combine. Gradually add 4 cups of water, stirring constantly, and bring the lentil mixture to a boil.

Reduce the heat to low.

Simmer, covered, for 1½ hours or until the lentils are soft and bursting open.

Season to taste with salt.

NIT'R QIBE (Ethiopian-Style Spiced Butter)

Active cooking time: 10 minutes | Total cooking time: 1 hour, 10 minutes | Yield: 1 cup

The basis for almost all Ethiopian dishes is the spiced, clarified butter known as *nit'r qibe*. Because Ethiopia has historically had a great deal of trade with India, many of the spices and cooking techniques used in Ethiopian food have Indian roots. *Nit'r qibe* is a spiced version of ghee, the clarified butter used in Indian cuisine.

1 pound unsalted butter

½ medium yellow onion, diced
    (about ⅓ cup)

3 cloves garlic, crushed

1 (1-inch) piece fresh ginger, peeled
    and cut into ¼-inch slices

6 green cardamom pods

1 4-inch cinnamon stick

4 whole cloves

1 teaspoon fenugreek seeds

1 teaspoon nigella seeds

½ teaspoon turmeric

12 coriander seeds

In a medium saucepan, melt the butter over medium heat, stirring constantly to prevent browning.

Once the butter has melted, increase the heat to medium-high and bring the butter to a boil.

Add the remaining ingredients. Immediately reduce the heat to low and allow the butter to simmer, uncovered and without stirring, for 1 hour.

Remove the butter from the heat. All the solids in the butter should have settled to the bottom with the spices. You should have a top layer of clear golden liquid.

Strain this liquid into a container with a fine mesh sieve lined with cheesecloth. There should be no solids in the final product.

Nit'r qibe can be refrigerated in a sealed container for up to 3 months.

Kitchen Passport The *nit'r qibe* recipe provided here will make more than you will need for the lentil stew. This spiced clarified butter can add exotic flavor to other dishes as well. Try using it for scrambled eggs or sautéed vegetables, drizzled over rice or greens, or as a base for a dipping sauce for bread. Just add *berbere* or *mitmita* (a different Ethiopian spice blend) to a small dish of melted *nit'r qibe* and stir before dipping any wheat or sourdough bread.

Elizabeth Kizito has become a well-known presence in Louisville, Kentucky. They call her the cookie lady, and she can be found at cultural and sporting events throughout the city, carrying on her head a basket full of her delicious cookies from her bakery, Kizito Cookies.

Elizabeth immigrated to the United States from Uganda in 1972. She came for her education, but she was also escaping the Idi Amin regime and the war that brought tragedy to her family. It would be easy for her to look back at that time and feel nothing but sorrow, but her own strength of character doesn't allow her to focus only on the suffering of her family. "Well, it changed their life, but everybody in the world, I think, suffers. My family suffered. I lost a brother in the war. I came here during the war. My family lost everything, but they rebuilt and they did well."

Elizabeth herself found a unique niche in her new home. Cookies are not part of Ugandan culture, but Elizabeth fell in love with them. "I got interested in making cookies because when I was in Africa, my father owned a bakery there. But we never really had cookies or chocolate chip cookies. Somebody gave me some when I came to America, and I liked them so much that I said, 'I'm going to make myself some cookies.' So I made chocolate chip cookies, and I ate them."

That first batch of cookies led to more, and before she knew it, Elizabeth's cookies had turned into a cottage industry. "I was working in a restaurant as a waitress, and I would bake cookies, and I would bring them up to work. And people were like, 'You bake good.' And sometimes I don't bake them at all, so they say, 'Why don't you bring us those cookies? We'll buy them.' Because you don't want to spend all your money baking cookies and give them away all the time. So they say, 'Bring them and we'll buy them.' So I used to take them to work and sell them to my coworkers."

Word about her cookies spread, and soon she was selling too many cookies to keep working as a waitress or to keep the business in her home. "I thought it would be harder starting a business here in America. But for me, I started out really simple, and I used a lot of African techniques, and I didn't worry about it. I did it for fun, then it caught on."

She learned those African techniques from her father, and her own cookie-baking experience has brought Elizabeth a new understanding of his life as a baker. "My father really worked hard in the bakery in Uganda when I was young. I saw him get up really early in the morning, and I didn't really understand it," she recalls. "And then I got here and was able to follow in the same footsteps like he did. I get up early and you work hard in the bakery. It's not something easy. It seems like bak-

Elizabeth
Namusoke
Kizito,
Louisville,
Kentucky

Elizabeth Kizito at
Kizito Cookies.

ing cookies—everybody likes baking cookies when they're little—but
when you have a bakery, it's a lot of demands, timing and producing
your product. You have to produce it to sell."

Elizabeth also sends her family American spices and plants to sell
in Uganda. "In my country, we don't use a lot of spices. We are more
influenced by Indian cuisine, because we use curry a lot. So for me, I
never had a lot of spices until I came here. Now I try to introduce a lot
of spices in my country, and I take a few plants or seeds with me. And
I tell my family these seeds are really, really good, like rosemary and
different things. So you can make money." While the spices aren't very
popular in Uganda, Elizabeth believes they will be if people will just try
them.

She also brings the flavors of Uganda into the cookies for which
she's become famous. She feels that the simplicity of Ugandan cuisine
has helped her be a better baker. "The flavors show up in the cookies
because I like a lot of things homemade. I'm always looking for the
good taste where you don't have other things cover up the taste. And

my cookies are really successful because they're homemade like you would make them at home. And I use all the best ingredients in my cookies."

Elizabeth doesn't have much trouble getting people to try her cookies. She doesn't have to advertise because the aroma of baking cookies can be smelled along the entire block where her bakery operates, beckoning anyone who passes by to come in for a taste. It's also impossible to resist her joyful smile when she talks about her cookies and her homeland.

She acts as an unofficial ambassador for Uganda in Louisville. In her bakery's retail shop, she sells not only her cookies and brownies but also handcrafted goods that she brings back from Uganda and the surrounding area on her annual trips to her homeland. She also encourages her friends to visit Uganda. "Uganda is a beautiful country. It averages, like, sixty degrees all year round. It's very lush. People who go there tell me they love it. Life is simple. A lot of people are poor, but they're happy."

And really, happiness is what Elizabeth's success here is based on. She's happy baking her cookies and being a part of a vibrant southern community. And she loves making other people feel the same way. "I like cooking because it makes people happy when they eat something good and it's homemade." 🍪

MATO KE NABINYEBWA (Ugandan-Style Plantains in Peanut Sauce)

Active cooking time: 30 minutes | Total cooking time: 1 hour, 30 minutes | Yield: 6 side dish servings

There aren't too many dishes more southern than peanut butter and banana sandwiches. Elvis certainly liked them. While it's true that many southern dishes have African roots, it's not likely that the peanut butter and banana sandwich is one of them. But this traditional dish does use that same flavor combination.

Elizabeth remembers eating bananas with peanuts in Uganda as a child. "In my country, we eat bananas. That's like eating meat and potatoes, because they eat them every day for lunch and dinner. If there's no food, like if you say people are poor—they have no food—what they mean is they have no bananas."

"We ate bananas with peanut gravy. And you take raw peanuts, and you put them in a pestle, a big pestle, and you pound it. And you can hear the pestle in the village when people are pounding their nuts. You know what they're going to eat. Then you cook that peanut, let it thicken like oats. And then you make the banana to be like a mashed potato, and you dip it in the peanut and eat it, and it's so yummy."

In this version of the dish, plantains are used because they are closer to the variety of bananas that grow in Uganda than are the bananas sold in American supermarkets. We also use peanut butter as the sauce instead of mashing and cooking peanuts. Still, the flavors blend beautifully, and the final dish is close to a pudding.

This dish doesn't even need a plate or bowl. It does just fine spread on toasted bread.

6 plantains, medium ripe
1½ cups unsweetened peanut butter
2 cups water

Preheat the oven to 350 degrees.

Peel the plantains by cutting off the ends and cutting a slit through the length of the skin. With the peel removed, slice the plantains into ¼-inch-thick pieces. Layer the slices evenly in a baking dish.

In a medium mixing bowl, stir the peanut butter until it is soft. Add the water slowly, stirring constantly until a thin sauce is formed. Pour the peanut sauce over the plantains in the baking dish.

Cover the dish with aluminum foil.

Bake the plantains in the oven for 1 hour or until softened enough to mash with a fork.

Mash the plantains in the baking dish and then spoon into bowls to serve.

Kitchen Passport This is such a simple recipe that it's easy to vary. Add chocolate to the mixture or honey for extra sweetness. Cinnamon or nutmeg would also be nice additions.

Leftovers can make a great filling for stuffed French toast. Simply spread a thin layer of the plantain mixture between two thin slices of bread before soaking them in the egg batter. Add a sprinkle of cinnamon and a drizzle of maple syrup when it's cooked, and you'll have a delicious breakfast.

Plantains

No one knows exactly where plantains originated, but historians generally believe that they first grew in Southeast Asia, then spread to Africa. In Africa, the trade of plantains became one of the primary factors in the wealth of the Bantu kingdom, which included most of central and southern Africa. Through that trade, plantains found their way to Portuguese Franciscan monks in the Canary Islands in the early sixteenth century. Those monks spread the fruit to the Caribbean and other parts of the Americas.

But what are plantains? It's easy to confuse plantains with the fruit we know as bananas in the United States because of their similar appearance. Unlike sweet bananas, green or unripe plantains are starchy and have a neutral flavor, much like potatoes. Ripe or overripe plantains are sweeter. Also, plantains are normally cooked instead of eaten raw. But just to make things more complicated, in many countries plantains are often referred to as bananas.

In Africa, plantains are a staple food, and there are as many ways to cook plantains as there are people to eat them. Fried plantain chips are a popular snack all over West Africa. In some parts, green plantains are boiled and pounded into a thick paste resembling mashed potatoes. This paste is known as *fufu* and is served with stews.

In Côte d'Ivoire, fried plantains are served with an onion and tomato sauce, often with fish. In Nigeria, they're roasted under hot coals to make a dish called *boli*, a common midday meal among the working class.

Plantains are also a common food in East Africa. In Ethiopia, even the root is sometimes used as food. In Uganda, plantains are wrapped in the plant's leaves and cooked over a fire before being mashed and served with a sauce. There, plantains cooked in this way are eaten with almost every meal nearly every day.

While plantains flourish all over the tropics, Uganda is the top producer of the fruit. Not only are plantains a staple for the people of Uganda, but their export is a vital part of the national economy.

From a nutritional standpoint, plantains are one of the healthiest foods in the world. They are high in fiber and potassium while low in carbohydrates and sodium. They are believed to be more easily digested than bananas, and in many countries, mashed ripe plantains are the first solid food given to babies as they are weaned.

You can find plantains at many supermarkets, but they are always available in Hispanic and Asian markets. Consider using ripe plantains in any recipe where bananas will be cooked. Not only will you be preparing a nutritious dish, but you'll also be bringing a flavor of Africa into your kitchen.

On a corner in one of Richmond's less revitalized sections of downtown, there is a restaurant. It's a small one, easy to miss if you're not looking for it. And yet, it's a place that is alive, a place where hopes and dreams have come to live, a place where a community has formed. Few restaurants succeed in creating such an environment, but Africanne on Main is one.

Chef MaMusu is the heart of this special place. She immigrated to the United States from Liberia in 1980, leaving behind civil war and bringing with her a history of southern food unlike any other. Liberia is a country founded by freed American slaves. They named their streets after southern street and city names. They spoke English as their primary language. And they ate the foods they had eaten in the South. "When the slaves went back, they took that, and they kind of mixed it with what was already there. So they took the soul food with them and blended it with the African spices."

Chef MaMusu doesn't feed customers. Instead, she feeds a community. When recession came to Richmond, she tackled it more as the head of a family than as a restaurateur. "I talked to my customers, and I said, 'Look, there will be a lot of things that we used to have that we might not have all the time, because we can't afford it. So all of us are going to be tightening together. I know you can't eat here as you used to. So if you come here and ask for lamb and all that stuff all the time, you might not see it like you used to, but the standards of being treated with love will always be there. The quality will always be there.'"

That quality is the basis of her success in Richmond. She has consistently provided healthy, great-tasting food to her community, and in return, she has become a part of their families. She sees that relationship in the way people appreciate it when she cooks a special dish for the daily buffet. "Sometimes I'll surprise them and make something and they'll be, 'You got this on the buffet today, okay!' It's like mom. You know every now and then, mom gives you something good. So that's how it is."

It took time to build this sort of relationship with her customers. She puts it all down to one simple yet huge concept. "I have to keep it real with them. These are people that trust me. It's trust. It's really, really about trust. Richmond is the type of city that doesn't like anything new, seriously. Don't like anything different. Don't like anything new. And they're about, 'If you're going to come and give me something different, you have to be here forever.' That's how they feel, you know. You're going to be here for a while."

Trust has allowed her to introduce the flavors of Africa to Richmond. "It's like taking soul food and adding African spices. We did a twist

Chef MaMusu at Africanne on Main.

to it. We're doing it this way as opposed to taking the African food and making it southern. I'm taking the southern food and making it African-style," she says. "They're familiar with collard greens in the South, but we cook it African-style, using African spices. The reason why I do it is for them to recognize what they eat, but they taste it differently."

She learned to cook from her grandmother, a professional chef in Liberia and the daughter of one of the original settlers. "She had two restaurants and was a total entrepreneur—a very talented woman. I learned all my skills from her."

The skills she learned from her grandmother were more than just the skills of cooking. She recalls the last conversation she ever had with her grandmother. "When I was leaving my hometown in 1980, I went to my grandmother's bedside to say goodbye. And then she said to me, 'I'm never going to see you again.' And I said, 'Oh, you'll see me again. I'll be back.' And she said, 'No, this is the end for both of us.' And I said, 'You'll live forever.' And she said, 'No, I'll only live forever on one condition. If you promise me that everything that I've taught you, you'll pass it on, then the essence of me will never die. What I have taught you is not yours to keep. You'll only be blessed if you can pass it on to someone else.'"

And so Chef MaMusu has passed it on. While she cooks for her community, she also teaches them to cook for themselves. "I needed to continue passing it on. And so as I got older, there was an urgency to start a school, and so I decided to." She opened Chef MaMusu's Cultural Cooking School in 2006. Then came the harder part—deciding whom she should teach. "I had to find a medium where they were not adolescent and not too old as teenagers, so eleven to sixteen, it seemed, was just that middle age that they are ready to accept new things."

The school has been a great success. Not only has she taught girls the skills of the kitchen, but she has also inspired some of them to seek careers in food. She can't help but smile with pride when talking about the girls she has taught. "So far, I have graduated seventy-eight girls. Two of them are going on to culinary school."

But even the girls who don't pursue a career in food have been given a gift that will benefit them for their entire lives. "I've been getting kids from the battered women's shelter programs, the projects, underprivileged neighborhoods. That's what I really wanted. It's been working very well, because not only do they have nutrition problems, they have behavioral problems. And then most of them are obese, and they're not eating well. So we have this whole rite of passage that I'm dealing with and not just cooking. I'm dealing with their health issues and their emotional issues, so I try to make it a total balance for them."

In a similar side venture, she helps women using food stamps to buy healthy groceries on a limited budget. "I told the first woman, 'This is the deal. I'm not going to do this forever, but I'm going to train you well, so that you can be the prototype to help your friends and pass that on.'" That woman now works with twenty-four other women in the community, and all because Chef MaMusu took the time to teach her the basics of healthy cooking on a tight budget.

She teaches them the same basics that her grandmother taught her. "There are three things: the temperature of the food they are going to cook, the pots that they're going to cook it in, and the seasonings. When you can master those three things, you can cook anything."

It sounds so simple, and yet the combinations of flavors are endless. And once again, it all goes back to her memories of being a child and watching her grandmother cook in Liberia. "On Saturday, she would make this pot of soup that had every imaginable thing in it—all types of meats and vegetables and everything. She would start this as a soup on Saturday," she recalls. "On Sunday, it would be like stew. On

Monday, it would be like gravy. On Wednesday, it would be something else. And that same pot went through the whole week, but she created something different with the ingredients all week. So that was my memorable time with her—starting off with her on Saturday and ending up with something different by the end of the week from the same concept." 🍲

JOLLOF RICE (West African-Style Rice and Vegetables)

Active cooking time: 1 hour | Total cooking time: 1 hour, 30 minutes | Yield: 8 main dish servings

Jollof rice is a popular dish throughout western Africa. This dish is also called *benachin*, which, in the Wolof language, means "one pot." This dish is believed to be the inspiration for another one-pot dish, jambalaya. This recipe is simple, but there are as many variations as there are cooks making the dish. The keys are the rice and the ingredients you add to that one pot to flavor it.

Chef MaMusu calls *jollof* rice a universal dish "because it can be prepared any way—vegetarian or non-vegetarian." It varies in preparation across western Africa. "The Liberians prepare a more southern-style *jollof* rice, with the mixed vegetables and the ham hocks and all that stuff, because they took that from slavery times. Because Liberia had so much southern influence, we kind of added to the *jollof* rice. We add different meats to it, depending on what you eat."

Regardless of the meats or vegetables used, *jollof* rice is a deliciously savory dish. The tomato, onion, and pepper add piquant flavor to the rice. The meat adds richness but, as Chef MaMusu said, is optional. For the best results, use vegetables that are at their seasonal peak during spring and summer. Frozen vegetables work well in winter, though.

¼ cup vegetable oil

1 fryer chicken, cut into pieces
   (about 2 pounds)

Salt

Freshly ground black pepper

2 large onions, diced (about 1⅓ cups)

1 red bell pepper, seeded and chopped
   (about 1 cup)

3 cloves garlic, minced (about
   1½ teaspoons)

2 hot chile peppers, seeded and diced

3 cups uncooked white rice

¼ cup tomato paste (about ⅓ of a
   6-ounce can)

Heat the oil in a large pot over medium-high heat.

Season the chicken pieces with salt and black pepper and cook them in the hot oil until they are brown on all sides, about 5 minutes per side. Work in batches if necessary to prevent crowding in the pot.

Remove the pot from the heat and transfer the browned chicken into a large stockpot. Add 5 cups of water to the chicken in the stockpot. Bring the water to a boil.

Reduce the heat to low and simmer for 20 minutes.

3 medium tomatoes, chopped
(about 3 cups)

2 medium carrots, peeled and chopped
(about 1½ cups)

1 cup fresh green beans, cut into 1-inch
pieces (about 4 ounces)

1 cup cabbage, shredded (about ¼ of a
small head of cabbage)

TO SERVE
Parsley or cilantro, chopped

Kitchen Passport You can substitute any meat for the chicken.
Beef or lamb work especially well
in the dish. In Senegal, fish is
the meat of choice for *jollof* rice;
shrimp would be very nice, too.
If you are using fish or shrimp,
add them at the end so they don't
overcook.

As with the meat, don't hesi-
tate to vary the vegetables. Add
fresh green peas or new potatoes.
Try thinly sliced okra, squash, or
shredded young collard or mustard greens. Substitute bok choy
or Napa cabbage for the regular
green cabbage used in the recipe.

While the chicken is simmering, drain all but
2 to 3 tablespoons oil from the pot and return
the pot to medium heat.

Add the onions and bell pepper to the hot
oil and cook, stirring frequently, until the onions
are translucent, about 5 minutes.

Add the garlic and hot chiles to the pot and
continue cooking for 1 to 2 minutes.

Stir the rice into the onion mixture and cook,
stirring frequently, for another 1 to 2 minutes.

Add the tomato paste and stir into the rice
mixture, coating the rice and cooking until the
rice has a pink to reddish hue. Add the tomatoes and continue cooking for 2 to 3 minutes.

Carefully pour the chicken and its simmering liquid into the rice mixture. Add the carrots,
green beans, and cabbage.

Bring the mixture to a boil.

Reduce the heat to low and simmer, covered, for 20 minutes.

Remove the rice mixture from the heat and
allow it to rest for 10 minutes before serving.

Season to taste with salt and black pepper.

Serve hot, garnished with parsley or cilantro.

PRESIDENT OBAMA'S CASSEROLE

Active cooking time: 1 hour | Total cooking time: 1 hour, 30 minutes | Yield: 6 to 8 main dish servings

A casserole may not seem to be a particularly African dish, and yet the herbs
and spices used here give this simple
casserole an exotic flavor. This is one of
Chef MaMusu's original recipes, developed

to celebrate the inauguration of President
Barack Obama.

The herbs and spices are key here.
Chef MaMusu chose these herbs not just
for their flavors but also for their healing

properties. "All the spices I use are healing spices. Cloves are good for bad breath, and they help people that have stomach problems or intestinal problems. Ginger is one of the main spices that I use a lot because it has multiple benefits in the body."

The combination of sweet plantains and spicy, smoky sausage is paired with creamy eggs and the tang of sharp cheddar. The parsley and thyme form a soft background for the stronger flavors of ginger and clove. Chef MaMusu recommends serving this dish as either supper or breakfast. Either way, you won't be able to eat it without tasting food that was created from love.

2 tablespoons olive oil

4 medium red potatoes, diced
   (about 1 pound)

¼ teaspoon salt

3 ripe plantains, diced

1 large yellow onion, diced (about 1 cup)

1 red bell pepper, diced (about 1 cup)

1 pound smoked sausage, preferably
   turkey, diced

6 large eggs

1 teaspoon fresh Italian parsley

1 teaspoon fresh thyme

1 (¼-inch) piece fresh ginger, peeled
   and grated (about ½ teaspoon)

¼ teaspoon ground cloves

1 cup sharp cheddar cheese, shredded
   (about 4 ounces)

Preheat the oven to 350 degrees.

Heat the oil in a large skillet over medium heat.

Add the potatoes and salt and cook, stirring constantly, for 10 minutes.

Add the plantains to the potatoes and continue cooking until the potatoes are soft, about 10 minutes more.

Add the onion and pepper and continue cooking until the onion is just translucent, about 7 minutes more.

Stir in the smoked sausage and remove the skillet from the heat.

In a large mixing bowl, beat the eggs lightly. Add the parsley, thyme, ginger, and cloves, stirring to combine. Add the potato and sausage mixture, stirring until thoroughly blended.

Pour the mixture into a casserole dish and top with the cheddar cheese.

Bake in the oven for 30 minutes or until the eggs have set and are firm.

Kitchen Passport Either salmon or cubed chicken would be great replacements for the smoked sausage in this recipe. Allow the meat to cook in the skillet for 5 minutes before adding it and the vegetables to the egg mixture. You could also crumble in cooked bacon as either a replacement meat or an addition.

By no means can this book or any other capture all of the immigrant stories from today's South. Nor does it cover all the immigrant groups who have come to share the South with us. What we have tried to do with this book is to open a small window onto a side of the South that you might not have seen or thought about before.

If we have any one wish for this book, it is that it will carry you beyond its pages and out into the world. Rather than serve as a full helping of the evolving foodways of the South, this book is meant to whet your appetite and lead you to meet the people who are making your part of the world just a little bit bigger and tastier.

The restaurants and people included here are a good place to start. Since we began writing this book, we have returned to as many of them as possible to enjoy wonderful meals and company. One thing to keep in mind, however, is that the restaurant business is a very difficult one. Even in a good economy, restaurants can fail. While we hope they're enjoying success, check ahead if you plan to visit any of these folks.

Best wishes and bon appétit.

Abarca, Meredith. *Voices in the Kitchen: Views of Food and the World from Working-Class Mexican and Mexican-American Women.* College Station: Texas A&M University Press, 2006.

Anderson, Lynne Christy. *Breaking Bread: Recipes and Stories from Immigrant Kitchens.* Berkeley: University of California Press, 2010.

Bienvenu, Marcelle. *Who's Your Mama, Are You Catholic, and Can You Make a Roux?* Lafayette, La.: Acadian House Publishing, 2006.

———. *Who's Your Mama, Are You Catholic, and Can You Make a Roux? Book 2.* Lafayette, La.: Acadian House Publishing, 2008.

Coe, Andrew. *Chop Suey: A Cultural History of Chinese Food in the United States.* New York: Oxford University Press, 2009.

Dabney, Joseph Earl. *The Food, Folklore, and Art of Lowcountry Cooking: A Celebration of the Foods, History, and Romance Handed Down from England, Africa, the Caribbean, France, Germany, and Scotland.* Nashville, Tenn.: Cumberland House, 2010.

———. *Smokehouse Ham, Spoon Bread, and Scuppernong Wine: The Folklore and Art of Southern Appalachian Cooking.* Nashville, Tenn.: Cumberland House, 1998.

Edge, John T. *Apple Pie: An American Story.* New York: Putnam Adult, 2004.

———. *Donuts: An American Passion.* New York: Putnam Adult, 2006.

———. *Fried Chicken: An American Story.* New York: Putnam Adult, 2004.

———. *Hamburgers and Fries: An American Story.* New York: Putnam Adult, 2005.

———. *Southern Belly: The Ultimate Food Lover's Companion to the South.* Chapel Hill: Algonquin Books, 2007.

———, ed. *Foodways.* Vol. 7 of *The New Encyclopedia of Southern Culture.* Chapel Hill: University of North Carolina Press, 2007.

Egerton, John. *Southern Food: At Home, on the Road, in History.* Chapel Hill: University of North Carolina Press, 1993.

Elie, Lolis Eric. *Smokestack Lightning: Adventures in the Heart of Barbecue Country.* Berkeley, Calif.: Ten Speed Press, 2005.

Fair, C. Christine. *Cuisines of the Axis of Evil and Other Irritating States: A Dinner Party Approach to International Relations.* Guilford, Conn.: Globe Pequot Press, 2008.

Ferris, Marcie Cohen. *Matzoh Ball Gumbo: Culinary Tales of the Jewish South.* Chapel Hill: University of North Carolina Press, 2005.

Harris, Jessica. *Iron Pots and Wooden Spoons: Africa's Gifts to New World Cooking.* New York: Simon and Schuster, 1999.

Jordan, Michele Anna, and Susan Brady. *The World Is a Kitchen: Cooking Your Way through Culture.* Palo Alto, Calif.: Travelers' Tales, 2006.

Kaplan, Anne R., Marjorie Hoover, and Willard Moore. *The Minnesota Ethnic Food Book.* St. Paul, Minn.: Minnesota Historical Society Press, 1986.

Lee, Jennifer 8. *The Fortune Cookie Chronicles: Adventures in the World of Chinese Food.* New York: Twelve, 2008.

Loewen, James W. *The Mississippi Chinese: Between Black and White.* 2nd ed. Long Grove, Ill.: Waveland Press, 1988.

Nathan, Joan. *The New American Cooking.* New York: Knopf, 2005.

Paddleford, Clementine. *How America Eats.* New York: Charles Scribner's Sons, 1960.

Parsons, Anne Snape, and Alexandra Greeley. *Kitchen Memories: A Legacy of Family Recipes from around the World.* Sterling, Va.: Capital Books, 2007.

Patout, Alex. *Patout's Cajun Home Cooking.* New York: Random House, 1986.

Puckette, Charlotte, and Olivia Kiang-Snaije. *The Ethnic Paris Cookbook.* New York: DK Adult, 2007.

Ray, Celeste, ed. *Ethnicity.* Vol. 6 of *The New Encyclopedia of Southern Culture.* Chapel Hill: University of North Carolina Press, 2007.

Roahen, Sara. *Gumbo Tales: Finding My Place at the New Orleans Table.* New York: W. W. Norton, 2008.

Sauceman, Fred. *The Place Setting: Timeless Tastes of the Mountain South, from Bright Hope to Frog Level.* Macon, Ga.: Mercer University Press, 2006.

Shortridge, Barbara G., and James R. Shortridge, ed. *The Taste of American Place: A Reader on Regional and Ethnic Foods.* Lanham, Md.: Rowman and Littlefield, 2008.

Silva, Nikki, and Davia Nelson. *Hidden Kitchens: Stories, Recipes and More from NPR's The Kitchen Sisters.* New York: Rodale Books, 2006.

Tannahill, Reay. *Food in History.* New York: Broadway, 1995.

Tilson, Jake. *A Tale of 12 Kitchens: Family Cooking in Four Countries.* New York: Artisan, 2006.

Willard, Pat. *America Eats!: On the Road with the WPA—the Fish Fries, Box Supper Socials, and Chitlin Feasts That Define Real American Food.* New York: Bloomsbury USA, 2009.

Thank you to everyone who took the time to share stories with us. This book also owes its existence to all those wonderful people whose stories we were unable to include in this book. Knowing that there were so many stories to be told drove us to do the best we could to let readers know just how much of the world is at their door.

This book would not have been possible without several people. First of all, Martha Foose assured us that, yes, we might be crazy, but the book was a good idea. John T. Edge gave us invaluable advice and helped us define the scope of the project. Nancie McDermott listened to us babble at all hours of the day and night. She offered us limitless encouragement and is still our biggest cheerleader.

Melissa and Kjeld Petersen gave us our first forum as honest-to-goodness writers in the pages of *Edible Memphis* magazine. What's more, Melissa told us just how nice *Edible Piedmont* publisher Fred Thompson was. We introduced ourselves to Fred at the Southern Food-ways Alliance Symposium and told him our idea. The next day, we not only had his advice but had an introduction to our editor as well.

Elaine Maisner, our editor at the University of North Carolina Press, has been superb. With her guidance, we wrote a much better book.

Our friend and neighbor Kerry Vaughan has been so important to us. She helped us get these stories onto paper, then edited our manuscript with great thoughtfulness and a keen eye.

Kelly Alexander gave us wonderful feedback on our manuscript. And there are not enough words to express what John Egerton has meant to us. Beyond being the inspiration for so much of what we do, he was a tremendous help in shaping the final outcome of this project.

Finally, Kelly English, Jeff Frisby, Andrew Armstrong, Jaime Ware, and the rest of the great folks at Restaurant Iris in Memphis, Tennessee, provided us a home away from home while we were writing the book. We appreciate them more than they know.